"It seems to us that *'The Penobscot Man'* should in twenty-five years, be a valuable 'human document,' for the life, the men, and the deeds, ring true. To those who would know a strong and fine side of New England manhood, this book is to be heartily commended for present reading – and, what is more for preservation."

Bliss Carman, *The Literary World*, (1904)

Nearly **125 years** since that review was written,
'*The Penobscot Man*'
is still a valuable human document, that describes a way of life, a period of time, and the fabric of a man.

Burnt Jacket Publishing
is pleased to bring you this new edition based on:

The Penobscot Man

by

Fannie Hardy Eckstorm

New Content and Annotated Edition by
Maine Author
Tommy Carbone

A

Burnt Jacket Publishing

Classic Release

BURNT JACKET MOUNTAIN - MAINE

THE PENOBSCOT MAN

Life and Death

on a

Maine River

Tommy Carbone, PhD

Copyright 2022

Burnt Jacket Publishing

an Annotated, New Content Edition

based on

THE PENOBSCOT MAN

by

FANNIE HARDY ECKSTORM

Original Printing 1904

With a 1924 Private Printing by Fannie Hardy Eckstorm

A BURNT JACKET PUBLISHING CLASSIC RELEASE

Books from Tommy Carbone

The Lobster Lake Bandits
Mystery at Moosehead

The Elephant Mountain Gang
Mystery at Maine's Moosehead Lake

Woods and Lakes of Maine - Annotated Edition:
A Trip from Moosehead Lake to New Brunswick in a Birch-Bark Canoe

Hubbard's Guide to Moosehead Lake and Northern Maine
Annotated Edition

Exploring the Maine Woods
The Hardy Family Expedition to the Machias Lakes

I Am Penobscot
A Novel

RUNNING A LOG

A BURNT JACKET PUBLISHING CLASSIC RELEASE

THE PENOBSCOT MAN
LIFE AND DEATH ON A MAINE RIVER
ANNOTATED EDITION

Newly added interior illustrations, and photos from the collection of Tommy Carbone, or as otherwise noted.

Author of new material and edition editor, Tommy Carbone.

Use of all newly added material (text, footnotes, and photos) from this book, other than short passages for review purposes or used within quotations, requires prior written permission be obtained by contacting the publisher at info@tommycarbone.com. Thank you for your support.

Original footnotes have been prefaced with Eckstorm's initials, FHE.

Front cover photo of the Seboomook rapids, at the start of the West Branch of the Penobscot River, courtesy of **Cheryl Derico** (*cderico photography*).

Photo of Ripogenus Gorge courtesy of **Mary Louise Osborne**.

Select back cover and public domain photos of logging operations, courtesy of Special Collections, Raymond H. Fogler Library, University of Maine.

20230501-5.5x8.5ISDJHC

ISBN: 978-1-954048-21-8

Burnt Jacket Publishing
Greenville, Maine

1. Maine woods - 2. Penobscot River - 3. Logging - 4. Expeditions and adventure - 5. Memoir - 6. Naturalist – 7. Hunting and fishing. - 8. Woodsmen 9. 19th Century History - 10. Katahdin. - 11. Lumbering - 12. Maine History

www.tommycarbone.com

CONTENTS

EDITION PHOTOGRAPHS ix

EDITION INTRODUCTION 1

FANNIE HARDY ECKSTORM 15

INTRODUCTORY 21

LUMBERMAN & RIVER-DRIVER TERMS 24

I   — THE LOGGER'S BOAST 27

II   — LUGGING BOAT ON SOWADNEHUNK 31

III   — JACK MANN 45

IV   — THE GRIM TALE OF LARRY CONNORS 53

V   — HYMNS BEFORE BATTLE 67

VI   — THE JAM AT GERRY'S ROCK 75

VII   — THE DROWNING OF JOHN ROBERTS, 1852 .. 81

VIII — DEATH OF THOREAU'S GUIDE –

        JOSEPH ATTIEN 85

IX   — THE WEST BRANCH SONG 125

X   — THE GRAY ROCK OF ABOL 127

XI	— THE LUMBERMAN'S ALPHABET	155
XII	— A CLUMP OF POSIES	157
XIII	— THE BURNING OF HENRY K. ROBINSON'S CAMP	191
XIV	— WORKING NIGHTS	195
XV	— LAKE CHEMO	219
XVI	— THE NAUGHTY PRIDE OF BLACK SEBAT AND OTHERS	223
XVII	— A BALLAD ABOUT JOHN ROSS	253
XVIII	— RESCUE	261
XIX	— DRIVERS' LUNCH	291
XX	— "JOYFULLY"	293
XXI	— 'TIS TWENTY YEARS SINCE	303
APPENDIX	— THE PENOBSCOT RIVER	323
APPENDIX	— A CLUMP OF POSIES	326

EDITION PHOTOGRAPHS

RUNNING A LOG v

PENOBSCOT RIVER - MAINE 13

FANNIE HARDY ECKSTORM, 1888. 15

1924 EDITION COVER 20

A BOOM 30

HAULING A BATTEAU ON RIPOGENUS CARRY 43

LUMBER CREW WITH TIN DIPPERS 47

LOG YARD FROM BREWER TO BANGOR SHORE 52

EAST MILLINOCKET DOLBY DAM, 1906 74

BREAKING A JAM 80

CLEARING A JAM 84

MAP AREA OF GRAND FALLS AND SHAD POND 94

JOSEPH ATTEAN 108

DAVID STONE LIBBEY 124

MT. KATAHDIN, FROM NEAR ABOL STREAM 154

RIPOGENUS GORGE – LOOKING WEST 159

BREAKING A JAM AT THE ARCHES 172

"RIPOGENUS, 1891" 179

WILBUR WEBSTER 183

GREENVILLE WHARF AT HIGH WATER 190

MEN TURNING A CAPSTAN ON A HEAD-WORKS RAFT 206

HORSE POWERING THE CAPSTAN. 207

THE STEAMSHIP KATAHDIN 217

RIPOGENUS RAPIDS 218

THE SOCIAL HOUR 222

THE CAMBRIDGE STEAMSHIP 233

PORTRAIT OF MANLY HARDY – 1905 252

PORTRAIT OF JOHN ROSS 257

BIG SEBATTIS MITCHELL 295

FOUR *TERRIBLY ABLE* RIVER-DRIVERS 316

LOG MARKS 320

THE PEIRCE MEMORIAL 322

EDITION INTRODUCTION

THE West Branch of the Penobscot River took the lives of many river-drivers. It took their lives in a yearly call for them to return to the Maine woods, to place their lives in cadence with the flow of the river. It took their lives in a way that their loved ones could not understand, for these men loved that river. In the most tragic way, lives were taken from men who took a wrong step, misjudged a log, or according to legend, the river would take the life from any man who had the moxie to curse her.

These were the men who knew this river long before she joined the East Branch at Medway, from where she became deep and predictable. They knew her when she roared her icy-cold water though narrow canyons and rapids between Ripogenus and Shad Pond. They knew her water strewn with boulders larger than horses, deep swirling eddies, and the swiftest of currents which could, according to one woodsman, "float a brick." But the river was indifferent to the men, and she could strike with an unpredictable vengeance, or be as stubborn as an ox by forming a jam behind a single key log. Yet, the river was not always to blame; for could the water be at fault in taking the lives of men who appeared to live more for the danger of the drive, than surviving to make it back home? It was those rivermen who were their own worst enemies in their attempts to run the rushing rapids, or when deciding to go over the falls for which batteaus were never intended. They took these risks in many cases for nothing more than bragging rights. It was those times when the river merely obliged and either granted them their glory, or through some weakness, or error, she claimed the life of another Penobscot man.

These Penobscot men went to the woods where they labored from ice-out in the spring, and if the water level held sometimes through the Autumn. They would sluice, boom, and pick jams from before daylight until late in the night when they could see no more, or no longer could hold themselves upright due to sheer exhaustion. But, day after day, week after week, they would rise again in the dark hours before the next dawn to keep the logs floating towards Bangor. In the days before the steamers reached these waters, they moved millions of board-feet of logs by their own human power turning a capstan across the open water of Chesuncook, Ambajejus, North Twins, and Quakish Lakes. This was their river, it belonged to the two-hundred-plus men of the West Branch Drive, and, as the reader will discover, not even an armed poacher with a vendetta could stand in their way.

These Penobscot men survived on beans, salt pork, and hard bread – a meal they lived with four times a day and washed it down with the strongest of tea. They slept in open tents during the height of the Maine black fly season. They wore the same clothes on their backs from Chesuncook to Bangor, where they turned up thread-bare, bug-bitten, sunbaked, and exhausted after their laboring on the river had taken yet another season of their lives. Yet, to a man, even if christened with the name '*Dingbat*,' they were terribly able characters who helped build the economy of Maine and delivered the logs that built a nation through their sentence to the river. Their conviction was a pride – they were the men of the West Branch Drive - they did not *think* they were the best men, they *knew* no one was better on any river, and their river was the meanest, roughest, most unforgiving river there was – and they loved her.

The stories in this book represent an important part of Maine history and the people who made that history. Eckstorm knew this when she was writing, and she anticipated that documenting this way of life would be important before it was lost. She was correct. The men of these stories weren't celebrated as American folk heroes, yet they kept doing this dangerous work that had to be done. These river-drivers went to the woods for months at a time to drag, push, pull, and float logs from deep in the Maine woods to the cities of Old Town and Bangor. Sure, they did this to earn a living, or a part of their living, if you could call it that. Life was difficult for these early inhabitants of the state, and most had multiple jobs in order to support a family. A less-skilled, or unprepared riverman often arrived in Bangor further in debt, or barely breaking even at the end of the Drive. It was these men who had spent a good portion of their expected pay on boots, shirts, wool underwear, and supplies that the *Company* conveniently sold to them while deep in the woods. These *on-credit sales* were made at a significant markup for the convenience and monopoly that was to be had at such a distance from any store. Luckily for these men, river driving wasn't the only way to put food on the table, for at other times of the year they were farmers, potato diggers, boat builders, mill workers, and fur traders. But driving logs was the most dangerous of their professions. It was dangerous for the kind of work it was, and it was dangerous for at times the men were their own worst enemies. They were a proud bunch, proud of the work they were doing, proud to work for men the likes of John Ross, and proud to a fault for belief in their skills as men of the Penobscot. No one, nowhere, was going to tell them rapids couldn't be run, or a river couldn't be demanded to move logs even in un-runnable low water. And certainly, no other man was better than them with a pole, cant-dog, or peavey.

Songs would be written about them. They themselves would sing ballads of their bosses, and the men they left behind, taken by the river from friends, wives, and mothers. These are their stories, not of one Penobscot *man*, but of the men who made up the fabric of the legendary man. Their lives were captured in these stories by Maine's best woods-history writer of the period, Fannie Hardy Eckstorm, and only she could have written about these men in this way. She knew the Penobscot Man, she knew the character that made the man; she knew these woods, she knew the river, she knew many of these men personally; and most of all, she herself was Penobscot. She also knew the *man* was dying. Eckstorm understood that while the river would continue year after year, and for nearly a half-century more men would drive logs down the foaming current, the Penobscot man would no longer be the one steering his batteau for Bangor. She knew others would take their place, men who would introduce steam power to move the logs, men who would mechanize the operation, but those men would not be made of the same thread as *The Penobscot Man* she was honoring in this book.

A few of these stories might seem to be about the work of river-driving, but don't be fooled. There is no doubt Eckstorm knew the methods and could describe the daily operations of a log drive, but that was not her purpose in writing this book. Rather, she was immortalizing the character of the men, and not the mechanics of breaking a jam, or handling a boat in the rapids. With a flair for telling a story, Eckstorm created this historical documentary of fascinating river occurrences the way they happened, or as close as anyone ever described them in writing. While the stories may seem independent from one another, for they happened over a forty-year timeframe, this was life as it was on the Penobscot in the mid to late 1800s, when such happenings were nearly yearly occurrences on the river, with only some of the men who played these parts being different each season. Although she was not on the river for all but one of the stories, Eckstorm in her methodical and fact-finding way brings to life these days on the Penobscot so that the reader may experience a period of time when river-drivers and lumbermen in the hundreds marched through the north woods.

While the title of the book is *The Penobscot Man*, the focus is not on a singular man, nor is it focused on the main branch of the river known as, *The Penobscot*. The Penobscot is not a single thread of water that runs cleanly through Maine. When Mainers speak of The Penobscot, you have to know the speaker and the context of a story to know where on the river you might be. If you visit Maine and what you experience is the waterfront of the Penobscot River near Bangor, or the river below as you drive over it on I-95, or from the high vantage point of the Penobscot River Observatory, what you see is not the character of the river where the stories in this book take place. By the time the river reaches those locations, she has been tamed by the wide swath of land she long ago claimed as her own. To discover the river of these stories the reader must travel upriver, nearly two hundred miles, deep in the Maine north woods.

The Penobscot River is made up of four branches – the North, South, East, and West. When added together the branches form the 270-mile-long river, making it the longest river that is entirely within the borders of Maine. The majority of the stories in this book, as far as definitive locations can be ascertained, occur on the West Branch. This branch, the longest of all four, runs from Seboomook Lake, then north of Moosehead Lake, and south of Katahdin where the river's character is one of canyons, rapids, and waterfalls, and on to Medway where it joins its sister, the East Branch. The branches of the river are detailed with a corresponding map in the Appendix. While the rivermen and lumbermen were not opposed to working the other branches, it was the West Branch, for its location to the prime lumbering, that became a famous highway for the river drives of the 19th and first half of the 20th centuries.

In the early years, and up until the turn of the 1900s, the lumber industry in this region of Maine was comprised mostly of independent lumber operators. These businesses formed the consortium known as the Penobscot Log-Driving Association (P.L.D.). Originally, the P. L. D. held the charter for log drives on the Penobscot river, granted by the State of Maine. Men from various companies would work alongside one another as contractors, moving logs which were marked for sorting at the booms down river. Those who worked on the West Branch were part of the fraternity known as **The West Branch Drive**. This Drive was made up of the A-Team, they were the best men, or in woodsmen terms – terribly-able men. They had to be, for this branch of the river was the most unforgiving, or in their view, the most challenging, and so, to their sense of adventure – the only river to drive on.

As the title of this new edition indicates, this is a book about life and death, and as such, not all of the stories have happy endings. It was not Eckstorm's purpose to write a love story about the men of the river, nor was she intending to make heroes of these men through fictionalized accounts. Oh, these stories may read like fiction with the elements of danger, excitement, mystery, and the unknown, but these are all true stories. And aren't those the types of stories which make the most interesting of reading when written correctly? For this type of writing Eckstorm had a gift, and she left to us through her words a way to remember, well beyond the handful of men she mentions, an entire class of men who did a job because the job had to be done, regardless of the danger. For that, Maine depended on the men of the West Branch Drive, and they all were the *Penobscot Man*.

Before this new edition, *The Penobscot Man* had been re-released by other publishers. However, the prior releases did nothing more than reprint copies of the pages of the original work, with no attempt to enhance the book for the current generation of readers. In this edition, the editor has provided a quality version with new material, information, and photographs. Although the writing of Eckstorm is not well known, and while there may not be a wide reader audience for a book of this topic, the writing and history deserved a new life. And so began a year-long project to research the original work, the stories, and further delve into the writer that Eckstorm was, all resulting in this commemorative annotated edition of a classic Maine book.

When originally released in 1904, this book received many positive reviews, but like most books, Eckstorm weathered her share of negative criticism, a topic she will cover herself later in this edition. Even following Eckstorm's passing there have been unfair characterizations of her work by some who have claimed that she was not a true historian, but an amateur folklorist. Had she had the opportunity, this mis-characterization would have been directly addressed by Eckstorm, who had written of herself in her essay on Katahdin legends, "Without pretending to be a student of folklore, and so passing no judgments in a field not my own, I wish to collate the versions of the Katahdin myths drawn from aboriginal sources, to make as clear as I can the Indian conceptions, and to add a little that I have gleaned in a long acquaintance with the Penobscot Indians."[1] By her own account, she was not writing folklore, she was writing history, legends, and experiences of others. Academics and critics who place her solely as a folklorist do not know her work enough to make such judgements.

Eckstorm may not have gone to college as a history major, but her broad knowledge of the world, literature, the arts, and her surroundings more than qualify her as a person who could write about Maine history. In fact, since she was interviewing and writing about people who had lived in her lifetime, it can be argued she was writing about current events, making her exponentially more qualified than a modern-day professor whose only experience with life in the 1800s is based on the work of others. Fannie Hardy Eckstorm did not write these accounts based on newspaper stories, journal articles, or other books. No, she went directly to the source, to the woodsmen, to the river-driver, to the lumbermen, and to the river. Mind you, this was the late 1800s, a time when having a woman visit a lumber camp, or a log drive, was unheard of. A number of the other stories she compiled by listening to the men who visited the home of her father, Manly Hardy, or directly from her father who knew a good number of the men depicted in these accounts. Her writings are interesting, informative, and she preserved a good deal of valuable knowledge on Maine Native American place-names, culture, and in this book the lives of many brave and hard-working Mainers and those who came to Maine to do this work. Her words and books are worth

---

[1] In, *Katahdin, Pamola, & Whiskey Jack – Stories and Legends from the Maine Woods*, Burnt Jacket Publishing, (2021).

the effort to preserve for readers of a new generation and I am pleased to bring the river-drivers to life again.

In the end we must remember that while Eckstorm was writing to capture history, and to make history interesting, she wanted these stories to be widely read, and her intent never was an academic research treatise. With this in mind, she brought these men to life with her characterizations and dialogue. In a paper by Edward D. Ives (1925-2009), a respected and fair University of Maine Professor, who was considered an expert on folklore, especially in Maine, wrote this about Eckstorm's story, *Lugging Boat on Sowadnehunk*, "The style is literary, and Mrs. Eckstorm is not above imagining a conversation or two, but my experience is that she can be depended on when it comes to "what really happened," especially on the level of the general story. She was far too concerned that readers in the know — among them the great John Ross himself — would approve her story to have fudged her facts."[2]

And there you have it. No matter if some 'literary critic' did not 'get' the book, the stories, or her purpose, Ives made two important points in his summary. First, Eckstorm could be depended on; and second, these stories were published when many of the men were still alive to read them, the men who were there, on the days these events actually occurred. These were the true Penobscot Men, men who understood the essence of the story, even if the conversations were not exactly as they occurred. Eckstorm **was** an historian and she was terribly able to tell a wicked good story.

---

[2] In, "The Only Man": Skill and Bravado on the River-Drive, Edward D. Ives, Maine History, Vol 41. No. 1, (2002).

There is one significant change in this edition to the original text, a change I considered long and hard about that I must inform the reader. Eckstorm had written her dialogue as the characters pronunciation sounded at the time. This meant the book included some sentences that were written as: "And by Judas' hemp, an' two selectmen, a yoke of oxen, an' an old snag throwed in, but p'raps that wa'n't no sight to see!" And this example is a sentence *light* on such pronounced-typing. I discovered that this dialogue was troublesome to the flow of the text to some readers. While I appreciate the historical context of the pronunciation, and the diligence it must have taken Eckstorm to accurately transcribe the language, I decided to edit select dialogue into a more readable format, which in no way changes the meaning of the stories. First, this change is made so that more readers will enjoy the stories. Second, the original book, without the new material of this annotated edition is available through an internet search, and the interested reader can reference those copies to compare the original to this edited version.

An exciting change to this annotated edition is the inclusion of Maine woods ballads. These ballads are old songs of the 1800s, many of which have unknown authorship, dates, and varying lyrics. A ballad, while often sung, wasn't always written to rhyme, for the telling of a story came before the need to perfect lyrical rhythm. But the men who crafted the verses had a pride in their poetry, not unlike the well-kept edge of their axes. As Eckstorm spent a good number of years in her later life documenting ballads of the woodsmen, the editor felt it was fitting to include a selection of these songs in this edition. The book, *Minstrelsy of Maine*, by Fannie Hardy Eckstorm and Mary Winslow Smyth includes background and notes on the origination of many woodsmen ballads that may interest the reader and researcher. When the men were in the woods, the singing of ballads was their entertainment. It should be no surprise then, that a boss of the drive would pay a woodsman a higher wage if he could carry a tune, for a crew that was happy with the food from the cook, and kept busy singing in the evenings, kept out of trouble.

This book has been my largest undertaking to date to publish an annotated edition of a classic book. Eckstorm's writing certainly needed little editing, but I found the topics so engaging, and her own drive for detail so specific, that I dug deeper, researched wider, and agonized over some of the notes compiled for these stories. No project such as this gets done without assistance. Again, I acknowledge the staff at the University of Maine Fogler Library, Special Collections Department, particularly, Ms. Desiree Butterfield-Nagy. From Ms. Butterfield-Nagy, no question ever went unanswered and she even went so far as to prepare research materials prior to my library visit. I appreciate that she dug deep in the archives for requested photos and was always a wealth of knowledge. I thank my wife, Meredith, for proofreading assistance; her input is always spot on where improvements are needed.

In publishing this book, I had the pleasure of making several new acquaintances who helped bring this edition to print. First, to Cheryl Derico, a lover of the Maine outdoors, goes the credit for the beautiful cover photo. Cheryl took this picture at the exact spot where the West Branch of the Penobscot River begins. Thank you, Cheryl for seeing where those roads would take you and sharing your art.

The photo on the back cover of the Ripogenus rapids just after the dam is courtesy of Mary Louise Osborne. That picture shows the torrent of water through the narrow canyon, and provides an idea of the power of the water along Ripogenus Gorge.

For those readers who have read my other works, both fiction and non-fiction, you will know that the region for these stories is for me a special place. The West Branch of the Penobscot River, and particularly the Ripogenus Dam location, are close to where I have spent many of my own days exploring the north woods around Moosehead Lake and northern Maine. The Eckstorm personal story "Clump of Posies," takes place between Greenville and Ripogenus and was of particular interest to the editor. That chapter required additional research and was an enjoyable challenge to piece together various sources of information.

If you ever get the chance to visit this beautiful and vast region of Maine, drive the Golden Road and take opportunities to stop along the way to view the falls, rapids, and canyons of the West Branch.[3] As you stand there listening to the torrent of water, feeling the powerful vibrations sending shock waves through the bedrock, maybe feeling the icy spray on your cheeks, try to imagine hundreds of men, moving millions of board-feet of logs through those narrow passes, breaking jams, riding logs, poling batteaus over falls and swirling rapids. As you stand there, imagine how some of them would be stranded on a log jam, maybe even thrown into the water, their life depending on the skill of their fellow rivermen to save them from the power of the West Branch of the Penobscot River.

Tommy Carbone

Greenville, Maine
January 2022

---

[3] Note: The Golden Road is a graded gravel road with no vehicle services. Visitors are advised to prepare and plan accordingly.

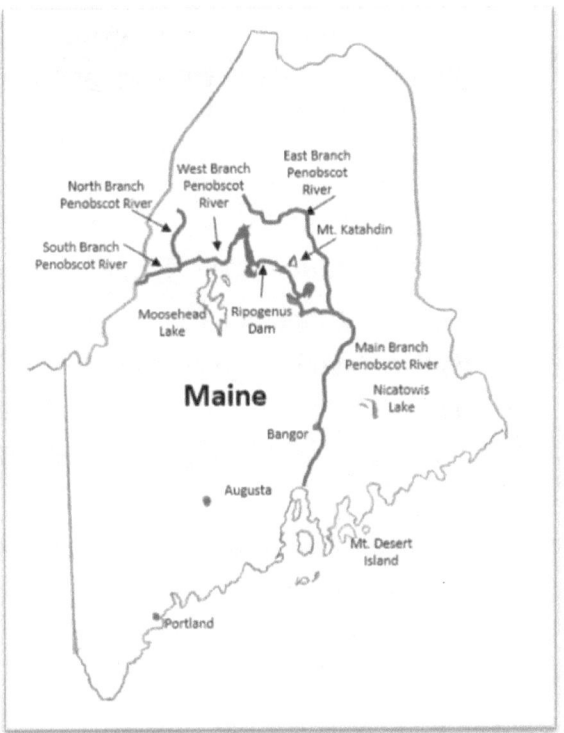

PENOBSCOT RIVER - MAINE

The area of Maine described by the stories in this book extends from Greenville at the south end of Moosehead Lake, and mainly along the West Branch of the Penobscot River, with certain references to the East Branch and of course at the end of the log drive in Bangor. One story, for which it will be obvious, takes place in another New England State.

The Penobscot River is comprised of four branches, the South, North, East, and West. The appendix includes details on each branch.

Selected books by and about
FANNIE HARDY ECKSTORM

- The Bird Book (1901)
- Woodpeckers (1901)
- The Penobscot Man (1904, 1924)
- David Libbey: Penobscot Woodsman and River Driver. True American types. (1907)
- Minstrelsy of Maine: Folk-songs and Ballads of the Woods and the Coast *with* Mary Winslow Smyth (1927)
- British Ballads from Maine *with* Mary Winslow Smyth and Barry, Phillips (1929)
- The Handicrafts of the Modern Indians of Maine (1932)
- Indian Place-Names of the Penobscot Valley and the Maine Coast (1941)
- Old John Neptune and Other Maine Indian Shamans (1945)
- Katahdin Pamola & Whiskey Jack – Stories and Legends from the Maine Woods – Tommy Carbone (2021)
- Exploring the Maine Woods – The Hardy Family Expedition to the Machias Lakes – Tommy Carbone (2021)
- David Stone Libbey - He Was Penobscot – Tommy Carbone (2022)

FANNIE HARDY ECKSTORM

(1865 – 1946)

FANNIE HARDY ECKSTORM, 1888.
Photo taken the year of her college graduation.
Image courtesy of Special Collections, Raymond H. Fogler Library, University of Maine

Fannie Pearson Hardy Eckstorm was born on June 18, 1865, in Brewer, Maine to Manly Hardy and Emmeline Wheeler Hardy. She was the oldest of their six children and attended the public schools in Brewer, Maine and Abbot Academy (Andover, MA). In 1888, she graduated from Smith

College (North Hampton, MA), was subsequently employed as the superintendent of schools in Brewer, and for a time worked in the book department of the D.C. Heath Publishing Company in Boston.

In 1893 she married Rev. Jacob A. Eckstorm of Chicago. Seven years later, following the passing of her husband, Fannie Eckstorm and her two children relocated from Providence R.I., back to Brewer, Maine.

Throughout her life, Eckstorm studied Maine Indians, folklore and natural history. It was an area she knew well, based on her experiences with her father in the woods and her personal acquaintance with the Native Americans and woodsmen. This book is only one example of her deep knowledge in these subjects.

In 1886 she became an associate member of the American Ornithologists Union, the first woman admitted as such. Before graduating Smith College, she co-founded the college chapter of the Audubon Society. Her interest in birds would be a lifelong pursuit, from which she published two books, *The Woodpeckers* (1901) and *The Bird Book* (1901).

She had a deep interest in documenting Maine folksongs and woods songs, and in collaboration with others, two books resulted from her efforts, *Minstrelsy of Maine* (1927) and *British Ballads from Maine* (1929).

Eckstorm had many other community interests, among them, she was a founder and vice-president of the Folk-Song Society of the Northeast, a founding member of the public library in Brewer, and was an honorary member of the Maine Historical Society. Through her association with the local Penobscot Indians, many of whom were friends of her father's, and her grandfather's, she studied and documented Native American culture. Her interest was in preserving their history, their way of life and how they shaped Maine.

Eckstorm wrote three books on the subject:

- Of Indian Place-Names of the Penobscot Valley and the Maine Coast (1941).
- Old John Neptune and Other Maine Indian Shamans (1945).
- The Handicrafts of the Modern Indians of Maine (1932)

Eckstorm also wrote for magazines such as *Forest and Stream, Sprague's Journal of Maine History, The Northern, The New England Quarterly, The Atlantic Monthly* and other publications and newspapers. Her knowledge was well respected by readers and she was never one to shy away from controversy in dealing with facts in her writing, or correcting others. The style of her writing is genuine and her documenting of Maine history has been trusted for over a century.

On December 31, 1946 Fannie Hardy Eckstorm passed away. She had been residing in the same home in Brewer since moving there in 1900. She was 81 years young.

DEDICATION

To

John Ross

And

The West Branch Drive

"That you and yours may know

From me and mine, how dear a debt

We owed you, and are owing yet

To you and yours, and still would owe."

Annotated Edition Note:

This dedication may seem on the surface to be thanking John Ross and the men of the West Branch Drive for taking risks, doing what had to be done on the river, in all sorts of weather and conditions, to get the logs to market. And maybe on one level it is. But in this small dedication, Fannie Hardy Eckstorm is thanking the Drive on a much deeper level for protecting her life, and the life of her father. The gratitude expressed here is no small matter. Revenge in the woods is a dangerous enemy and Eckstorm, when she was still Hardy, and a young woman, had made an enemy from writing the truth, and an 'accident' in the forests of 1891 would have been a hard thing to prove. Eckstorm will have more to write about this dedication in the final chapter of this book, which was not published in the original 1904 edition, but added only to the 1924 re-release.

"For something about them, and the idea of them, smote my American heart, and I have never forgotten it, nor ever shall, as long as I live. In their flesh our natural passions ran tumultuous; but in their spirit sat hidden a true nobility, and often beneath its unexpected shining their figures took on heroic stature.
— Owen Wister, The Virginian.

"And when I went to bid him welcome home, he told me that the history of your worship was already printed in books, under the title of 'Don Quixote de la Mancha;' and he says it mentions me too by my very name of Sancho Panza, and also the Lady Dulcinea del Toboso, and several other private matters which passed between us two only; insomuch that I crossed myself out of pure amazement, to think how the historian who wrote it should come to know them."
— The Adventures of Don Quixote de la Mancha, Part II. book i. chap. 2.

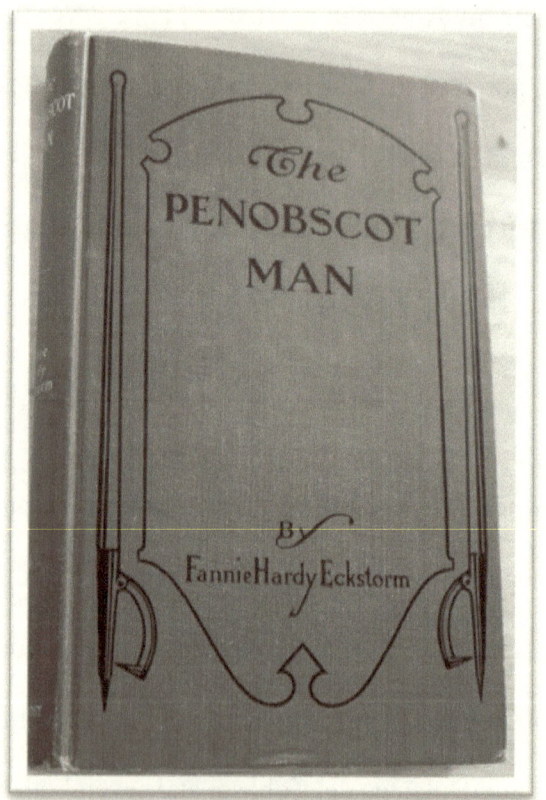

1924 EDITION COVER

(Editor's Collection)

Notice the Peavey marking the right and left border.

INTRODUCTORY

THE question is sometimes asked why a state like Maine, so sparsely settled, poor, weak in all external aids, can send forth such throngs of masterful men, who, east and west, step to the front to lead, direct, and do. We who were brought up among pine-trees and granite know the secret of their success. It comes not wholly by taking thought: it is in the blood.

Here are stories of men, the kind we have yet a-plenty, who die unknown and unnoticed; and every tale is a true one, — not the chance report of strangers, the gleanings of recent acquaintance, the aftermath of hearsay, the enlargements of a fading tradition; but the tales of men who tended me in babyhood, who crooned to me old slumber-songs, who brought me gifts from the woods, who wrought me little keepsakes, or amused my childish hours, — stories which, having gathered them from this one and that one who saw the deed, I have bound into a garland to lay upon their graves.[4]

---

[4] The tribute of this paragraph is to the men who are the subject of the stories. It is not only a tribute to those she knew, or her family knew, but to an entire class of woodsmen, river-drivers, hunters, guides, and the like who Eckstorm had a great respect for and crowned them all, *The Penobscot Man*.

Such tales are numberless; choice becomes invidious unless rigidly limited, and therefore, since the old West Branch Drive is no more, I have chosen solely among its members, and have strung these tales, like beads of remembrance, upon one thread, — of which we who love it never tire, — the River.

These are stories told with little art. In the long run, the books that lie closest to the facts have the advantage. It is lovely to be beautiful, but it is essential to be true. The events are actual occurrences; the names, real names; the places anyone may see at any time. Yet each story is not merely personal and solitary, but illustrates typically some trait of the whole class. Their virtues are not magnified, their faults are not denied; in black and white, for good or evil, they stand here as they lived, — as they themselves would prefer to stand on record. So they acted, thus they felt, these were their thoughts upon grave subjects: and it may be that the Penobscot man is a better, wiser, more serious man than even his contemporaries have judged him to be.

But one thing, from which we may glimpse the secret of the Maine man's success, cannot fail to impress whoever reads these tales, and that is that he dies so cheerfully. He is not concerned about himself, nor about his future in another world, so much as about his work here. For Death, he does not fear it. Sometimes he courts it, sometimes he scoffs it, sometimes he defies it; but always, always his work comes first. And however low it may seem, however crude, however inferior to that of the man of more culture, finer perception, larger opportunity, he likewise lives for an Ideal. For honor, for friendship, for emulation, for sport, for duty, for grim, stern, granite obstinacy, he risks his life and wills his will into achievement, or dies for his failure.

His morals — we will not speak of them; his aspirations — he rarely talks of them; his religion — well. Heaven send that there be many of us as sound in the righteousness of charity as he! But his real strength is in his devotion to what he sets out to do. As Stevenson says of our late lamented Alan Breck: "Alan's morals were all tail-first; but he was ready to give his life for them, such as they were."[5] And this is ever the litany of brave men the world over: A clear conscience, a good cause, O Lord, and, if it need me, the chance to die for it.

Fannie Pearson Hardy Eckstorm

Brewer, Maine
1904

---

[5] Alan Breck Stewart (1711 – 1791) was a Scottish soldier wrongly accused of the 1752 murder of a royal agent. He inspired the character of the name Alan Breck, the adventurer in the novel *Kidnapped* by Robert Louis Stevenson.

LUMBERMAN & RIVER-DRIVER TERMS

The following are wood-terms of interest with many additional terms defined within the chapter footnotes as appropriate.

- Bar-room – The bunk room at the logging camp. Also called, the ram-pasture.
- Batteau – The long double-ended boat of similar appearance used on the log drives. Usually with a crew of five to eight men. Sometimes spelled *bateau,* or *bateaux*.
- Boom – A string of logs that when chained together can contain the logs being floated across a lake. These booms could be many acres in diameter when being dragged across lakes such as Chesuncook or Moosehead. The same term was used for a boom location where logs were held and sorting according to log marks. Often there was a boom house at these locations. The Ambajejus Lake boom house was built circa 1907, and is on the National Register of Historic Places.
- Cant-dog, or cant-hook – Similar to a peavey except the end has a blunt tip, or right angle tip. It also has a rotating metal hook, the dog.
- Capstan – the wooden spool set on a raft about which an anchor line was wound on when booming logs.
- Carry – the path or narrow tote road along the river, or around a dam, that is used to carry boats and supplies when the river can not be run due to falls or rapids. Also a road connecting one waterbody to another. The most infamous in Maine is the Mud Pond Carry at Chamberlain Lake.
- Caulks – Or spelled *calks*, or *corks*, these are the spikes set in the soles of the lumberman's boots. Boots such as these are still worn today by those in the lumbering and forestry industry.
- Deacon Seat – The log bench that ran along the bunks in the lumberman's cabin.

- Deadwater – area of a river or stream where little to no current is apparent.
- Depot Camp – a place where supplies and equipment are stored.
- Drive – A log drive with no specific reference to any river.
- Handled boat – the dialect used by a riverman who was in charge of a boat. If one said, including the article, "I handled *a* boat on the West Branch," the speaker was deemed greener than moss on the north side of a tree.
- Hull-cook – is the cook's assistant; also called a 'cookee.'
- Jack Mann Load – an accumulation of things to carry of odd and inconvenient sizes.
- Logon – a loggers term, a derivative of lagoon. A deadwater, or a shallow place with no outlet, where sometimes logs were floated to hold or be sorted. Sometimes spelled as logan, or poke-logan.
- Peavey – a cant-hook (or cant-dog) with a point at the end.

- Picaroon – A steel hook with large handle. Mainly was used to pull the shorter pulpwood logs to the handler.
- Pike-pole – A long pole with a sharp spike at the end. This tool saw significant use in sluicing logs over a dam.
- P. L. D. – was the Penobscot Log-Driving Association, a formation of independent lumbermen. The P.L.D. held the charter to the Penobscot River from the State of Maine. This preceded Great Northern and the court battles.
- Pulpwood – the smaller logs, usually four-feet in length used for pulp at the mills to make paper.
- Roll dam – or 'rolling dam' is a dam without gates, built at the head of falls or rough water, on the smaller rivers and streams. It cannot retain any head of water, like a dam with gates, but by increasing the depth of water above the falls and presenting a smooth lip to the current, keeps the logs from stranding at the head of a 'pitch.' The purpose is to help prevent jams from

forming. The logs ride up an incline of smooth timber and slide down a similar incline, making the 'roll.' Jams still formed at these locations, but it did reduce the frequency.
- Run dam – logs built into the bank of a river at a curve so that the logs "run into" the bank and continue downstream instead of jamming.
- Sluice – the act of getting the logs over a dam; or 'sluiced' through the chute or gate.
- The Rear – means the up-stream end of the log-drive. The down-stream end was 'the head of the drive,' and the logs between were 'the main drive.'
- Scaler – The person who measured the board-feet of logs.
- Tote-road – The road used to reach the woods and the rivers where the logging operations occurred. Called so because the supplies and equipment were 'toted' over these roads.
- Turkeys – 'grips,' 'suitcases,' bags of clothing. The 'Kennebecker' was a name given to a particular fashion of a luggage bag.
- Wangan – the camp store of supplies. Could include anything the operation would need while in the woods, from beans to boots, and everything in between. Could refer to the boats used to lug the supplies, the company store at the camp, or even the lumberman's outfit of his personal supplies. The men of the lumbering operations would often complain about the prices the company charged, since purchases from the wangan were their only choice. By the end of the drive much of their pay was owed to the company for new boots, tobacco, shirts, buttons, and other items lost or needed, that they had to buy while out in the woods.
- Yard – the place where lumber was stored, sometimes the location next to a river where lumber was piled during the winter to wait the spring drive.

I — THE LOGGER'S BOAST

THIS edition fittingly begins with a ballad that sums up the feelings of the Maine lumbermen and river-drivers, who retire to become story-tellers.

The Logger's Boast
Published 1851, Author Unknown

Come, all ye sons of freedom throughout the State of Maine,
Come, all ye gallant lumbermen, and listen to my strain;
On the banks of the Penobscot, where the rapid waters flow,
O! we'll range the wild woods over, and a lumbering will go;
And a lumbering we'll go, so a lumbering will go,
O! we'll range the wild woods over while a lumbering we go.

When the white frost gilds the valleys, the cold congeals the flood;
When many men have naught to do to earn their families bread;
When the swollen streams are frozen, and the hills are clad with snow,
O! we'll range the wild woods over, and a lumbering we will go;
And a lumbering we'll go, so a lumbering we will go,
O! we'll range the wild woods over, while a lumbering we go.

When you pass through the dense city, and pity all you meet,
To hear their teeth chattering as they hurry down the street;
In the red frost-proof flannel we're encased from top to toe,
While we range the wild woods over, and a lumbering we go;
And a lumbering we'll go, so a lumbering will go,
O! we'll range the wild woods over while a lumbering we go.

You may boast of your gay parties, your pleasures, and your plays,
And pity us poor lumbermen while dashing in your sleighs;
We want no better pastime than to chase the buck and doe;
O! we'll range the wild woods over, and a lumbering we will go;
And a lumbering we'll go, so a lumbering will go,
O! we'll range the wild woods over while a lumbering we go.

The music of our burnished ax shall make the woods resound,
And many a lofty ancient Pine will tumble to the ground;
At night, ho! round our good camp-fire we will sing while rude winds blow:
O! we'll range the wild woods over while a lumbering we go.
And a lumbering we'll go, so a lumbering will go,
O! we'll range the wild woods over while a lumbering we go.

When winter's snows are melted, and the ice-bound streams are free,
We'll run our logs to market, then haste our friends to see;
How kindly true hearts welcome us, our wives and children too,
We will spend with these the summer, and once more a lumbering go;
And a lumbering we'll go, so a lumbering we will go,
We will spend with these the summer, and once more a lumbering go.

And when upon the long-hid soil the white Pines disappear,
We will cut the other forest trees, and sow whereon we clear;
Our grain shall wave o'er valleys rich, our herds bedot the hills,
When our feet no more are hurried on to tend the driving mills;
Then no more a lumbering go, so no more a lumbering go,
When our feet no more are hurried on to tend the driving mills.

When our youthful days are ended, we will cease from winter toil,
And each one through the summer warm will till the virgin soil;
We've enough to eat, to drink, to wear, content through life to go,
Then we'll tell our wild adventures o'er, and no more a lumbering go;
And no more a lumbering go, so no more a lumbering go,
O! we'll tell our wild adventures o'er, so no more a lumbering go.

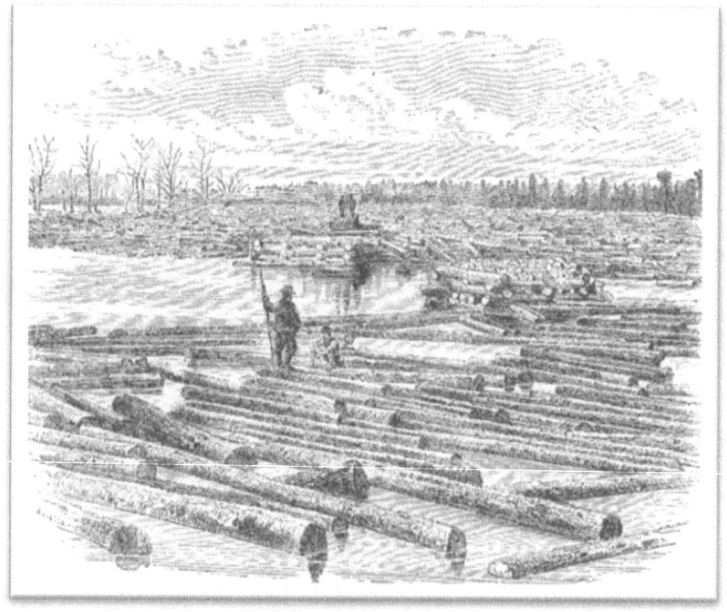

A BOOM

From, Thomas S. Steele's *Canoe and Camera*
Annotated Edition from Burnt Jacket Publishing (2020)

II — LUGGING BOAT ON SOWADNEHUNK

By water we are surrounded,
But from it we are protected,
And if we don't get wrecked
All trouble we resign;
For the rapids that we run
Seem to us no more than fun,
For our troubles are all done
When we're on our rafts of Pine.

from, The Falling of the Pine

This is a Penobscot story.

WHEN the campfire is lighted, and the smoke draws straight up without baffling, and the branches overhead move only as the rising current of heat fans them; and then if the talk veers round to stories of crack watermen, and the guides — speaking more to each other than to you — declare that it was Big Sebattis Mitchell who first ran the falls at Sowadnehunk, (though full twenty years before, John Ross himself had put a boat over and come out right side up), do not, while they are debating whose is the credit of being first, let slip your chance to hear a better tale. Bid them go on and tell you how Joe Attien, who was

Thoreau's guide, and his men who followed after and who failed, were the ones who made that day memorable.

And if your guides are Penobscot men, they will tell it as Penobscot men should, as if there were no merit in the deed beyond what any man might attain to, as if the least a man should do was to throw away his life on a reckless dare, and count it well spent when so lavished. For so are these men made, and as it was in those days of the beginning, so is it yet even to the present among us.

You will have heard, no doubt, of Sebattis, he who from his bulk was called by the whites Big Sebat, and from his lazy shrewdness was nicknamed by his tribesmen Ahwassus the Bear. Huge and round he was, like the beast he was named for, but strong and wise, and in his dark, flat face and small, twinkling eyes there were resources, ambitions, schemes.

Scores of you who read this will recollect the place. In memory you will again pass down the West Branch in your canoe, past Ripogenus, past Ambajemackomas, past the Horse Race, into the welcome deadwater above Nesowadnehunk.[6] There, waiting in expectancy for that glorious revelation of Katahdin which bursts upon you above Abol, that marvelous picture of the giant towering in majestic isolation, with its white "slide" ascending like a ladder to the heavens, you forgot yourself, did not hear the tumult of falling waters, did not see the smooth lip of the fall sucking down, were unconscious that just before you were the falls of Sowadnehunk. Then, where the river veers sharply to the right, you felt the guide spring on his

---

[6] For further information on Maine place names given in this book, the reader is referred to the following text for cross references, information, and the original meanings for the words. *Woods and Lakes of Maine – A Trip from Moosehead Lake to New Brunswick in a Birch-Bark Canoe. Annotated Edition*, Burnt Jacket Publishing, (2020).

paddle as he made the carry by a margin, and you realized what it would have been to drift unguided over those falls.

So it has always been, — the sharp bend of the river to the right, blue, smooth, dazzling; the carry at the left, bare, broad, yellow-earthed. Crossing it forty rods, you cut off the river again, and see above you to the right the straight fall, both upper and lower pitches almost as sheer as mill-dams, and in front the angry boil of a swift current among great and thickset rocks. So it always stays in memory, — at one end the blue river, smooth and placid, and the yellow carry; at the other, the white hubbub of tossing rapids below perpendicular falls.

One May day long ago, two boats' crews came down to the carry and lugged across. They had already lugged three miles on Ripogenus, and a half mile on Ambajemackomas, besides the shorter carry past Chesuncook Dam; they had begun to know what lugging a boat meant. The day was hot, — no breeze, no shade; it was getting along toward noon, and they had turned out, as usual, at three in the morning. They were tired, — tired, faint, hot; weary with the fatigue that stiffens the back and makes the feet hang heavy; weary, too, with the monotony of weeks of dangerous toil without a single day of rest, the weariness that gets upon the brain and makes the eyes go blurry; weary because they were just where they were, and that old river would keep flowing on to Doomsday, always drowning men and making them chafe their shoulders lugging heavy boats. There was not a man of them who could not show upon his shoulder a great red spot where the pole used in lugging boat, or the end of an oar on which barrels of pork or flour had been slung in carrying wangan,[7] had bruised and abraded it. And now it was more lugging, and ahead were Abol and Pockwockamus and Debsconeag and Passangamet and Ambajejus and Fowler's and

---

[7] Wangan – see lumbering and river-driver terms.

— there are, indeed, how many of them! The over-weary always add to present burdens that mountain of future toil.

So it was in silence that they took out the oars and seats, the paddles and peavies and pickaroons, drew the boats up and drained them of all water, then, resting a moment, straightened their backs, rubbed the sore shoulders that so soon must take up the burden again, and ran their fingers through their damp hair. One or two swore a little as relieving their minds, and when they bent to lift the boat, one spoke for all the others.

"By jinkey-boy!" said he, creating a new and fantastic oath, "but I do believe I'd rather be in hell today, with ninety devils around me, than sole-carting on this carry."

That was the way they all felt. It is mighty weary business to lug on carries. For a driving-boat is a heavy lady to carry. The great Maynards,[8] wet, weigh eight to nine hundred pounds, and they put on twelve men, a double crew, to carry one. The old two-streakers (that is, boats with two boards to a side where the big Maynards had three) were not nearly so heavy, and on short carries like Sowadnehunk were lugged by their own crews, whether of four men or six; but diminishing the crew left each man with as great a burden. A short man at the bow, another at the stern, with the taller ones amidships under the curve of the gunwale if they were lugging without poles, or by twos fore, aft, and amidships for six men lugging with poles, was the usual way they carried their boats; and it was "Steady, boys, steady; now hoist her!" — "Easy, now, easy; hold hard!" for going downhill she overrode John and Jim at the bow, and going up a rise Jack and Joe at the stern felt her crushing their shoulders, and when the ground was uneven with rocks and cradle-knolls, and she reeled and sagged, then the men at the sides caught the

---

[8] Maynard boats were designed and built by Hosea B. Maynard. These boats were over thirty feet long and were the favorite of the West Branch Drive.

whole weight on one or the other of them. Nothing on the drive speaks so eloquently of hard work as the purple, sweat-stained cross on the backs of the men's red shirts, where the suspenders have made their mark; they get this in lugging boat on carries.

But they bent their backs to it, wriggled the boat up and forward to her place, each crew its own boat, and staggered on, feet bracing out, and spike-soled shoes ploughing the dirt and scratching on the rocks. They looked like huge hundred-leggers, Brobdingnagian insects,[9] that were crawling over that yellow carry with all their legs clawing uncertainly and bracing for a foothold. The head boat crowded Bill Halpin upon a rock so hard that he fell and barked his shins on the granite; that dropped the weight suddenly upon Jerry Durgan's shoulder, so that a good two inches of skin was rasped off clean where it had been blistered before; little Tomah Soc stumbled in a hole, and not letting go his grip, threw up the other gunwale so that it half broke his partner's jaw. Those boats took all the mean revenges wherewith a driving-boat on land settles scores for the rough treatment it receives in the water.

They were lugging that May morning only because no boat could run those falls with any reasonable expectation of coming out right side up. For up to that time they had chiefly used the Wallace boat, built low and straight in the gunwale, raking only moderately at the bow and low in the side. It is related that when the great high-bowed Maynard batteaus were first put on the river, short old Jack Mann,[10] who was pensioned in his latter

---

[9] Brobdingnag is the fictional land of giants, in Gulliver's Travels by Jonathan Swift (1726). Here we can image human-sized insects carrying the boat across the carry.

[10] Jack Mann was a lumberman of some local fame. Eckstorm makes several references to him in her writing in this book as well as her essays compiled in, *Exploring the Maine Woods – The Hardy Family Expedition to the Machias Lakes*. A short story on

days by P. L. D.,[11] looked with high disfavor on the big, handsome craft, and then, rushing into the boat-shop, demanded an axe, an auger, and a handsaw.

"What's that for?" asked the foreman, suspecting that it was but one of Jack's devices for unburdening his mind in some memorable saying.

"Want 'em to cut armholes in that blasted boat," growled Jack, insinuating that the bows were above the head of a short man like himself.

But the old boat, — you may yet sometimes see the bones of one of them bleaching about the shores of inland ponds, or lying sun-cracked in the back yards of country farms, — stable and serviceable as she was, was no match for this handsome lady of today. They run the Arches of Ripogenus now with all their boats, and have done it for years; but at the time when Sebattis came down to Sowadnehunk, such water no man ever dreamed of running. It is likely enough that Sebattis, just back from a sixteen years' residence at Quoddy, did not know that it had ever been run successfully.

Be that as it may, when Sebattis and his bowman came down, the last of three boats, and held their batteau at the taking-out place a moment before they dragged her out and stripped her ready to lug, what Sebattis, as he sat in the stern with his paddle across his knees, said in Indian to his bowman was simply revolutionary.

---

placenames further immortalizing Jack Mann is added to the end of this chapter.

[11] FHE: The Penobscot Log-Driving Association, known as P. L. D. to distinguish it from P. L. A., the Penobscot Lumbering Association. It is always called either *P. L. D.* or *The Company*. It owns all dams, booms, etc., and annually sells the drive at auction to the bidder contracting to take the logs down at the lowest rate per thousand.

"Huh?" grunted his dark-faced partner, turning in great surprise; "You thought you wanted to run those falls? Plenty of rapid water on those there falls!"

The bowman had stated the case conservatively. That carry was there merely because men were not expected to run those falls and come out alive.

But the bowman's objection was not meant as a refusal: he knew Sebattis, that he was a good waterman, few better. A big, slow man, of tremendous momentum when once in motion, it was likely enough that all the years of his exile at Quoddy he had been planning just how he could run those falls, and if he spoke now, it was because this was the hour striking. In his own mind he had already performed the feat, and was receiving the congratulations of the crowd. It was no small advantage that he knew an audience of two boats' crews was waiting at the lower carry-end to testify, however grudgingly, to the authenticity of what he claimed to have done.

The bowman had faith in Sebattis; as he listened to the smooth stream of soft-cadenced Indian that cast silvery bonds about his reluctance and left him helpless to refuse (Sebattis being both an orator in a public and a powerful pleader in a private cause), the bowman caught the rhythm of the deed. It was all so easy to take their boat out into midstream, where the current favored them a little, to shoot her bow far out over the fall, and, as the crews ashore gaped in horrified amazement, to make her leap clear, as a horse leaps a hurdle. And then to fight their way through the smother of the whirlpool below, man against water, but such men as not every boat can put in bow and stern, such strong arms as do not hold every paddle, such great heads for management, such skill in water-craft as few attain.

This was the oration, with its Indian appeal to personal glory. It was, as Sebattis said, "Big thing" and he fired his bowman with the desire for glory. The Penobscot man, white man or Indian, dies with astonishing alacrity when he sees anything worth dying for. And the name of "crack waterman" is a shining mark to strive for.

Thus, at the upper end of the carry Sebattis and his bowman talked over at their leisure the chances of dying within five minutes. At the other end the two boats' crews lay among the blueberry bushes in the shade of shivering birch saplings and waited for Sebattis. It did not worry them that he was long in coming; they knew the leisurely Indian ways, and how unwilling, though he weighed hard upon two hundred and sixty, and had strength to correspond, was Big Sebattis to lug an extra pound. They pictured him draining his boat and sopping out with a swab of bracken the last dispensable ounce of water, then tilting her to the sun for a few minutes to steam out a trifle more before he whooped to them to come across and help him. It did not worry them to wait, — it was all one in the end: there would be carries to lug on long after they were dead and gone.

So, looking at the logs ricked up along the shores and cross-piled on the ledges, looking at the others drifting past, wallowing and thrashing in the wicked boil below the falls, they lounged and chaffed one another. Jerry Durgan was surreptitiously laying cool birch leaves on his abraded shoulder, and Bill Halpin was attentively, though silently, regarding his shins: there had been none too much stocking between him and that "big gray." The Indians, stretched out on their backs, gazed at the sky; nothing fretted them much. On one side, an Indian and an Irishman were having a passage at wit; on the other, two or three were arguing the ins and outs of a big fight up at 'Suncook[12] the winter before, and a Province man was

---

[12] Abbreviation for Chesuncook. The village on the shores of Chesuncook Lake was a north woods outpost and location of a supply farm.

colloguing with a Yankee on points of scriptural interpretation. It was such talk as might be overheard almost any time on the drive when men are resting at their ease.

"It was French Joe that nailed Billy; Billy he told me so," came from the group under the birches.

From among the Indians out in the sunlight arose a persuasive Irish voice.

"Why is it, Tomah, that when your folks are good Catholics, and our folks are good Catholics, you don't ever name your children Patrick and Bridget?"

And the reply came quick: "'Cause we hate the Irish so bad, you know!"

Off at the right they were wrangling about the construction of the Ark.

"And I'd just like to have seen that boat when they got her done," said the Yankee; "just one door an' one winder, and ventilated like Harvey Doane's school house. They caught him nailing all the windows down. How are you goin' to ventilate?' says they. 'Oh,' says he, 'the fresh air's a powerful circulatin' stuff; I calculate they'll carry the old air out in their pockets, and bring in enough fresh air in their caps to keep 'em goin'; 'And that was all they ever did get; as long as he was school agent. My scissors – and that ark! Three stories and all full of live-stock, and only one window, and that all battened down! Tell you what! I'd a hated to be Mr. Noah's family and had to stay in that ole Ark ten months and a half before they took the cover off! Fact! I read it all up once!"

Said another: "I don't seem to remember how she was built, except the way they run her seams. She must have been a jim-dickey house with the pitch all on the inside as well as on the outside o' her. Seems to me a boat ain't bettered none by a daub o'pitch where there ain't none needed."

"'T ain't the Ark as bothers me some," put in the Province man; "I reckon that flood business is pretty nigh straight, but I couldn't ever cipher out about that Tower of Babel thing. Man ask for a hod o' mortar,[13] an' like enough they'd send him up a barrel of gaspereau;[14] that's" —

The religious discussion broke off abruptly.

"Holy Hell! — Look a-comin'!" gasped the Yankee.

Man! but that was a sight to see! They got up and devoured it with their eyes.

On the verge of the fall hovered the batteau about to leap. Big Sebat and his bowman crouched to help her, like a rider lifting his horse to a leap. And their eyes were set with fierce excitement, their hands cleaved to their paddle handles, they felt the thrill that ran through the boat as they shot her clear, and, flying out beyond the curtain of the fall, they landed her in the yeasty rapids below.

Both on their feet then! And how they bent their paddles and whipped them from side to side, as it was "In!" — "Out!" — "Right!" — "Left!" to avoid the logs caught on the ledges and the great rocks that lay beneath the boils and snapped at them with their ugly fangs as they went flying past. The spray was on them; the surges crested over their gunwales; they sheered from the rock, but cut the wave that covered it and carried it inboard. And always it was "Right!" — "Left!" — "In!" — "Out!" as the greater danger drove them to seek the less.

But finally they ran her out through the tail of the boil, and fetched her ashore in a cove below the carry-end, out of sight of the men. She was full of water, barely afloat.

---

[13] A 'hod' is a tray, or three-sided box that has a pole to carry over the shoulder.

[14] Gaspereau, or Gasparot. Name of a common salt-water fish, as called by Acadian French. Also called alewife.

Would Sebattis own to the boys who were hurrying down through the bushes that he had escaped with his life only by the greatest luck? Not Sebattis!

"Now you bail her out with the paddles," said he to his bowman, and they swept her with their paddles as one might with a broom.

"Now you drain her out," commanded Sebattis, when they could lift the remaining weight, and they raised the bow and let the water run out over the slanting stern, all but a few pailfuls. "Better you let that stay," said the shrewd Sebattis.

It was quick work, but when the crew broke through the bushes, there stood Sebattis and his bowman leaning on their paddles like bronze caryatids,[15] one on either side of the boat. They might have been standing thus since the days of the Pharaohs, they were so at ease.

"Well, boys, how did you make it?" queried the first to arrive on the spot.

Sebattis smiled his simple, vacuous smile. "Oh, very good; she took in lil' water maybe."

"By gee, that ain't much water! Did she strike anything?"

Sebattis helped to turn her over. She had not a scratch upon her.

Then the men all looked again at the boat that had been over Sowadnehunk, and they all trooped back to the carry-end without saying much, two full batteau crews and Sebattis and his bowman. They did not talk. No man would have gained anything new by exchanging thoughts with his neighbor.

And when they came to the two boats drying in the sun, they looked one another in the eyes again. It was a foregone conclusion. Without a word they put their galled shoulders under the gunwales, lifted the heavy batteaus to their places, and

---

[15] Caryatids – a stone carving used as a support pillar; as in a Greek-style building

started back across that carry forty rods to the end they had just come from.

What for? It was that in his own esteem a Penobscot man will not stand second to any other man. They would not have it said that Sebattis Mitchell was the only man of them who had tried to run Sowadnehunk Falls.

So they put in again, six men to a boat, full crews, and in the stern of one stood Joe Attien, who was Thoreau's guide, and in the bow Steve Stanislaus, his cousin. That sets the date, — that it was back in 1870, — for it became the occasion for another and a sadder tale. If only Steve Stanislaus had held that place for the rest of the drive, it is little likely that we should have to tell the story of the death of Thoreau's guide.[16]

And they pushed out with their two boats and ran the falls.

But the luck that bore Sebattis safely through was not theirs. Both boats were swamped, battered on the rocks into kindling wood. Twelve men were thrown into the water, and pounded and swashed about among logs and rocks. Some by swimming, some by the aid of Sebattis and his boat, eleven of them got ashore, "a little damp," as no doubt the least exaggerative of them were willing to admit. The unlucky twelfth man they picked up later, quite undeniably drowned. And the boats were irretrievably smashed. Indeed, that was the part of the tale that rankled with Sebattis when he used to tell it.

"Very much she blamed it on us" (that is, himself) "that time John Ross." (Always to the Indian mind John Ross, the head contractor of the drive, was the power that commanded wind, logs, and weather.) "She don't care so much 'cause drowned a man, 'cause she can get plenty of men; but those there boats, she talk about very hard."

---

[16] On July 4th 1870, Joe Attien was drowned at Grand Falls, on the Penobscot near Millinocket. This story is told in a later chapter. Attien was sometimes spelled Aitteon, and currently as Attean.

That is how they look at such little deeds themselves. The man who led off gets the credit and the blame; he is the only one remembered. But to an outsider, what wins more than passing admiration is not the one man who succeeded, but the many who followed after and failed, who could not let well enough alone when there was a possible better to be achieved, but, on the welcome end of the carry, the end where all their troubles of galls and bruises and heavy burdens in the heat are over, pick up their boats without a word, not one man of them falling out, and lug them back a weary forty rods to fight another round with Death sooner than own themselves outdone.

HAULING A BATTEAU ON RIPOGENUS CARRY

Photo by Fannie Hardy Eckstorm, 1891.

In her journal, Eckstorm had noted that was the first year horses were used on the carry.

Image courtesy of Special Collections, Raymond H. Fogler Library, University of Maine

RIPOGENUS LAKE CAMPS

HUNTING, FISHING, RECREATION
Send for Booklet

A New Country is here opened up for Sportsmen just half way down the "West Branch" Canoe Trip; 40 miles by steamer from Greenville to Northeast Carry; twenty miles to Chesuncook by canoe, twenty miles more to camps by large motor boat making 15 miles an hour. Fine trip made in a day and a half from Greenville. **Home Camps** comfortable with spring beds, etc. **Back Camps and Lean-tos** cover a great tract of Wilderness, for Sportsmen desiring to go far back in the woods. **Good living every where, Grouse, Ducks** and **Black Bear.** We guarantee to give you **Trout Fishing** that is **unequalled** and **Moose** and **Deer Hunting** that is **unsurpassed.** Choice of the sportiest quick water in Maine, for the stream fisherman, or the most placid of pond and lake fishing for those who prefer it, where brook trout up to 6 pounds (larger if you know how) rise to the fly all summer.

Ralph Bisbee, May 1 to December 1, **CHESUNCOOK P. O., MAINE**
December 1 to May 1, **GRANT FARM P. O., MAINE**

Old Advertisement for a Sporting Camp.

III — JACK MANN

THIS chapter about Jack Mann was not included in Eckstorm's book *The Penobscot Man*. However, since Jack is mentioned many times in this book, and other Eckstorm writings, a chapter has been deemed appropriate to include for this famous Penobscot Man. These notes about Jack Mann are based in part on Eckstorm's journals, as well as, news articles that also documented the legend of Jack.

JACK MANN was from East Eddington, a tiny spot on the map that is part of Eddington, and lies north east of Brewer. For much of his life, he lived on the road to the lower end of Chemo Pond, near the Air Line Road, or what is now known to those not from the area as, Route 9. The Air Line Road, predated any air travel, of course, but was named for the stage company that ran the transportation line in this region.

Interestingly Jack was not his name, but rather it was William. His father was the one-armed Robert Mann. William's nickname was originally, 'Jackknife,' because as a boy he stole a jackknife from a man who was known as Old Eben Davis. Eventually, his nickname was shortened to Jack, and he was called by that name for the rest of his life by those who knew him, heard of him, or wrote about him.

Mann enlisted for service in the Civil War. Within a short time, he deserted, and was subsequently caught and carried back to the line. In Maine, he worked on the log drives as long as any boss would hire him.

Jack had a reputation as a ladies' man, and this may have been supported by, or started on, a particular Fourth of July when he was drunk. On that day, exact year unknown, he was seen walking down Bangor's Exchange Street with a girl on each arm. It was recorded he went along pushing the crowd aside with his hands saying, "Look out, Jack Mann and his women are coming."

On a different Fourth of July (for Jack was not one to hang back on the drive when a celebration was occurring), Jack, who was in the same state of inebriety as most holidays, and another lumberman decided to show the spectators what it was like to '*handle boat*' on the West Branch. Seeing the festivities took place several blocks from the waterfront, and neither the Kenduskeag Stream or the Penobscot around Bangor afforded any quick water for said demonstration, they lugged a batteau on a four-wheeled cart up Hammond Street hill. This hill remains and if you start at the intersection of High Street (or Ohio Street) and Hammond Street, where the 1833 Congregational Church is today, as it was in Mann's time, and point your direction down the hill towards the Kenduskeag, you will get a feel for this historic Jack Mann demonstration. They handled that 'boat-on-wheels' full tilt down the hill only stopping because the window of Wheelwright and Clark's department store got in the way. The boat, Jack, and his sternman were decorated in the neckties that had been on display. At the bottom of the hill, the 1859 Wheelwright and Clark building which is on the National Register of Historic Places, not only survived Jack Mann, but also the 1911 Bangor fire and much of the urban renewal of the last century. As of 2021, the building housed a clothing store.

One of Jack's most enduring legends is in what Eckstorm had referred to as a "Jack Mann load." In, *"Exploring the Maine Woods – The Hardy Family Expedition to the Machias Lakes,"* she told of what she herself was given for one of the carries, "True, I got Jack Mann's load — two axes, a fish-pole, a frying-pan, a bundle of ropes, my heavy jacket and the two grape baskets— not much in pounds but a fine assortment for inconvenience." This was her nod to Jack's often complaining of what he was assigned to carry when on the drive. One of his most complained about loads was a recollection of his early days as a luncheon boy when he had to carry, "A ton of loose hay and fifty pint-dippers *without handles* against a *head wind.*" On the drive, the cooky, or luncheon boy, used to bring the dippers strung by the handles, and hanging in a great loop down his back, so many of which, they'd almost touch the ground. Jack, of course, had it worse, he always did, since on that day the dippers he was forced to carry had no handles.

When Jack was too old to go river driving, he was pensioned by the Penobscot Log-Driving Association, with his board at the Bangor Alms House. It is said Mann died about 1880.

LUMBER CREW WITH TIN DIPPERS
Image courtesy of Special Collections, Raymond H. Fogler Library, University of Maine

Jack Mann's Fate as Read Between the Lines of a Maine Central Time Table

The following play-on-words story, appeared in the January 1924 edition of *The Northern*, a newsletter of the Great Northern Paper Company. It was written by A. L. Grover who signed himself as, "Professor Engineering Drawing." He wrote this piece on his train travels from Orono to Boston, taking the placenames from the train time tables and adding them to his verse.

And did you tell me that you never heard what finally became of Jack Mann? Then I invite you, for just a minute, to stop, look and listen. It happened like this:

Hermon Pond and-Ross-Goggin were stuck on *Biddy-Ford* and the *Widder-Pitlock*. These two couples had just returned from a joy ride to *Rum-Ford* and *Pass-a-Dum-Keag* and had now decided to *Live-r-more* quiet life and, having taken a *Bath* in the stream were now sunning themselves on the *Fair-banks* of the *Dead River*, which after plunging over the strong water of *Steep Falls*, flows silently on down to *Dark Harbor*.

Back of them lay a *Greene Intervale* at the far edge of which was a *Forest* that sloped upward to a *Highmoor*, the summit of *Mt. Hope*.

The two couples were so interested in each other that they did not notice *Jack Mann* and his *Pal-Myra* as they *Drew* nearer to them from the distant *Maplewood,* all the time keeping behind a *Green-bush* that was close to the unobserved lovers. Behind this *Green-bush, Jack Mann* and his *Pal- Myra* stood and gazed at the unsuspecting quartette.

"Who are they?" asked *Pal-Myra* in a whisper.

"It's *Hermon Pond And-Ross-Goggin* huggin' *Biddy-Ford* and the *Widder-Pitlock,*" replied Jack-Mann.

"I didn't know but it might be *Bemis Brooks* and *Mattie-Wam-Keag,*" said *Pal-Myra.*

"I know *Mattie-Wam-Keag* is pretty 'hot stuff,' but I'm sure this is *Biddy* and the *Widder,*" retorted Jack.

Just then they saw *Biddy-Ford's* head *Wilt-on Hermon Pond's* shoulder.

"Oh, wouldn't that make yer sick!" said *Jack* in a stage whisper. At this point, he jumped out from behind the *Greenbush* and shouted, "Oh, you *Jay*! you *Olamon*! Is this *Hartland* or *Unity*?"

Hermon Pond And-Ross-Goggin were on their feet in an instant. *Hermon,* who was the more impetuous of the two, cried: "It's none of your business whether this is *Hartland* or *Unity*; but I'll show you there can be no *Harmony* on the *Fair-banks* of this stream when you, *Jack Mann,* or any of your *Frye,* undertake to insult our ladies."

Now Jack Mann was a super-man, a *Harri-son* of the *King-man* of the Forest. He also had the reputation of being a bad man in a scrap. He had one vulnerable spot, however, which was known only to *Hermon Pond. Hermon* took advantage of this knowledge and as he *Drew* near to *Jack Mann* he hit him a quick, sharp blow in his *Oquossoc.* Jack reeled and, with an amphibious splash, fell into the *Dead River* and floated slowly down to *Dark Harbor.*

"Oh, *Hermon Pond,* what have you done!" gasped *Biddi-Ford.*

"I don't *Carratunk*," replied *Her-mon*;

And-Ross-Goggin shouted, "I don't *Cari-bou* since you *Winn* and we've *Concord*."

"*Great Works*," said *Wytipitlock*.

In this last statement, the author used *Wytipitlock* in place of *Widder-Pitlock*, in case readers missed his meaning in his use of Widow Pitlock. See the below list of placenames for explanations.

Key to sample of character and location names that may not be obvious for those 'from-away,' or not familiar with Maine's old train depots as some of these locations were stops on the railroad line which no longer exist.

- *and-Ross-Goggin* - read as, Andro-sgoggin for the Androscoggin River.
- *Bemis Brooks* – Bemis Railroad stop at Rangeley Plantation, Maine.
- *Biddy-Ford* – Betty Ford – Biddeford, Maine.
- *Brooks* – Railroad stop at Brooks, Maine.
- *Dark Harbor* – a village located on the southern end of the town of Islesboro in Waldo County, Maine.
- *Dead River* – Rail stop near what was once a Maine town, Dead River Plantation. The town, along with Flagstaff Village, was flooded when the dam was built in the 1950s.

- *Forest* – Railroad stop at North Washington, Maine.
- *Great Works* – Railroad stop at Old Town, Maine.
- *Greene* – Railroad stop at Greene, Maine.
- *Intervale* – Railroad stop at Conway, New Hampshire; this was the junction point between the Maine Central and the Boston & Maine railroads.
- *Jack Mann* – Jack played himself in this story, but of course there is the town of Jackman, Maine.
- *Mattie-Wam-Keag* – Railroad stop at Mattawamkeag.
- *Pal-Myra* – Jack's pal, Myra for Palmyra, Maine.
- *Pass-a-Dum-Keag* – Passadumkeag is a town on the east bank of the Penobscot River at the confluence with the Passadumkeag River in Penobscot County, Maine.
- *Rum-Ford* – Rumford, Maine.
- *Widder-Pitlock (or as Wytipitlock for the Widow Pitlock)* – Wytopitlock is an unincorporated village along the Mattawamkeag River in Aroostook County, Maine and was a Railroad stop at Reed Plantation, Maine.
- *Winn* – Railroad stop at Winn, Maine.

LOG YARD FROM BREWER TO BANGOR SHORE

Men are walking on the logs which have been sorted.

Fannie Eckstorm Collection. Taken around the year 1900.

Image courtesy of Special Collections, Raymond H. Fogler Library, University of Maine

IV — THE GRIM TALE OF LARRY CONNORS

The choppers and the sawyers, they lay the timber low,
The swampers and the skidders, they hustle to and fro;
Along comes the teams all at the break of day,
'Load up your teams with a thousand feet, to the river haste away.'
from, The Shanty Boys

IT is hardly conceivable that at noon of a hot summer day, in clear sight and clear sunshine, not a cloud nor a shadow to suggest a mystery, a keen, shrewd, practical business man, one of the head contractors of a big concern like the West Branch Drive, should think he saw a ghost, more especially when the apparition was topped by a flaming hat of scarlet felt and accompanied by two manifestly flesh-and-blood woodsmen not unknown to him. But so it fell out at the Dry Way of Ripogenus. And "Jim" owned up to his scare.

"By gum," said he, when he met me afterwards, "but you had me that time." And there would have been no sense in denying it, for he had given a snort like a startled buck, and even at ten rods away his attitude of surprise and consternation betrayed him. "Seeing you come up out of that hole with that red hat on, I thought for sure you must be the ghost of Larry Connors. I'd passed there not half a minute before, and not seen nothin', the bank's so steep there. Then I looked back over my shoulder and up pops that red hat; thought for a second that the everlastin' haunts had got me sure!"

Years afterward I was talking with a riverman of the old school. "And have you been up *there!* And do you know the Big Heater, and the Little Heater, and the Big Arches, and the Little Arches! And say, now, do you *know* about Larry Connors! Well, I want t' know, you *do* know all about Larry Connors! Smartest man ever was on the West Branch Drive!" And then the rosy sunset of his recollection burned away to ashen thoughts. "But they never found nothin' of him," he said slowly and sombrely.

"Lewey Ketchum," — said I, for I knew from Father, Lewey had come across what happened.

"Yes — Lewey Ketchum — that's so — down to the Big Eddy," said he, and stopped. It was plain he knew the story.

But this was long since, by virtue of being taken in broad daylight for the ghost of Larry Connors, I came into possession of the facts about his death. One and another told it, each one adding something; bit by bit I patched the whole together till I made the story out.

"Yes, old Jim he got his hoops started all right enough," said one of the men. "He wouldn't have owned up to it, if there had been any other way out. You see, Larry was killed right about that very spot. And the drive had all gone along, and Jim he'd just come down, — hadn't even heard of your being here, — an' most like's he was just sauntering along the driving-path, not expectin' to see no one, and he got to thinkin' about Larry. Then he seen your red hat, and that fixed him. You see, Larry always wore something red on his head; that red topknot was his trademark; didn't seem to make much difference what it was, a cap, or a handkerchief, or a red band round his hat, or the end of an old comforter pulled on, — just as far as you could see him, there would be Larry's red comb sticking up, and him just whelting into the logs and swearin' to beat seven of a kind. There's no mistakin' but Larry was a terrible able man."

But what was there about Larry Connors that, so many years after his death, could conjure up his ghost in broad day, bright sunlight, open spaces, to affright a sober, shrewd, hard-headed business man? Not, certainly, that he wore a fantastic headdress and died in the Dry Way of Ripogenus. Many are the men that have gone down in the morning to work on the logs in that gorge, men of blood and bone, who at evening, as thin, impalpable ghosts, have stolen up from Ripogenus to whatever land of shades and twilight duskiness — growing, let us hope, to brighter dawning — is allotted to men, not righteous, nor moral, nor admirable altogether, but yet dying ungrudgingly for their work. Throngs of such have traveled up the gorge of Ripogenus since Larry Connors died there thirty years ago, and yet of them all you will hear no name so often repeated, no story so many times rehearsed, as the grim tale of Larry's going. Somehow the men do not seem to forget Larry Connors. He stands for somewhat more than fantastic headgear and spectacular annihilation.

Larry Connors was an Exchange Street[17] Irishman, and the best of his education he acquired upon the logs at City Point.[18] By the time he was graduated from the supervision of the truant officer, he was capable of doing anything on logs. He was utterly fearless, thoroughly efficient, a lighting Irishman of the old bulldog type, close-haired, crop-eared, bullet-headed, ready

---

[17] A street near the waterfront in Bangor, Maine running along the Kenduskeag Stream to the Penobscot River. The area near here was known during the time as the, "Devil's Half Acre." Lumbermen came to these streets for the numerous bars, brothels, and gambling establishments. Many Irish immigrants found themselves living in the tenements of this area.

[18] City Point was an area where the logs being driven down the Penobscot were held for the mills and shipping.

always to show his teeth —less only the front one knocked out in a fight — with reason or without. Yet the men liked him. My father, for whom he worked all one winter in the woods, always had a good word for Larry, that he was a hard worker, a quiet man in camp, and — which is perhaps the most remarkable thing ever said of Larry Connors — that he never heard him swear.

This commendation must stand unique. For I have heard it said by one of his mates that Larry was "the wickedest man that ever went on the West Branch Drive."

"And you hadn't better not believe," my informant went on, sowing his negatives with so lavish a hand that it was doubtful whether the crop would grow up odd or even, "you hadn't better not believe that this West Branch Drive ain't not no holy Sunday-school!"

Being bred up to the Maine woods and its speech, I understood him to imply that Larry was notoriously profane; that was certainly his meaning. Yet had Larry killed a man, or been of vicious and irreclaimable temper, or of bestial cruelty, or implacable in revenge, — even then, though he might have been avoided as a "bad" man, he would hardly have been condemned as a "wicked" one. No, the wicked man is the profane swearer, the unprovoked blasphemer.

How does it happen, inquires the stranger, that in a country where neither dog, horse, ox, nor log will move till it is prodded with an oath, where profanity is general rather than the exception, and there is a variety and ingenuity and artistic finish about even the commonplace cursing that marks it as the work of no unpracticed tongue, how does it happen that this commonest vice of all is selected as the most censurable?

In its common forms it is neither censured nor censurable especially, nor is it a vice; it is a vulgarity. There is no harm intended by the pleasant maledictions of every-day life, the oath of emphasis, the oath of affection, the oath of good-fellowship just to make you feel at home, the picturesque and kindly cursing of the fellow of scanty vocabulary. But now and then arises a man of different temper, who blasphemes violently, who studies it as an art, who, not using it as a neighborly by-path of speech, so lavishes his energies on purely rhetorical anathemas that he chills the blood of even these seasoned woodsmen and rivermen. Such men, they say, will sometimes swear five minutes at a time without stopping, and swear "most horrid;" and these they say are "wicked men," because, as they know from dread experience, no man can thus defy the Almighty and come out scatheless. Hence the overpowering impiousness of those like Larry Connors, upon whom the judgment was swift and sure. This is why the man is still remembered.

Yet if you dare assume that it was not a judgment, no man agrees with you. There were enough that day who heard him say that he would break that jam or go to hell doing it. How many of those who have spoken to me have spoken as eyewitnesses!

"I was right there!" —

"I should have been with him on the logs, but I had just gone ashore for my axe." —

"I saw the whole thing." —

"I didn't see it, but I could hear it all, and the man next to me he said, 'There's some poor fellow gone; guess it must be Larry.'" —

"Yes, he did say just them very words, for I was right by and heard it."

One after another, though it is thirty years since and the ranks are thinning, has rehearsed the scene and his words. For they all know how Larry Connors died at the Dry Way of Ripogenus.

In those days the Dry Way was not a dry way, but a waterway. They have tamed the River since then, and this is one of the places where it wears the curb. Rough as it is today, the

River is a chained beast beside what it once was. Today, where channels divide, wing-dams throw all the water into one thoroughfare; today there is a great dam at the head of Ripogenus Gorge, with gates to control the water and the sluicing; today, by night and by light, men stand on every commanding point, waving a firebrand if it is dark, their hands by day (unless already the telephone has superseded these), watching and signaling if the logs catch on; in two minutes word goes up from the Little Arches three miles below, and the sluicing stops till the jam is cleared. No longer do the great sticks come leaping up on the backs of those already stranded, uncounted and uncontrollable. And today, if a jam does form, there is a little shed by the dam where dynamite is kept; enough of that will remove the stubbornest obstruction. But the older men will tell you how in their youth, that is, in Larry Connors' day, they were let down by ropes from the cliffs at the Big Heater, to hang like dangling spiders from a thread when the jam broke under them; how they watched and warred on the Arches; how they held the perilous pass by the Little Heater against leaping timbers; how they fought for life with the wild logs below the Dry Way. In Larry Connors' day it was "We who are about to *die*, salute you." They died, — they never surrendered, — that is why the River has been conquered.

There is three miles of this turbulent water, the roughest that the will of man ever brought to heel and made to carry his freights for him. Those who have seen it in the drought of August, when the lakes are emptied and the current is weak and lagging, have no conception of the grandeur of the spring torrent. "Three miles of Niagara," a lumberman once called it, and the phrase well describes this canyon, ripped out of the solid rock, with sheer and often inaccessible walls, and the rock-ribbed, boulder-studded river-bed, falling more than seventy feet to the mile, down which rushes a boiling, seething, smoking flood of water, all a-lather in its haste.

The worst place upon it is just at the head of the gorge as the waters leave the lake. Here an island divides the channel, and a great dam is stretched across both branches of the river. The part of the dam on the north is pierced for sluice and gate ways; the southern portion is a side-dam, without gates, to cut the water off entirely from the lesser channel. Down one side of the island race the white horses of the falls, tossing their manes, thundering, smashing, flying in a smother of foam as they press through the Gorge of the Perpetual Rainbow. Down the other side lies the Dry Way, and here the former river-bed is scraped to the bone, bare of all water but a silvery trickle, with beetling sides of bare and shining rock. What a contrast between this and the waterway the other side of the island!

There they never attempt to clear a jam; they let it catch and grow, and soon the pressure of the water behind it tears all away, snapping the largest logs like willow wands, tossing them thirty feet in air. "We never put a man on there to clear a jam," Joe Francis told me, and he was boss of the whole drive that year; "we let it form and pile up, and the water tears it all away." Nor would he even let us go to look at it until they were done sluicing, on account of the danger from leaping logs.

Once, before the dam was built, the Dry Way was like that, too. In Larry Connors' day, it was not dry but a waterway like the other. It was just here by the foot of the island, where the southern shore sweeps round like an amphitheatre, that a jam had formed that day when Larry made his last bid against death, for the glory of being looked at.

It was not a big jam, only a hundred and fifty or two hundred thousand feet of pine; but it was a bad one, held by a single key-log. The boss of that crew had been on it and sounded it. He had come ashore with his hand on his chin. He was a Spencer, and if anyone knows logs and water it ought to be a Spencer, — Veazie, or Old Town,[19] or Argyle, they are all rivermen. Thirteen springs this one worked on the West Branch Drive, and it rested with him to say what was to be done now.

"What d' ye think of it, Steve?" asked one of the men.

"Think? — 1 think it is a devil of a jam for a little one," said he; "I'm still thinking."

An old riverman had undertaken to tell the tale, and he went on: —

"Course the fellows was all hangin' round waiting to be ordered on. They had their peavies with them, and was just a-holdin' for the word how to take it.

"It's all right for a jam,' said Steve; 'when she hauls, she'll go clearn to thunder, and it won't cost the Company a red for pickin' up the pieces; whole thing hangs on one key-log, is neat and pretty as a basket of chips, and just about as safe as a barrel of gunpowder on the Fourth O'July; when she goes, she'll go tearin'. Sorry to disappoint ye, boys, but I guess I won't drown any of you today. We'll dog-warp this off. Get the tackle and take a hitch around that key-log, and we'll put on men enough to send her flukin'."

The riverman continued, "Well, boss is boss, and boss is supposed to have things his own way; but there was boys there that wouldn't listen to this. Safe ways of doing things wasn't what they was crying for. Out steps Larry, and he did look the able man for sure, calked shoes and a blue shirt, his trousers cut off at the knees and more rags 'n patches. And he had a red handkerchief tied round his head kind o' cocky, so the tails of it flew out. He just swung his peavey up on his shoulder and planted himself, with one hand held out — well, they don't make abler men to look at."

---

[19] Oldtown, is a former spelling of Old Town, Maine.

"So, Larry says, 'Look a-here, Steve,' says he, 'I'm beggin' the chance.'

" 'I know you are a crack man, Larry,' says Steve, 'but I'd rather drown a poorer one; mine's the best way, Larry,' says he, kind o' coaxing him.

"Then Larry turns round to the boys, and sorter smiled at 'em. It was the big dare he was givin' 'em, but he didn't speak it loud, only smiling; like as if he thought they was an easy crew to beat out.

" 'It's my job, boys,' says he, sort of satisfied; and he says, 'I'll go a step beyond any man in *this* crew.'

"And he hadn't not got the words out of his mouth when out steps Charley Rollins of Veazie. Rollins says, 'The man that goes a step ahead of me — he goes to hell!'

"Well, that fixed it. Larry sprung his knees a little's as if to limber 'em, and he says, 'That's all right, Charley; that's a bully bluff, but I'll raise you.'

"There wouldn't have been any holding them back after that. Them two was in the same boat together, and they'd been running races all the spring to see which could get into the most bad places. No matter who else had volunteered, after that it was between them two to cut that key-log.

"So the rest of the crew took their peavies, and they got their axes, and they all went out on the logs. I suppose it was long about here that Larry went back to camp and got a luncheon, because it was Rollins's turn to go first. Anyway, Larry goes up to camp, and he sets down under the bushes and commences to fire bits of waste biscuit at a squirrel that was around filling up his wangan on soda bread, and says he, 'Say, cooky,' — Furbish was cook that year, he told us all what Larry said afterwards, — 'say, cooky, gimme a hatful o' biscuit an' a hunk o' hoss; I'm hungrier 'n an owl on Friday. Just been down to the foot o' the

Island, an' they've got the' — well, he said they had the — the — donno's I can justly remember what it was that he *did* say."

There was a bland ingenuousness about the evasion which I admired as coming from one whose phonographic memory was never known to blur a record.

"But he told cook, says he, 'I'm goin' to break that jam, if I go to hell doing it.' Them's just his words; maybe he said more afterwards, I don't know, Larry was quite a hand to talk, he didn't know no better; but he did say that he would break that jam or go to hell doing it, all the boys testified to that.

"Well, it was Rollins's turn to go on first, as I was saying. You see, in a bad place they spell men; that's the custom. It don't do to have a man get all tuckered out with hard work and then have to run for his life when he ain't neither lungs nor limbs to help him; for the minute she cracks he's got to jump and run like thunder. So when the boss thinks that the first one's done all that's good for him, he calls him back and sends out another man. O' course the last one has the worst chance. Now Larry made the dare, and he was the one that raised it, and it was his right to get in the last clip at that log — that's what he was biddin' for. And that's why Rollins went on first.

"Often in a bad place they would have ropes around the men and pull them out, right up above the danger. But this time the boys knew they'd got to leg it on their own hook; and let me tell you, when you've got five hundred thousand — *feet* that is, board feet — of big pine pitch-poling after you, why you can run all right if there's any run in you. Just heave away your axe and strike a beeline for the shore, and you won't get there then none too soon for your peace o' mind. Breakin' jams is some uncertain work.

"Well, 'twas Rollins's turn to go first, as I was saying. He looked at that key-log and bit his axe in full clip. Did ye ever hear an axe take into wood that's under busting strain? Never did? Well, you listen someday, if ever you get the chance.

"And Rollins begun his scarf on the under side of the log. That was a right enough thing to do; that was good play; more than that, it was fair by Larry. After Rollins got his scarf in good shape, Spencer calls him back and sends out Larry.

"Out runs Larry, skippin' and swear-in', his kerchief tails flying, and all the boys looking on to see him go. A terrible reckless fellow was that Larry. And either he didn't stop to think, or else he didn't care, for the first thing that he done was to put in his scarf on the *upper* side of that log.

"What's the trouble with *that*? All the trouble in the *worlds*, I tell you, seeing his life might hang on a quarter of a second! If he'd a kept on in Rollins's scarf, that log when it cracked would have cr-r-r-a-a-*acked*! He'd have heard it splitting long enough to have got a start before the jam did. Cutting in on the top-side weakened it too sudden. When the log broke, it just *bust*.

"Well, then she hauled!

"And by Judas' hemp, an' two selectmen, a yoke of oxen, and an old snag throwed in, but perhaps that wasn't no sight to see! And to hear, too! Every lad in sight raised a yell, and those on shore danced and flung up their hats. And those on the logs they cut and run like the recess bell had rung and they didn't want to be late in. *And* the logs they started, jumping and squealing and thrashing and grinding, like seventeen sawmills running full-blast of a Sunday. You never heard anything in *your* life like a big jam of logs let loose. You ain't no idea of the noise and hubbub one of them will make when she hauls.

"The men got a pretty good start, but for all of that, they was tumbled in amongst the logs and used pretty rough. Two or three of them had to lay down in the cracks of the ledge and let the logs roll over them; but they managed to cling a-hold of the alders, and they all got out, — all except Larry.

"He was quicker than *three* cats, Larry was, but he wasn't quite up to the gait them logs set him, just flying through the air and up-ending every which way. And of course he had the worst chance; that's what he bid for. They tell the story different about Larry. Some says that he made a ledge all right, and a big log squirreled and caught him, and they see a red streak just like you'd hit a mosquito there. But what *I* see was that he was on the jam a-running, and a big pine lept and struck him in the back. Head and heels met in the air as it flung him clean. And he fell amongst the logs and they rode over him. But we never saw no more of Larry Connors. He said he was going to break that jam, if he went to hell for it, and he broke it all right enough."

So that was all there was to it. A brave man — a great dare — a wager won, or lost, as you will — and then all is snuffed out as irrecoverably as the flame of a candle.

They told me they looked for the body far and near, but there was nothing to be found. Babb was the head contractor of the drive that year, and he took charge of the dead man's kit. I have been told that when it was overhauled before being packed to send out to his friends, the men stood round in silence, not so much curious as respectful, wondering how that little bag of worthless duffle turned out on a blanket to be sorted by the head man kneeling beside it could be all that was left of so brave a man as Larry; silent for the most part, or when they did speak, speaking briefly and to the point; for they could not forget that saying of old Jack Mann's, that "Larry was so fond of stealing that when he couldn't get anything else he would steal the stocking off from one foot and put it on the other."

My riverman finished the story with:

"Says one: 'If you find a knife with a boot-leg sheath, it's mine; Larry borrowed it maybe.'

"And another says: 'I'm short two pair o' socks, blue yarn footed down with gray, lookin' like that pair there.'

"And another and another steps up with his claim.

"So they laid out all the things that was called for. And there was a cardigan marked 'Newell,' and a vest with a handkerchief in it marked 'Myra Spencer' and other things that didn't seem rightly to belong to his folks. And all the boys looked on it as a judgment on swearing.

"You see there *is* such things as judgments. Never knew a man to say that God Almighty couldn't drown him but he went and got drowned within the hour. There was one up to Telos Cut was rode under by two logs just as soon as he said it. And there was one down to the Gray Rock of Abol, slipped off in a perfectly safe place and went downstream like lead, and him a good swimmer. And there was John Goddard's barn that he said he built so firm that the Almighty couldn't fetch wind enough to shake it. He'd had two blown down before that, and he built that one to stand. And then there came a hurricane that just sifted that barn into toothpicks, and eight good driving-bolts in it, but they never found hide nor hair of them. And then there was Larry. Them's judgments.

"Didn't no one ever find no sign of him? M-m-m-no! That is, we didn't. He just went out like the smoke of a dandelion blossom; didn't leave no trace. But next spring, when Lewey Ketchum and Joe Dimon was up on their spring hunt after bears, down by the Big Eddy, — that's a good three miles below the Dry Way; you know, you been there times enough, — in back maybe a quarter of a mile from the eddy, in open second growth, I heard tell that they found a human skull, and it had the marks of bears' teeth on it.

"They was skinning a bear at the time that they'd just taken out of their trap, and Joe he sauntered off in the woods while Lewey finished off the skin. And bime-by he sung out, 'Lewey — Lewey, there's the funniest skull here you ever seen; awful round it is.'

" 'Lucivee,[20] I guess,' says Lewey, keepin' right on at the skin; 'they've got the roundest skull of anything.'

" 'But its front teeth are flat,' sings out Joe.

" 'Then it's a man,' says Lewey, and he goes and looks.

"And he saw that it had one front tooth gone just like Larry, so they hadn't no great of a doubt who it was to. They stuck it up in the fork of a tree and spotted a line in to it, so's his friends could find it again if they wanted it, and that's the last that ever I heard of it."

After this manner the man who broke the jam at the Dry Way came finally, as a bare and eyeless skull, — that blaspheming skull that once had a tongue in it, — to sit like some foul bird in a tree-fork through wintry storms; wherefore the men who had known him felt that even the judgment which had fallen upon him was insufficient, and this strange dismemberment was by the hand of God ordained as a warning against profane swearing. No wonder that they thought his ghost un-quiet, and that even on a hot June day it might be out in a red felt hat for a stroll along the Dry Way.

---

[20] Lucivee, or *loucerfee*, was applied by the Maine woodsmen, such as Lewey Ketchum and Manly Hardy to the wolverine. It was also known as the *Indian devil, lunksoos, skunk bear*, and other terms. Not to be confused with the Canada lynx. For a comparison of the older names applied to various animals, see, *David Stone Libbey – He Was Penobscot. Maine Woodsman and River-Driver*, Burnt Jacket Publishing, (2022).

V — HYMNS BEFORE BATTLE

This story is reprinted from the Bangor Daily Commercial, 1897, at the request of several who have desired its republication among these later stories. Though true in spirit, it does not deal with an actual occurrence at the place named, and therefore is not entitled to admission among these matter-of-fact stories. And yet the owner of another "Nancy," the late Roderick R. Park, when contractor of the Mattawamkeag Drive, used sometimes to call his men off for a dance just like this one, and the good old tune of "Roy's Wife" was known wherever he and his fiddle went.[21] *FHE*

THE GOLDEN noon of a young June day, and fourteen strong men swinging down the carry-path to the "putting-in place;" on each man's shoulder his heavy peavey, clanking its iron jaw as he jolted over rocks and hollows; on each man's feet heavy shoes, studded, heel and sole, with inch-long calks of sharpened steel; on each man's body rags and tatters, worn and weathered from their first monotony of aniline[22] and shoddy into gear indescribably barbarous and fantastic.

---

[21] "Nancy," as you will discover is the name given to the boss's fiddle. Eckstorm's opening note to this story, shows her transparency with these stories as to the chapters that are directly factual, or what we would now classify as historical fiction. It is no doubt that a few of the book's early critics, of whom she mentions in the final chapter added at the second printing, had latched onto this note and incorrectly placed the entire book as a work of fiction.
[22] Aniline was a chemical compound used for dye. Here the author means the harmonious / monotonous color of their clothes is no longer.

There was a jam forming below on the Horse Race, — a great upreared mass of logs, like a pile of gigantean jackstraws or the side-swath of a cyclone, where all the wreck is flung, up-ended, interlaced, triply bound and welded, a confusion which seemed inextricable. And volunteers were called to pick the jam.

These were the men, whose armed heels smote fire from the rocks, whose peavies jangled a battle-note, whose short step lengthened to a stride as they saw the river sweeping past and their boats before them, saw the rapids race at the tail of Ambajemackomas and heard on the upstream draught of air the ominous war of a full flood growling on the Horse Race below, and (either you dread it or it draws you, when you hear the River calling so) came swinging down the carry in haste to meet their foe. It is a pretty sight to see a phalanx[23] of picked watermen rally, as if by bugle call, to face their ancient enemy, the River.

Yet there, in sight of the river, one of them fell out.

"Ho, hi! See here!" he called to those ahead.

The fourteen men with peavies on their shoulders, clustering together, stood stock-still, like old herons round a fishing-pool, their necks craned over, and gazed at something in the damp, black soil.

"Gee whipperty!" said one, "that there's a woman's track!"

Then, as if contradicted, though no one spoke, — "Yes, sir, that is! There's been a woman here."

Women were unknown in that place at that season. Yet there, under the over-arch of an alder, was a slender footprint. They could tell you today, those men, though it is twenty years since, just how long and how wide was that woman's track, carelessly imprinted in the mud beside the carry-path.

Very unchivalrous the world counts these woodsmen; — very little the world knows about their ways and romances, for

---

[23] Phalanx in ancient Greece was an infantry formed in close ranks with shields and long spears overlapping.

nowhere does romance bear a more fragrant blossom or bloom so long. The sprig of cedar, many years preserved, because with it a woman crowned an act of daring; the wild flower, pressed in the crumpled corner of a greasy pocketbook, because a woman called it beautiful; the chance track in the roadway where a week before an unknown woman stepped, kept from obliteration just because she was a woman, — no line of life that men follow today comes so close to the high mark of mediaeval chivalry with its superb faith in womankind, regardless of the faults of individual women.

But the life is rough? So surely was chivalry! Rougher than we know for. Its faith saved it; and what grew into mariolatry in the past is still, in the unromantic present, the better part of many other rough men's religion.

"Yes, sir," said the bearded man, "there was a woman here. Jee-e-e-roozlum, there wuz!"

Confronted by this evidence of a woman's presence, his speech underwent a sudden censorship, and, like rags in a broken window, any inoffensive word was stuffed in to fill the gaps.

"There was; gee-e-e-whittaker, there wuz! It's somethin' to make account of. The wangan chest is this end the carry, and there ain't nothin' can't wait. Hike out old Nancy, and let's break her down."

The speaker was boss of his crew, a man possessed of a little authority over those below him and of more over those above him, who had learned to let him take his own way without meddling; for he was one of those men who, discountenancing the maritime maxim, can break orders and defy owners. It has always been the glory of the West Branch Drive that it had so many such men, every one of whom placed the welfare of those logs above his own life, could have handled the whole drive if there were need, and whose insubordination would never have gone so far as to endanger the least part of their trust. No matter how mutinously they spoke, they never failed to be where they were needed, and that was all P. L. D. asked of them.

There is neither time nor room for fiddles on the drive, but this man had wanted Nancy, and he carried Nancy. If he had wanted the moon, he would have put it in the wangan chest just as boldly. And now, when called to pick off a jam, he coolly halts his men in the face of danger and death — because the occasion is notable — to have a scrape at the old fiddle.

In the faces of some there is questioning what John Ross will say. Whom he rebukes.

"What'll John Ross say? Don't care what John Ross'll say! Ain't this a free country? What did old Jack Mann say to his boss when he knocked off at noon with all his crew because it looked like sprinklin'? — that he'd 'a sight rather have the good-will of a whole crew than of one man, any day.' And so'd I! John Ross ain't a-runnin' this crew now; *I* be! There ain't nothin' in particular about a little side jam that can't wait. Stick up your darts, boys; rowse a boat out, an' all hands bow to partners."

In a trice they were ready. The peavies plunged their iron beaks into the earth, the driving-boat turned bottom up in a twinkling, and while the boss was still groping in the wangan chest for his fiddle case, the two supplest men had unbuckled and cast aside their spiked driving-shoes. It was a dance on the drive — a dance by-proxy; for the pitchy, flat bottom of a driving-boat is an area too limited for a general engagement. So while the fiddler sawed and tightened his strings, and the barefooted dancers sprung their knees to get them in condition, the audience disposed itself to watch.

The fiddle tuned, the fiddler seated, he touches the horse-hair to his cheek, then holds the bow upright and Nancy tucked beneath his chin, waiting for them to call the tune.

"Money Musk!"

"Fisher's Hornpipe!"

"Irish Washerwoman!"

"Something we sing out in the States," cries a dissenting basso; "give us a real Christian tune!"

There is rough water below them and a jam to pick; and — are they moved to sing hymns of prayer and praise?

O innocent, the fiddler knows them better. He bends his head a moment to catch the humor of his audience moved to retrospection by the sight of a woman's footprint, and away whisk jigs and "penny- royals" while the expectant dancers stand agape.

Up and down plays his wrist, in and out works his elbow, forward and back sways his body; he treads his foot; a musical ecstasy carries him beyond the bounds of his own mean accomplishments, and he plays with fervor what his men have called for — a most Christian song. It begins, —

> *"I'm lonesome since I crossed the hill.*
> *And o'er the moor and valley."*

And they sang.

Of course they sang, — bass and tenor, how they sang, for they all knew that, — sang till the clearer voices floated high above the slender birch-tops and the bass swam midway in the clear June sunshine, and beneath, mingling with the roll of the rapids, rumbled the undertone of those who could not sing, yet would not refuse to try.

It came like rain in drought, freshening dusty foliage and slaking the thirst of parching hillsides — this most Christian song of women remembered in the face of danger.

"The bee shall honey taste no more,
The dove become a ranger,
The falling waves shall cease to roar,
Ere I shall seek to change her.
The vows we register'd above
Shall ever cheer and bind me,
In constancy to her I love,
The girl I've left behind me."

The logs slipped past by twos and threes and half-dozens, going to throw themselves upon the abattis of the ever-increasing jam below. And still the fiddler bent above, his fiddle. Young men have sweethearts, older men have wives, and once more the bow is laid to the catgut, to draw from it a tribute to the wives at home.

"Roy's Wife of Valdevally" nods the bow-paddle to the stroke-oar. They did not know the words, nor that it had words, nor that they were not altogether a compliment, — that lay all in the title, — but the fine old tune of "Roy's Wife of Aldivalloch"[24] was known wherever Nancy felt the bow. It had been played many times before on that river, though never when John Ross was waiting for a crew.

That ended, once more the bow hugged the fiddle. To young men, sweethearts; to their seniors, wives; but men old enough to handle the bow of a driving-boat have children and homes as well, and the fiddler played once more while John Ross waited.

Up through the tangle of undergrowth by the river's edge, hastening from the jam below, jingling his dippers as he ran, puffed and sweated the luncheon-boy, with orders to "swear them into a two-forty; for it had caught on at the middle and

---

[24] Roy's Wife of Aldivalloch is a traditional Scots melody from the late 1700s. The lyrics are available on the internet.

formed clear across the river, was rolling up all the time, and would hold till everything underground froze stiff" (so the message ran), "if they didn't shove a crew down double quick and break the jam; and why in — in all hemlock, hadn't they been there long before?"

An order enjoining unlimited, idiomatic, artistic swearing is a commission of honor to any luncheon-boy, and this one, as he posted up the drivers' path by the riverbank, was marshaling his vocabulary so as to do him credit, when, though full of his errand, he heard the fiddle, soft and sweet, — for the bow itself crooned the words to silent listeners, —

> *"In mansions or palaces, where'er I roam.*
> *Be it never so humble, there's no place like home."*

The luncheon-boy loitered along at a walk, then sauntered, and finally, in spite of his hot haste, waited till the last slow stave had sung itself away to an echo.

"Middle jam," said he, shamefully neglecting the opportunity for elegant profanity; "everything piling up chock-full. Run down lively; them's John Ross's orders."

Fourteen men sprang to their feet and ran out the batteaus; the fiddle shut itself up in the case; the peavies leaped into the boats; oars, axes, paddles, and all flew into position, and the two driving-boats, fully manned, with bowmen and steersmen standing in their places, darted out into the swirling current that tails down from Ambajemackomas. Behind them were songs of sweetheart, wife, and home; and ahead, around the bend whence the upstream draught of air brought the growl of the rapids. Death and Danger sat waiting for them on the middle jam. Were their chances for life and victory less for that quarter hour's devotion at the one shrine all woodsmen worshipfully recognize, — the memory of home and woman?

EAST MILLINOCKET DOLBY DAM, 1906

Image courtesy of Special Collections, Raymond H. Fogler Library, University of Maine

VI — THE JAM AT GERRY'S ROCK

THE BALLAD, "Jam at Gerry's Rock," has been recorded by many artists, with subtle variations in the lyrics. The song isn't only famous in Maine, for it has been sung across the United States and in other countries. One of the most well-known group to record it was The Limeliters on their folk song album, 'Our Men in San Francisco,' released in 1962 as, "The Jam at Jerry's Rock." It is is available through an internet search to listen too.

The following is but one version of the lyrics documented by Fannie Hardy Eckstorm. While the exact origin of the ballad is unknown, the tale is of a young river driver foreman by the name of Jack Monroe, who one Sunday morning takes to the logs with six of his men to clear a jam.

Come all you bold shanty boys, and listen while I relate
Concerning a young shanty boy and his untimely fate,
Concerning a young river man, so manly, true, and brave;
'T was on a jam at Gerry's Rock he met his watery grave.

  'T was on a Sunday morning as you will quickly hear,
  Our logs were piled up mountain high, we could not keep them clear.
  Our foreman said, 'Turn out brave boys, with hearts devoid of fear;
  We'll break the jam on Gerry's Rock and for Eganstown we'll steer.'

Now, some of them were willing while others they were not,
For to work on jams on Sunday they did not think we ought;
But six of our Canadian boys did volunteer to go
And break the jam on Gerry's Rock with their foreman, young Monroe.

They had not rolled off many logs when they heard his clear voice say,
'I'd have you boys be on your guard for the jam will soon give way.'
These words were scarcely spoken when the mass did break and go,
And it carried off those six brave youth and their foreman, Jack Monroe.

When the rest of our brave shanty boys the sad news came to hear,
In search of their dead comrades to the river they did steer;
Some of the mangled bodies a-floating down did go,
While crushed and bleeding near the bank was that of young Monroe.

They took him from his watery grave, brushed back his raven hair;
There was one fair form among them whose sad cries rent the air —
There was a fair form among them, a maid from Saginaw town,
Whose cries rose to the skies for her true love who'd gone down.

Fair Clara was a noble girl, the river-man's true friend;
She lived with her widowed mother dear, down at the river's bend;
The wages of her own true love the 'boss' to her did pay,
And the shanty boys for her made up a generous purse next day.

They buried him with sorrow deep, 'twas on the first of May;
'Come all of you, bold shanty boys, and for your comrade pray!'
Engraved upon the hemlock tree that by the grave did grow,
Was the name and date of the sad, sad fate of the shanty boy,
   Monroe.

Fair Clara did not long survive, her heart broke with her grief,
And scarcely two months afterward death came to her relief.
And when the time had passed away and she was called to go,
Her last request was granted, to be laid by young Monroe.

Come all you bold shanty boys, I would have you call and see
Two green mounds by the riverside, where grows the hemlock
   tree,
The shanty boys cleared off the wood by the lovers there laid
   low —
'Twas the handsome Clara Vernon, and her true love, Jack
   Monroe.

In Maine, many woodsmen of the early 1900s relayed to Eckstorm that this tale was a true story of a jam on the East Branch of the Penobscot, near what was once Hunt's Farm. They reported the rock was later blown up to prevent a recurrence of a jam. The stories seemed to be so true, that some reported even seeing the grave of Monroe and his lover, young Clara.

The myth of the ballad and its origins became a personal challenge to Eckstorm who wrote she, "never undertook so difficult a piece of historical research as 'Gerry's Rock.'" In, *Minstrelsy of Maine*, she devoted a section of twenty-two pages in her pursuit to determine the origins of the ballad and the location of the fatal rock that caused the jam. Through interviews she conducted, letters sent and received, and even pleas the editors of sporting journals posted in their papers for readers to submit what they knew about Gerry's Rock, Eckstorm accumulated a wealth of information that all turned out to be more myth than fact and she wrote, "Immediately after the song was printed in the 'Maine Sportsman,' in 1904, several experienced river-drivers, of a generation now passed away, located Gerry's Rock for me." However, the location of the rock, if it in fact existed, was much debated and Eckstorm diligently cataloged all the various myths of the ballad's namesake rock.

While river deaths certainly did happen, and jams along the rocks were the cause of a good number, she discovered that no one event matched the story of Jack Monroe, and no rock on any branch of the Penobscot, or any river in Maine for that matter, could be determined as existing, or once existing, where such a tragedy occurred. And while there are places near the East Branch named Jerry Brook and Jerry Pond, Eckstorm's research concluded the song was not written about any death that occurred near those waterbodies.

So just where was Gerry's Rock and where did Jack Monroe die? And why did so many Maine woodsmen believe the ballad was written about a river accident on the Penobscot?

The ballad, in various forms mentions the locations of: Saginaw, which is a town in Michigan; Eganstown, possibly referring to Eganville, a town founded by lumber baron John Egan on the Bonnechere River in Canada; and also Oldtown in Maine, but the latter was added in more recent versions after Mainers adopted Gerry's Rock to be on the Penobscot. In her research, Eckstorm documented where people reported to her the exact bend in the river and rock location the jam occurred, but upon further research she discovered they had placed the location of the jam based on the lyrics or some legend they had heard.

Following the clues and facts to where they led, Eckstorm concluded, "Nothing about the song, 'Jam on Gerry's Rock,' has been settled except that it did not occur at all the places where it has been located."

This conclusion troubled her, for she was a researcher who wanted to know correct answers. Her analysis ended with, "If I have failed, it is because oblivion has all but already closed over the origin of the song and the incident it was based upon, which can hardly lie back of the memory of men now living. So swift is Time the effacer!"

Some of the facts that contribute to the song being poetically composed for woodsmen's entertainment, and not one of actual fact, have to do with certain terms used in the ballad. One of the strongest reasons to know the lyrics did not originate in Maine is the use of the word 'shanty.' Eckstorm provided evidence that the term 'shanty' and 'shanty boy,' were prevailing Western terms, and had recent introductions at the time from the Provinces. In the West, 'shanty' was what in Maine was referred to as the 'wangan-boat' (the supply boat); and the 'shanty boy' of Canada was the Maine 'river-driver.' (In Maine, a 'shanty' was also rude woods tavern or a poorly built camp.) She concluded the use of the terms 'shanty' and 'shanty boy,' were more poetical, than truly words of the Maine woods. Eckstorm noted that she had never heard 'shanty' or 'shanty boy,' used in the Maine woods by woodsmen, until the use in ballads and songs, which were likely imported by travels of the lumberman or those who relocated to Maine. The lyrics appear to have morphed and been adopted depending on the singer and the region they were log driving, or where they had once lived. If the ballad was transported out west, or vice versa, from west to east, it appears the men took poetic license and retained the words in the lyrics that suited them best.

The fact that this jam occurred on a Sunday, and some of the men refused to work the Sabbath, will be a theme in the Chapter, "Joyfully," a story told by a Hardy family friend who worked driving logs in Canada.

BREAKING A JAM
Illustration from: *Forest Life and Forest Trees: Comprising Winter Camp-Life Among the Loggers, and Wild-Wood Adventure with Descriptions of Lumbering Operations on the Various Rivers of Maine and New Brunswick* (1851).

VII — THE DROWNING OF JOHN ROBERTS, 1852

John Roberts, as we understand,
It was the name of this young man,
And his fate we hope will a warning prove
To all who do these lines peruse.

It was on one morning, a cloudy sky,
This young man left his home to die;
While from his home he did depart,
A gleam of hope twined around his heart.

He hired out with David Brown
To help him drive his lumber down;
To the West Branch he quick did go,
Which soon did prove his overthrow.

He ventured out to break a jam
Which had commenced on the Roll Dam,
And as he started for the shore
He fell, alas! to rise no more.

He fell amidst the dashing spray,
Where foaming waters filled the way,
And by the current he was dragged along
Into a boil so fierce and strong.

We think he got his fatal blow
While struggling 'neath the undertow,
By some large rock beneath the wave,
Where he soon found a watery grave.

Our boats was left upon the rear,
We could not reach our object dear;
Three times he rose within our view
And seemed to bid us all adieu.

They swept the stream from shore to shore
His lifeless body to procure,
Trusting to God to course the way
Unto his tendermint of clay.

On the third day at three o'clock
Young Roswell Silsby took a boat,
And with a grapple all in his hand,
He dragged him from his bed of sand.

And then a bier was made,
And on it was John's body laid,
Drawn from the grave where he must lie
Till Gabriel's trumpet rends the sky.

May that good God who reigns on high,
Send his salvation through the sky,
And fit us all to see his face,
And dwell in Heaven that happy place.

Through the meticulous journal notes of Manly Hardy, Eckstorm to her great satisfaction was able to identify the man of this ballad and the correct location of the incident described. She discovered this ballad dated back to at least the 1850s and in *Minstrelsy of Maine, wrote*: "The senior editor recalled that in the fall of 1853 her father was deer-hunting at Williams's Pond, now called Great Pond, on Union River, and on looking up notes she found that in the spring of that year Charley Roberts, a river-driver, while sitting on the bank at the Hulling Machine Rapids on the inlet to the pond, eating his luncheon, had been killed by a dead tree falling on him, and that this happened at the same place where his brother John Roberts had been drowned the spring before. The roll dam was just above the Hulling Machine, on the West Branch of (the) Union River."

The Union River has an East Branch, West Branch, and Middle Branch, making the discovery of this location even more challenging due to the potential confusion with the West Branch of the Penobscot. Great Pond is just east of *The Horseback* near Greenfield, Maine, and the *Hulling Machine Rapids* she notes of the Union River is more recently called *Hells Gate Falls*. This finding for Eckstorm is significant as Roland Palmer Gray, in his 1925 book, *Songs and Ballads of the Maine Lumberjacks*, incorrectly placed a version of this ballad, which he titled, *The West Branch Song*, on the West Branch of the Penobscot River. When writing his book, Gray had requested information from Eckstorm on ballads, but it seems he made many errors in his book, which became apparent only after the diligence Eckstorm applied through her expert woods-knowledge in writing her own book about Maine ballads.

A BURNT JACKET PUBLISHING CLASSIC RELEASE

CLEARING A JAM

from

Thomas S. Steele's – Maine Adventures
Annotated Edition, Two-book Collection
Burnt Jacket Publishing (2021)

VIII — DEATH OF THOREAU'S GUIDE – JOSEPH ATTIEN[25]

ON July 4th, 1870, Eckstorm was not at the Blue Rock Pitch when this fatal accident happened, for she was only five years of age. There were no cameramen on the banks of the river to provide her with photographic evidence of the batteau being swamped. Yet, no other writer before her had ever documented the death of the man to be immortalized in this story.

Eckstorm wrote this tribute in honor of Joseph Attien, a man who died at way too young an age. Attien deserved then, as now, to be remembered as more than a guide to Thoreau. While Attien was certainly a prominent character in Maine's Penobscot tribe, in this story he is shown to be a Penobscot Man, a terribly able riverman, and a hero to those who witnessed his actions that day on the river.

This tale is so skillfully crafted by Eckstorm that the reader will also understand the pride of river bosses, subordinates, and company responsibility; and while those explanations are a secondary theme, that message should not be lost in the reading. At the conclusion of this chapter, further details are included on the tragedy, as well as a Maine placename that has been confounded with the history.

---

[25] The editor has added Joseph Attien's last name, spelled as Eckstorm had, to the title of this chapter. Eckstorm had her reason for why she titled the chapter the way she had, and it was a good one. However, it is now appropriate for Attien's name to appear in the title.

THE STRANGEST monument a man ever had in sacred memory, — a pair of old boots. For a token of respect and admiration, love and lasting grief, — just a pair of old river-driver's boots hung on the pin-knot of a pine. Big and buckled; bristling all over the sole with wrought steel calks; gashed at the toes to let the water out; slashed about the tops into fringes with the tally of his season's work, less only the day which saw him die; reddened by water; cracked by the sun, — worn-out, weather-rotting old boots, hanging for years on the pine-tree, disturbed by no one. The river-drivers tramped back and forth beneath them, a red-shirted multitude; they boated along the pond in front and drove their logs past, year after year; they looked at the tree with the big cross cut deep in its scaly bark, and always left the boots hanging on the limb. They were the Governor's boots, Joe Attien's boots, they belonged to Thoreau's guide.[26]

The pine-tree had seen the whole. It was old and it was tall. Its head stretched up so high that it could look over the crest of Grand Pitch, tremendous fall though it is, right up where Grand Falls come churning down to their final leap into Shad Pond. It had been looking up the river in the sunshine of that summer morning and had seen the whole, — the overloaded boat that set out to run the falls, the wreck in the rapids, the panic of the crew,

---

[26] FHE: Thoreau spells the name "Aitteon;" I have preferred the form found on his tombstone, "Attien," because it indicates both the pronunciation and the derivation. For it is not Indian, but the French Étienne, or Stephen.

the men struggling among logs and rocks, the brave attempt at rescue, and the dead, drowned bulk, which had once been the Governor, as it was tumbled down over the Grand Pitch into the pond below. The pine-tree had stood guard over it for days, and when, from its four days in the grave of the waters, it rose again, the pine-tree still kept watch over it, until, on the sixth morning, the searchers found it there. And when they found his body they cut a cross into a tree by the side of the pond, and they hung up his boots in the tree and they stayed there always, because everybody knew that they were the Governor's boots.

If ever Henry David Thoreau showed himself lacking in penetration, it was when he failed to get the measure of Joseph Attien.[27] True, Joe was young then — he never lived to be old; yet a man who, dying at forty-one, is so long remembered, must have shown some signs of promise at twenty-four.[28] But Thoreau hired an Indian to be aboriginal. One who said "By George!" and made remarks with a Yankee flavor was contrary to his hypothesis of what a barbarian ought to be. It did not matter that this was the sort of man who gave up his inside seat and rode sixty-miles on the top of the stage in the rain that a woman might be sheltered; — all the cardinal virtues without

---

[27] Eckstorm published a lengthy review of Thoreau's, The Maine Woods, for which she has been praised, as well as criticized. A summary with annotations is included in, *Exploring the Maine Woods – The Hardy Family Expedition to the Machias Lakes,* Burnt Jacket Publishing (2021).
[28] FHE: The newspapers said he was thirty-five when he died, but his gravestone says plainly, "forty years and seven months." It is interesting to learn that one who lived so well and died so generously was born on Christmas Day.

aboriginality would not have sufficed Mr. Thoreau for a text.[29] He missed his opportunity to tell us what manner of man this was, and so Joe Attien's best chance of being remembered lies, not in having been Henry Thoreau's guide on a brief excursion, but in being just brave, honest, upright Joseph Attien, a man who was loved and lamented because he had the quality of goodness. "His death just used the men all up," said a white riverman years afterward; "after that some of the best men wasn't good for anything all the rest of the drive."

I could give, as I have gleaned it here and there, the testimony to his worth, the statements of one and another that he was not only brave but good, an open-hearted, patient, forbearing sort of a man, renowned for his courage and skill in handling a boat, but loved for his mild justness. "He was just like a father to us," said a white man who had been in his boat. Thirty-three years after his death I heard a head lumberman, who also had served two years in his boat, a very silent man, break out into voluble reminiscence at merely seeing Joe Attien's picture.[30] But there is a story, indisputably authentic, which shows better than anything else the largeness of the man.

He had been slandered by a white man whom he had thought his friend, in a way which not only caused him distress of mind, but was calculated to interfere materially with his election to the office of tribal governor, the most coveted honor within an Indian's grasp, and that year elective for the first time.[31] The

---

[29] Eckstorm was quick to praise Thoreau when he deserved to be, but she was critical where she saw him lacking, especially in his missing several chances at learning from Maine Native Americans during his time in the Maine woods.

[30] In her journal notes, dated Oct. 1903, Eckstorm identifies this woodsman as, Rod Sutherland.

[31] FHE: His epitaph is wrong in asserting that he inherited the title of governor. The office had been a life-office, hereditary in the

incident occurred just before his first election in 1862, — for he was governor seven times. Hurt to the quick, he avoided his former friend, yet said nothing. When he discovered that the false accusation had arisen from a wholly innocent and most natural mistake, without a word in his own justification, leaving the charge to stand undenied, he renewed the old friendship, and his friend never knew what just cause he had given for resentment till, years after Joe's death, it was accidentally revealed by one who had heard the misunderstanding explained. Such was the man.[32]

Attien family, who were chiefs, but at Joseph's father's death it was made annual and elective. Joseph Attien won his elections by popular vote against great opposition, and he carried seven out of the eight elections held up to the time of his death. The eighth — by the intervention of the so-called "Special Law," passed by the state to reduce the friction between the parties — was the New Party's first election, none of Joseph Attien's party, the Old Party, or Conservatives, voting that year.

[32] The man that unintentionally offended Joseph Attien, was nonother than, Manly Hardy. Journal notes of Eckstorm indicate Manly once made a passing comment about the moral of electing a tribal governor who was known to drink. One can surmise by reading the Hardy journals, and Eckstorm's stories, that Manly was a teetotaler and he may have had high standards for not just himself, but others. The entire incident was a misunderstanding. Sometime before 1862, Steve Stanislaus, cousin to Attien, had gone to Manly's store to buy some otter traps. It was when Stanislaus had just come off the drive and was all sunbaked and travel-worn. While there, Steve offered Manly a drink. Turns out, Steve and Joe were similarly built and looked a good deal alike. In a case of mistaken identity, Manly took Steve for Joe in making his comment. Once Joe Attien understood the cause for the drinking remark, clarified by Stanislaus once he realized the misunderstanding, Attien renewed his friendship with Manly.

If you ask the men who were there at the time how Joseph Attien died, they will never suggest that it was an accident or the hand of God. More or less emphatically, according to their natures and the vividness of their recollection, they will say right out, "Dingbat Prouty did it; it was Dingbat Prouty drowned Joe Attien." They will cheerfully admit that this is not a man to be spoken of slightingly, because he is a great waterman; but upon this point there is only one opinion, — that he forced Joe Attien to run a bad place against his better judgment, for the mere sake of showing off.

"He pushed himself in." —

"He han't no business in that boat at all." —

"Prouty drowned Joe Attien, everybody who was there says so." —

"He hadn't no business in that boat and didn't belong there anyway, but he said he was going to run them falls, and he did run 'em.

It is very hard to tell a true story, and the more one knows about the facts, the harder it is to make a story of them. Here was a simple tale of how the inordinate ambition of one man to win a name for himself brought grief upon the whole drive. The next turn of the kaleidoscope gave a wholly different combination. For I took what I had gathered to John Ross himself.

"Is this straight?"

And he said: "No; you are all wrong there. Prouty belonged in that boat; he had been bowman of it about two days. It was my orders for them to go down and pick a jam on the Heater, and they were going. I was right there and saw the whole of it, and I never blamed Prouty."[33]

---

[33] In 1904, Eckstorm interviewed Ross for perspective stories she was planning for *The Atlantic*. A note from January 8, 1904 states,

But why, then, should the men have blamed him? No exculpation could be more complete than this. There is no appeal from what John Ross says he ordered and saw executed. Why do not the men know this? Instead of telling a simple tale, are we undertaking to square the mental circle? For, with nearly two hundred men close at hand, it seems preposterous that the facts should not have become generally known; it is still more incredible to suppose that, thinking independently, they could all have reached the same false conclusion; but that, having been cross-examined in all sorts of ways for four and thirty years, they should never have varied from their first error is inconceivable.

Why do the men still hold Charles Prouty responsible, if he was not to blame?

From being a study of facts, the story turns into a question of psychology. Why is it that when one has been looking at red too long he sees green and keeps on seeing green, even when there is no green there?[34]

That is the clue. A man does not get a name like "Dingbat" and keep it all his life for nothing. Therefore, after the men had gazed fixedly upon the commanding excellence of Joseph

---

"Interview with John Ross, his son Harry, and his daughter Mrs. C. Vey Holman. Ross at this time 71 years old; would be 72 in March." When Ross mentions "Heater" in the context of the Attien drowning, it must be clarified as to the meaning. The Big and Little Heaters on the West Branch are well known to be in Ripogenus Gorge. The falls between Quakish Lake and Shad Pond where Attien drowned were known as the *Blue Rock Pitch, Rhine Pitch* and *Grand Falls*. Woodsmen, such as Ross, generically called these places of rapids, falls, and narrow passes, 'heaters.' For example, the Slewgundy Heater is a ¼-mile-long dangerous gorge on the Mattawamkeag River and was recently the location of a drowning.

[34] In reference to how the cells in the eye process color. An experiment to try this can be found on the internet.

Attien; after they had seen him pass beyond their ken, "all the trumpets," as it were, "sounding for him on the other side;" when they turned away and looked at the man whom fate had elected to stand beside him that day, what would one expect them to see by contrast?

Green! very green! And to keep right on seeing — *green*!

Having affirmed the worth of Joseph Attien and the warm esteem in which all held him, it remains to show how, because he was placed in too sharp a contrast with such a man, Charles Prouty incurred a blame which his chief says was none of his.

We come now to the story. Chance gave to it a fitting frame — grand scenery, bright sunshine, a date of distinction, the eye of the master. You are never to forget that up on a log-jam, just below where this happened, stood himself — John Ross. He ordered the boat down; he saw it go; he sent another to the rescue; he reported this to me; it stands authenticated. But what the men saw and felt, that which is unofficial, that which represents the current of the story and carries us on to the end, I gathered for myself among them.

On the drive there is no distinction of days. Holidays or Sundays, the drivers know no difference; one week's end and the next one's beginning are all the same to them. The Fourth of July now is marked for them by no other suitable recognition than extremely early rising.

But it used not so to be. In the old days, when it was a point of pride to have the logs in boom by the last of June, the men were free to celebrate on the Fourth. To them the Fourth of July was the greatest day of all the year. Like boys just out of school, they were free from work, free from restraint, free to make just as much noise as they pleased, and, having plenty of money in their pockets wherewith to purchase all sorts of a good time, they enjoyed a glorious liberty. The Fourth was never a quiet day in Bangor, if the drives were in the boom.

However, the year of our Lord 1870 is distinctly chronicled as one of the most uneventful ever known; nothing at all going on but a church levee across the river in Brewer, so that the police loafed out the Fourth in weary and unwonted idleness. The drives were late that year, so very late that, though the head of the West Branch Drive was some miles downstream, the rear of it rested on the Grand Falls of the Indian Purchase.[35] The hands had been leaving the day before, so as to get home for the Fourth; the water was falling; the whole drive was belated and short-handed; the head men were worrying; no one had any time to remember that it was a legal holiday.

That is, no one remembered it except the Chronic Shirk. His rights had been assailed, and, having found a Temporary Cripple, who could not escape by flight from his unwelcome company, he insisted on arguing the case, and volleyed back his opinions of working on a legal holiday with an explosiveness which reminded one of the reports of a bunch of fire-crackers.

It was "Rip — rip — rip — bang! But he didn't like this; Workin' on a Fourth of July! The Declaration of Independence had said — that it was a man's right — on the Fourth of July — to get as tight as Lewey's cow; and he did rip — rip — rip — *object* — to being defrauded out of his constitutional rights!"

He was a sun-baked, stubble-faced fellow; less troubled with clothes than with the want of patches, but with shirt and skin about one color where the sun had toned them to each other around the more ancient rents; and he sat in a niche in the log-jam, expectorating tobacco forcibly and to great distances, and

---

[35] This refers to Township T3 Indian Purchase. This township is just of the Millinocket Township. It encompasses all of Quakish Lake, with the dividing line running down the center of the West Branch and through the center of Shad Pond.

swore voluminously about his ill-luck in not being somewhere else. Just then he had nothing to do. He was an expert at picking out jobs where there was nothing to do. This time he was waiting for his mate, who had gone for an axe, and not a stroke of work had he done since his mate left him. There it was, a bright sunny morning about seven o'clock, a good time to work, and the logs ricked up like jackstraws on both sides of the falls; the whole river in that confusion which the rear has to clean up and leave tidy; plenty of work for this fellow to do with his peavey in picking off singles and rolling in little handfuls caught along the edges, and helping to do his share of the setting to rights; but instead, he sat on a log-jam in the sun, and spat more vigorously and swore more violently as it grew upon him how ill the world was using him in making him work on the Fourth of July.

The Cripple, unable to escape, tried to divert him from his melancholy. "Well, Tobias Johnson's boat got down all right," he remarked.

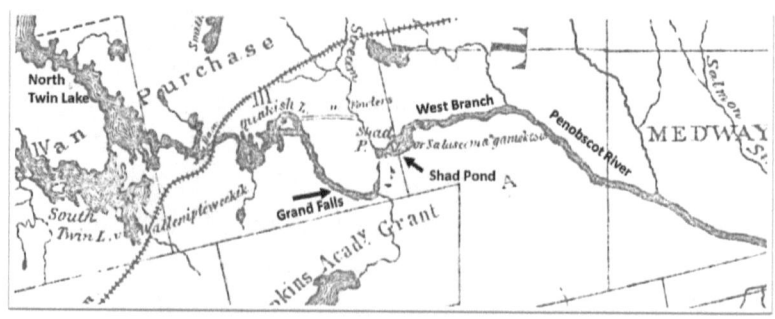

MAP AREA OF GRAND FALLS AND SHAD POND

from Hubbard's 1899 Map; predating the town of Millinocket.

Tobias Johnson and his crew had but just run the Blue Rock Pitch.[36] It was to see the boats go down that the Cripple had crawled out upon the logs. The water being very bad that morning, what Tobias Johnson had done was bound to be a topic of conversation all that hot day among little groups of men working on the logs. Even the Shirk ought to have whirled at such a glittering conversational lure. Instead he sulked.

"I'd be rip — rip — ripped, if I was seen runnin' these here falls to-day. It's a damned shame to have to work on the Fourth of July anyway. Head men that know beans from bedbugs would have had the whole jim-bang drive in long ago," and he exploded a whole bunch of crackers on the heads of the offending contractors of the drive. "Here we be a-swillin' sow-belly and Y. E. B.'s[37] an' down to Bangor, don't I know just as well as can be, Deacon Spooner has brought up a thousand pounds o' salmon to Low's Market, an' is reportin' all about the sun-stroke to the schoolhouse, an' the camp-meeting they are gettin' up down to Whisgig on Shoo-Fly, an' salmon enough for all hands an' the cook."

(Deacon Spooner was a sort of summer Santa Claus, who purveyed imaginary information and real Penobscot River salmon. He was held in high local esteem, but he went out of print about this time, and the great volley of oaths which the Shirk shot off at the merry and inoffensive deacon, though they

---

[36] Blue Rock Pitch is in the area of Grand Falls, on a bow of the West Branch between Quakish Lake and Shad Pond. Even as of the current day, this is a remote area of the river.

[37] FHE: Sow-belly is pork; Y. E. B.'s are yellow-eyed beans. Pork and beans are the river-driver's staple of diet, as well as the lumberman's, and not as much relished in midsummer as in the colder season.

may not account for his disappearance, would provide good reason for looking for him among the damned.)

The Cripple tried to get away, but he was too closely followed. Then, deciding that talking was better than listening, he took the reins of conversation. "Bi[38] must have found it awful rough water," said he. "Don't believe there'll be not another boat attempt it today, with the water slacking so. Say, did you hear that yesterday Joe Attien tried to get Con Murphy to leave Tobias's crew an' come into his boat? And Con said he liked his own crew, an' didn't want to change, not even to be in Joe's boat. I heard that he got Ed Conley out of Lewey Ketchum's boat, now Lewey's left the drive. Speaks pretty well for Tobias, though, don't it?"[39]

The discontented one turned impartially from Deacon Spooner and damned Tobias.

"Jim Hill!" said the other, "how them logs has took to runnin'! They're goin' it high, wide, an' lively. That stops all boat capers for one while. Any boat that had it in mind to rival Bi Johnson had better think twice about it before they get out into this mix-up on slack water. Guess our fun's up and I might's well be crawlin' back to camp."

"Guess I might's well stay right here where I be," said the Shirk. "John Ross is up there on that dry jam east side, an' I'd just as soon be where I can keep an eye on him."

The Cripple made a few painful, hobbling steps over the logs and had reached the crest of the jam, when he turned with his hand shading his eyes and looked down toward the Blue Rock

---

[38] Short for, Tobias Johnson.
[39] Con Murphy was an able river-driver in his own right. He would rise up the ranks to be a foreman. Murphy was one of the bosses in 1891 when Eckstorm documented the West Branch Drive. See chapter, *Clump of Posies*.

Pitch, where a boat was drawn up on the shore and the crew stood waiting.

"Say, though," he shouted to the Shirk, trying to make himself heard above the water, "looks like they was talkin' about runnin' after all! Who is it? make 'em out?"

The grumbler put up his head cautiously to make sure that John Ross was attending to his own business, before he ran briskly to the peak of the jam, and announced that it was that ding-ding-danged Injun, Joe Attien; could tell him by his bigness.

"Hain't he the perfect figure of a man, though!" broke in the other in admiration. "Pity his heft keeps him from his rightful place in the bow."

Joe Attien weighed two hundred and twenty-five and, because of his great weight and strength, always captained his boat from the stern, although in running down quick water the bow is the place of honor.[40]

The leisurely one, having made sure that he was getting the right man, proceeded to curse Joe Attien and all his forbears. Then he sat down upon the logs and resumed his original lamentation. "Now down to Bangor way today they'd be doin' somthin' worth lookin' at — boss races an' boat races an' —"

"Joe'd be in the canoe race sure," interrupted the other.

"Not by a long chalk!" said the grumbler. "Don't you see he's governor again? Don't you recollect that last time, when they made him a ding-danged, no-good judge, an' him one of the best

---

[40] Honor, in this context, refers to the position of great responsibility for boat and crew. Those boatmen in the bow who brought their crews safely through fast water were praised for their skill.

paddles in the tribe, a rip — rip — rip — splitting good man on a paddle, all because he was a ding-dang-donged governor?"[41]

The other man admitted the cogency of the argument. "But say," said he, "that's the real thing there. Ain't that Dingbat talkin' up to Joe?"

They watched the rapid, incisive movements of a slender, agile young fellow, outlined against Joe's bulk.

"Dinged little weasel," muttered the grumbler, identifying him; "so durn spry't he don't cast no shadow!"

Then he relapsed once more into his reflective mood. "Now down to Bangor way now, you bet, — oh, boss races and boat races an' canoe races, an' 'Torrent' and 'Delooge' a-squirtin' out in the Square, an' cirkiss an' greased pig, an' tub races an' velocerpede races, — there'll be somthin' down there today worth lookin' at, an' up here nothin' but this dod-blasted ol' river an' a ding-dang passel o' logs!"

"Say," said the other, "I can't quite make that out yet. I ain't a-catchin' on to that performance. There's McCausland an' Tomer an' Joe Solomon an' Curran an' Conley, they all belong — but where's Steve Stanislaus? An' that little Dingbat — what's he doin' with a paddle there?"

"Wants Joe to run the falls."

"Well, but he ain't in Joe's boat!"

"Course not, little rumscullion! That's it! He's failed to get his own crew in, most like, an' now he's stumpin' Joe to take him along on his crew. You watch an' see him do it. He ain't a-goin' to let Bi Johnson have the name of bein' the only man that dares to run these falls to-day, not if he can help it. He'll shake

---

[41] In Eckstorm's journal, she wrote, "Father says Joe Attien could not take part in the Fourth of July boat-races because he was governor and it was thought to be beneath the dignity of the governor."

the rafters o' heaven but he'll show us that he's every bit as good a waterman as Tobias Johnson."

"What makes him light on Joe? and where's Steve?"

The men did not know as yet that the day before, when the crews reorganized at the Lower Lakes, Steve Stanislaus, who was Joe Attien's friend and cousin and physical counterpart, had left Joe's boat. But all sorts of low cunning being readable to the Shirk, he was not at loss for an explanation.

"Well, don't you see, he's cut Steve out some ways. Joe handlin' stern, that gives him a chance to go in the bow, and that's right on the way to a boat of his own, and what he couldn't get with no other man. He don't ship to be no midshipman in the maulin' they are goin' to git. He's figgerin' how to put himself at a premium as a crack man."

"Reel Dingbat trick," muttered the other.

"Joe knows that this ain't no runnin' water today; just wicked to try to run here, the way things is now."

"Don't want to, don't have to," retorted the swearer, for once omitting the garnish of his speech. And it was more true than most epigrams. Joe's orders to go down with a boat did not imply that he was to run the Blue Rock Pitch against his judgment. A waterman of his reputation could dare to be prudent. All the spectators thought that he intended to take out above the pitch and carry by. Then they saw him pick up his long paddle.

The Shirk pricked up his ears and began to be more cheerful. "Looks like something was goin' to happen now!" he chippered. "There they are a-gettin' her ready. Now they're runnin' her out. There's Dingbat taking the bow. Wonder what they are goin' to do with that spare man? Which one of them rip — rip — rippin' galoots do you s'pose Joe'll be leavin' behind?"

That seventh man in the boat was what the men never understood; it gave the color to the accusation that Prouty pushed himself in. Seven men is a boat's crew when working on logs, but in running dangerous places they carry but six or even four men. It would seem as if, planning not to run, Joe had his log-working crew, and then, changing his mind suddenly, forgot to leave behind the extra man.

"Gosh! How rough the water is!" said the Cripple. "All choked up with jams both sides, and the logs running to beat hell. They don't stand one chance not in — My soul! — but he's puttin' that spare man in on the lazy seat! Well, what you must do you will do." It was the inbred fatalism of his class, which makes them stoical.

Simultaneously the grumbler fired off a volley of curses which made the air smoke. "Rip — rip — rip — bang! — bang!! If that Go-donged Injun ain't a-shippin' a Maddywamkeag crew!" (In the cant of the river a "Mattawamkeag crew" means all the men a boat will hold.)

The Shirk was fully alive now. He jumped up and took his peavey from the log side of him. "Guess I'll be moseyin' right along down now," he chirped. Then he set out running over the logs at a lively pace, trailing his peavey behind him. He anticipated seeing something fully equal to greased pig and velocipede races.

There was not much to see by that time. The catastrophe came at once, before they were fairly started. The water was very rough that morning — on a falling driving-pitch it is always roughest. There was that crowning current heaped up in the middle that would push a boat up on the shore; there were the log-jams making the channels narrow and crooked; there were the loose logs running free that would elbow and ram a boat and crowd her off when she tried to avoid them; there were the doubtful, treacherous channels, creatures of the log-jams along the banks and of the fickle current, new with every differing condition, never to be fully memorized; there were the rocks, not less cruel because cushioned with great boils of water; and there were the boat's own weight and tremendous momentum. No thorough-bred waterman will ever undertake to say how fast a boat can run in a rapid; for he does not know himself. He says, "Very fast," and turns the topic to all-day records.

Still the great sharp-nosed boat had as little cause to apprehend disaster as any boat could have had. She bore a picked crew; she obeyed Joe Attien; and she was a staunch and trusty boat, very wise about all the ways of water. She knew all kinds and how to take them. There were the huge boils, those frightful, brandy-colored boils, streaked full of yellow foam-threads spinning from a hissing centre; and there were the slicks, where a great rock betrayed his lurking-place only by the tail of glassy current below, — safe are such places, for the rock lies above them; and there were the ridgy manes of white water-curls, where the slopes of two great rocks met and rolled the water backward; — but she knew how to take them all; she was prepared for perils on all sides, danger unintermittent, whether she took it slick, or bit into the foam with her long beak, or caught it raw and crosswise beneath her flaring gunwales. What she did not expect was that her peril would come before she had caught the set of the current at all; no one looked for that, not even the Shirk, who was running fast so as to be right on hand when she swamped, and was addressing to them various select remarks not intended to be heard above the roar of the water, such as, "Guess you got your belly full this time, old fellow;" and, "Go it, boys, you'll get plumb to hell this trip."

It was nothing to one of his kind that seven men stood in deadly peril, and the show of the moment he was craftily neglecting that he might better witness the closing spectacle; but he never dreamed that it would come as it did.

It was a very simple accident; the dragon-fly, with bulging eyes, rustling in zigzag flight along the river's brink, might have reported what he saw as well as could a man. There was the long, lean boat, blue without and painted white within, lying with pointed stern and longer, tapering snout, steeving sharply, like a huge fish half out of water; within her the line of red-shirted men, their finny oars fringing her battered sides, the stripling Prouty high up in the bow, too eager to snatch the honors of which he has won so many fairly since; then the row of seated men — ragged red shirts, sorely weathered; hard red knuckles, tense on the oar-butts; sun-burned faces under torn brims, or hatless; sun-scorched eyes, winking through sun-bleached lashes; all, Yankee and Irishman and Province-man, black-eyed Indian and blue-eyed Indian, waiting on big Joe Attien towering in the stern, confident that what he did would be done right. Seven men, and four were looking backward to the shore and three were facing forward toward the water, four one way and three the other, as if emblematic of the coming moment when they should be divided by three and by four, for life, for death.

What they thought and how they felt, who could tell now?

But out of all those there, the man's heart which would have been best worth reading was that spare man's on the lazy seat, who knew rough water, and could see ahead, and who had nothing at all to do. If he unbuckled his stout, calked brogans, and slipped them off his feet, who could say whether it was done from fear or from foresight?

Then the poles dip, the long spruce iron-shod poles at bow and stern, the oars sweep shallow water, and, splashing and gritting gravel as they push off, the poles dipping one side and the other, abreast and backward, like the long legs of an uncertain-minded crane-fly, they shove her out.

And then was their black fate close upon them: she did not swing to the current; she was too heavy; the crew were raw to one another and to the boat; bow and stern did not respond as they always had done when Steve Stanislaus and Joe handled the boat, as their old crews still say, "just like one man."

Logy and bewildered, instead of turning promptly to the current, the old boat let the water catch her underneath her side. It shot her straight across the channel, right among the ugly rocks on the other shore, close above the Blue Rock Pitch. Before she could be straightened, the River took her in his giant hands and smashed her side against a rock, smote her down with such a crash that the men along the banks who saw and heard it cannot be convinced that she was not wrecked; and some who saw her fill so suddenly still declare that her whole bottom was torn off as you rip the peel from a mandarin orange. That is not true; she was not much hurt. But eighteen hundred pounds of boat and men were hurled upon that sunken rock with the full force of the River. The port side buckled fearfully; the ribs groaned and gave; the nails screamed as the sharp rock sheared off their heads, and a long yellow shaving, ploughed out of her side, went writhing down the foaming current.

Down to the water's edge dipped the upstream gunwale; in poured the water in a flood, and before she settled squarely, the lifted port side showed that long and ugly scar. What of the shock that sent the man upon the lazy seat reeling backward, that tumbled the men at the oars forward upon their faces, that wrenched their oars from their hands and threw the batteau seats from the cleats and sent the spare man's driving-shoes adrift among the litter of unshipped seats and useless men? Unmanned, unmanageable, full to the lips of water, and just on the brink of the Blue Rock Pitch, what could the old boat do?

Joe dropped his useless pole and took his paddle, but she could not answer to it, and bow-heavy with the weight of water running forward as she felt the incline of the fall, her stern reeling high in air, her crew, disarmed and helpless, crowding on the bowman, she wallowed down that wicked water among rocks and logs.

So much is fairly certain, but beyond this no one seems quite sure; for I can find no one who saw it. Tobias Johnson's crew could not, not having eyes in the backs of their heads, for they had sprung at once to the rescue in their own boat. The Shirk, who would have been glad to see, was out of the running. In his haste to be on hand, he had tripped himself on his peavey and had been plunged headforemost into a hole in the jam, where, kicking and clawing, he went off like Mother Hoyt's powder-horn. (Cursing his own awkwardness? No, not a bit! Damning the men who were struggling in the water, because they had tripped him up and hadn't given him a fair chance to see them die!)

Nor did John Ross on his log-jam see it, though he was so near, for he told: "I was on a dry jam right there, but I had kept Levi Hathorn's boat with me in case anyone should tumble in or anything should happen, and I sent it down to them — and I don't know any more. I saw that they were going to have a hard time, and — and I turned and looked the other way."[42] (*Ladies and gentlemen, — tender-hearted ladies, high-minded gentlemen, — pause and consider whether, standing there, yours would have been the transcendent grace that "turned and looked the other way!"*)

One thing everybody knows, — there were men in that boat who could not swim; there are such in every boat. The others leaped and swam; these clung to the boat. And Joe Attien stayed with them, — not clinging as they did, buried in water; not

---

[42] Although Ross had stated to Eckstorm that his order was to pick the jam, the crew needn't have run the falls; they could have carried around. Why they ran it, is only answered as to why many crews ran rapids and falls as they did. Not only did they decide to run the falls, but the boat was heavy with a crew numbering seven.

crouching and abject, waiting for the death that faced him, — not a coward now, never, but paddle in hand, because the water ran too deep for pole-hold, standing astride his sunken boat, a big, calked foot upon either gunwale, working to the last ounce that was in him to drive the sunken wreck and the men clinging to it into some eddy or cleft of the log-jams before they were carried down over the Heater and that thundering fall of the Grand Pitch. It is the last one sees of Joe Attien, no one has reported anything after that; one remembers him always as standing high in the stern of his boat, dying with and for his men.

The Humane Society gives no medals for rescues made along the river; our men have nothing to show for anything they have done; but when all the paeans of brave deeds are chanted, let someone remember to sing the praises of Tobias Johnson's crew. We do not speak of them — this is not their day. Enough that when they saw Joe Attien's boat swamp, they all leaped into their places and swept out to the rescue. Man after man they pulled in, heedless of their own safety. The last one they caught when they were just on the verge of the Heater, and then somehow, overloaded as they were, on the brink of sure death, they swung in and crept back to the landing-place.

Ashore they looked over the saved and called the names of the dead. They had three, McCausland and Joe Solomon and Curran. Joe Attien was gone, and Stephen Tomer, an Indian lad, and Edward Conley of Woodstock, and Dingbat Prouty. They still hoped for these, — hope dies hard, and they knew how difficult it is to drown a man who resolutely prefers to try his chances of being hanged. So they and all who had flocked in to them at the flying rumor of disaster took up pick-poles, pickaroons, peavies, whatever might be used to save a living man or to recover the body of a drowned one, and set off down the drivers' path which skirts the falls.

There was little hope of finding Joe. When they saw him go, they all understood that, dead or alive, they would find him with his men. But Dingbat had been seen swimming strongly. If the logs had not crushed him nor the rocks broken him, he might yet be picked up in some inshore cove, where the eddy played, clinging to the alders, too fordone to pull himself out, but still alive.

They searched well, and they searched some time before they found him, — for I had it from one who was there, — and when they did discover him, it was the rescuers who were scant of breath.

"Ga-w-d! but don't he seem to be takin' it easy!" said one.

For a man who had just been through what he had been through, he certainly was taking it very easy. He was sitting on a log out in an eddy, a great hulling-machine log, peeled by the rocks in rapids, with tatters of bark hanging to its scarred sides, bitten to the quick by the ledges, broomed at the ends by being tumbled over falls. There in the eddy it was drifting, because it was too big to be dislodged until some driver prodded it out and over the Grand Pitch. Unable to escape, it went sailing round and round, sometimes butting other logs and ramming the weaker ones out into the rapids, sometimes nosing up against the line of the current, and always drawing back again into its quiet haven, swimming slowly, but swinging often, ever a little beyond the line of the bushes, ever a little inside the line of the current. The falls-spume gathered in clots against the side farthest from the eddy's vortex, and the torrent, as it rushed past, threw up wavelets that lapped its flanks.

There in the warm morning sunshine, wet as a drowned rat, his hair plastered over his sharp-cut face, and the wrinkles round his nose showing clearer than common, sat the missing bowman, dripping from every edge and elbow, but stolidly sucking his pipe.

"Well, I call that nerve!" remarked one of the rescuers, viewing him from behind a screen of bushes. He appreciated the self-command it took for a man considerably more than half drowned and entirely soaked to get out his old pipe, dig her clean, and clamp her under his spiked shoe to dry while he peeled his wet tobacco down to the solid heart of it, got out his matches from his little water-tight vial, and filled and lit her up. They admired his young bravado and waited a moment watching him, as, theatrically unconscious of their presence, which he well enough observed, he drew at his pipe and swung with the eddy, his shadow now falling to the front, now to the rear.

"Ain't he a James Dickey-bird!" said another beneath his breath.

Then Dingbat overdid the matter. "Where's that damned Injun?" he demanded, suddenly acknowledging their presence.

The ichor of swift resentment coursed through their veins;[43] already it was settled in their minds who was responsible for this disaster. Here he was, safe enough, having saved himself; Joe Attien was dead trying to save his crew. As the lightning-flash sometimes photographs indelibly the objects nearest where it strikes, so on the minds of these men that unfeeling question branded forevermore the pictures that stood for those two lives, — Dingbat floating at his ease in the eddy, having looked out for himself, Joe Attien drowned and battered and lost among logs and ledges, willing to lose himself if he might save his crew. They have never forgotten, never will forget that difference. To this day, when you ask one of them who was there at the time how Joe Attien died, this contrast leaps before him, and he says that, "Dingbat Prouty did it."

---

[43] Ichor, from Greek mythology, meaning of fluid that runs through the veins of the gods.

The rapids give place to river meadows, the meadows grow into salt shore-marshes, the marshes lose themselves at the verge of ocean, and a mist creeps up out of the sea. Time levels and softens all, and draws a veil of haze across to hide what is unpleasantly harsh. So be it! Let all that is unworthy, low, or mean be blotted out, provided that the lights we steer by, the beacons across the wide waste waters, be not dimmed; — leave us, O Time, the memory of men like this!

JOSEPH ATTEAN
Penobscot Nation Governor, Guide, and River-Driver
(December 25, 1829 – July 4, 1870)
Labeled as, *Joseph Attien* – an undated photo from the *Fannie Hardy Eckstorm Papers.*
Image courtesy of Special Collections, Raymond H. Fogler Library, University of Maine, Orono.

I was a tiny child when Joe Attien died. He had been a familiar friend, and often, no doubt, he fondled me as he did his own babies. But I do not remember him. Instead, I recall — not clearly, though I somehow know that it was they — the delegation of Indians who came down to ask my father where they should go to look for his body. They were tall, and I looked through their legs as between tree-trunks, and the shadow of grief on their dark faces made them like the heavy tops of the pine-trees, trees of mournfulness and sighing.

"Spos'n' gov'nor could got pole-holt, she could saved 'em."

And, "She could saved it herself gov'nor, 'cause she strong man and could swim, but she want to preservation crew."

So my father pondered the problem, and told them where to look for the body. "A brick would swim in that water, it is so strong," said he. "The governor was a heavy man, but unless he is jammed under logs or wedged between rocks, he will be carried right down over Grand Pitch. As soon as the current slackens, it will drop him and he will sink in shallow water at the inlet to the pond. It is hot weather now, and the water being shoal there, by the time you can get up river the body will have risen; you will find it in the upper end of Shad Pond."

It all came out as he had predicted. The body of Edward Conley had been picked up above the falls several days before, but the two Indians they found together in Shad Pond on Sunday, the sixth day. They took both the bodies ashore, and where they landed they cut a deep cross into a tree; and because they could not treat lightly anything which had belonged to so brave a man, Joe Attien's boots they hung upon a limb of the tree. There the river-drivers left them till they wasted away, a strange but sincere memorial of a good man.

Was Prouty Exonerated?
Annotated Edition Commentary

"The bowman chooses the course with all his eyes about him, striking broad off with his paddle, and drawing the boat by main force into her course. The sternman faithfully follows the bow."
- Henry David Thoreau, *in* KTAADN, 1846.

On the pages of KTAADN from which this quote is taken, Thoreau subsequently described the region between Quakish Lake and Shad Pond. In fact, they had left their batteau above Grand Falls on this exact stretch of the river, waiting to be carried around.

- - - - -

IT would appear that the story in this chapter (somewhat) exonerates bowman Charles "Dingbat" Prouty. However, the editor has discovered notes in Eckstorm's journal files indicating she still had doubts about Prouty, even after John Ross had given her his version. In, *'Tis Twenty Years Since*, the chapter Eckstorm added at the end of the 1924 edition of *The Penobscot Man*, she tells how she re-wrote her story about the death of Attien before the original book release based on John Ross's account.[44] In fact, an article she submitted for the

---

[44] The chapter, *'Tis Twenty Years Since,* is included in this edition. The spelling as Attean, or Attien, is based on the source or journal notes.

Atlantic Monthly with this story, predating the book's release, was called back for editing in order that she could align to what Ross told her. The added chapter, published after John Ross, and everyone who had been on that drive had died, form the basis that led to additional research for this edition.

In the original published story, Eckstorm understood Ross had to answer her questions as a company man when he took the responsibility for assigning Prouty to Attien's boat, which he did; but all the while, she left some doubt for the reader as to why the crew ran the falls. She wrote, "Morally every man I ever talked with blamed Prouty in outspoken terms; and no doubt privately Ross felt with them. But so magnificent was the morale of the old West Branch Drive that the head of it was honor-bound to stand by the men who had stood by him." This is telling. The following notes, from the Eckstorm files, reveal a bit more about Prouty's character and what others thought of him. Eckstorm would not have left these notes if she had not felt they needed to be preserved, for her belief was a person's character rarely needed to be protected. When she did destroy letters or her notes, she gave valid reasons, as in the Sunday jottings of her own father's journals, for she understood those words were not meant for others to read. It is no doubt that Eckstorm knew her writings would prove valuable in the future, and luckily these have been preserved for analysis.

The first correspondence is from none other than *Penobscot Man* David Libbey.[45] In a 1904 letter, he wrote to Eckstorm:

"As for the Attean tragedy ..... I have an impression that Joe Solomon told me the boat came out without further injury; but am far from being certain of it. I remember every word of the terse sentence with which he dismissed the subject: "She lose his head. He think cause he have Joe Attean in the stern, that he

---

[45] From Eckstorm's journal section, *Woods Notes & Incidents* – and her correspondence with David Libbey.

could fly!" There you have it. You are all right anyway. John Ross' account goes, an no one will venture to dispute it."

In this case, Joe Solomon, used the pronoun '*she*' even for a masculine object. Here, Solomon told Libbey that Prouty had "lost his mind" in lobbying Attean to make the run of the falls. Even though Libbey knew that Prouty, as bowman, had some fault in the matter, he informed Eckstorm that no one will question her authority on the subject seeing she has the words of John Ross. The account from Ross may have appeased Eckstorm for the first publication of the book in 1904, but by the time she issued the second edition, she decided to set the record straight on what she knew, possibly because all the men involved had already passed on. However, even then she did not publish all she had discovered, for her journal held additional details, evidence she knew would be useful to the story, but not until after her own passing.

It seems, an earlier letter was received prior to the above from David Libbey, as if Eckstorm was pressing Libbey for further details. He wrote:

"What a host of memories your delightful letter did stir up! Attean and "Dingbat" Prouty. Both had faded wholly out of my mind. You see I came here, to Newport, in 1870, and as this river runs into the Kennebec, it seemed to sever all connection with the Penobscot waters;[46] and yet, even I had drove (that isn't good grammar but it's good dialect) 25 seasons, "handling

---

[46] From Newport, Maine, the Sebasticook River runs southwest to merge with the Kennebec River at Waterville. Libbey's locality reference of *severed ties* to *The Penobscot,* is more fully explained in the chapter, *The Naughty Pride Of Black Sebat And Others*, In that story, Eckstorm informs the reader of her own experience with an exchange between herself, a Penobscot woman, and a *less fortunate* woman who was a Kennebecker. Regional associations were, and in many cases still are, strong in Maine.

boat," 15 of them on Penobscot, St. Francis and Magaguadavic waters;[47] but I was on the East Branch when Attean was drowned; drove that spring from Chamberlain for Tom McDaniel. But I drove with Joe Solomon the next spring so I was well acquainted with the details. I never blamed Prouty for running the falls, because he didn't know any better. A boy, who had gained what experience he possessed on the Corporation drive![48] Governor Attean, admittedly the best sternman on the river and boss of the boat, was wholly wrong in running against his judgment. But there is a much graver charge against Prouty. When they swung out from the landing, they had to clear a rock just below them. When the bow had swung down as far as Prouty thought it ought to, instead of looking to see if the stern was clear, he threw his bow upriver, which of course forced the stern down river. Just the extreme end struck, but it was enough. The stern broke off like a pipestem. It was ..."

And here the letter from Libbey ended, at least what survived. This page of Eckstorm's journal has a typed note, indicating the rest is missing, where she wrote, "perhaps lost."

The conclusion of Libbey's letter is interesting, because the later dated letter, where he indicated Solomon told him, "The

---

[47] The Magaguadavic River is located in the province of New Brunswick, Canada. The name may translate to, "River of Eels." Maine river-drivers drove that river and another story of such is told in the chapter, *Joyfully*.

[48] This is a shot at the *'Corporation'* meaning the likes of large companies, and not the P.L.D. and West Branch Drive. The old-time West Branch Penobscot Men had little respect for the big company ways of doing things. This topic is covered further in the chapter, "Working Nights." As Attean drowned in 1870, and Prouty was a young man in his early twenties at the time, it is unknown what *'Corporation Drive'* Prouty had worked for. Prouty's birthplace was not definitively discovered by Eckstorm as some told her Canada, and others said he was born in Maine.

boat came out without further injury; but am far from being certain of it," but here, he noted, "the stern broke off like a pipestem." This is just one of many conflicting transcriptions of this tragedy.

When a boat is traveling over rapids, along a steeped bank river, at high speed, the rush of the water, and visibility from various places on the banks are questionable. We will of course never know the full details, and the color of these stories surely evolved over time. In these letters, we read how Libbey recalled, some thirty-four years following the accident, what someone told him about the rock and Prouty's handling of the boat. Libbey, an expert river driver may not have blamed Prouty for running the falls, but he certainly blamed him for his failure to handle the batteau properly, for the bow is the *place of honor* in running fast water.

Eckstorm's journal notes continued with correspondence from Mr. L. I. Flower, who lived in New Brunswick. Flower, was someone who, it seems, worked for a lumber company, maybe by the name of King's Company. As far back as 1891, Eckstorm had been corresponding with Flower on woods-terms. They discussed the terms 'dry kyle,' 'wangan,' 'gorbie,' and other woodsmen's words as meanings differ between Maine and New Brunswick. In a letter of Nov. 1, 1902, Eckstorm learned that Flower had some association with a David Cremins, who lived in Harvey, New Brunswick. Cremins had been working the Penobscot Drive in 1901, on a boat's crew commanded by Charles Prouty.[49] Flower 'interviewed' Cremins, on Eckstorm's behalf, in August of 1901.

---

[49] Note to future researchers: The typed notes in the Eckstorm files at the University of Maine Fogler Library, may appear, based on locality of the typing, that the 'David' named is David Libbey. It is not. The timelines do not line up for this to be possible. By August

"Any relation to Dingbat Prouty," asked Flower.

"Dingbat Prouty? What do you know about Dingbat Prouty? Why Charles is Dingbat. Dingbat is just a nickname," answered Cremins.

Flower continued, "I told Dave what I had heard about his late superior, and in turn asked if Prouty was really as good a man on lumber as he had been exploited. He said he was a very good man indeed, but added, 'If I were in the same crew as Prouty and were a better man than he, I would never let him know it. He would drown any man he considered better than himself, I believe, and not think twice about it.'

"I was very much surprised to hear this and said to David that, 'drowning all the men better than himself in a crew was truly an original way of keeping his place at the head, and that one would feel some delicacy about resorting to the counter-irritant of drowning him first, besides Dingbat might not stay drowned.'"

Based on the conclusion of the letter, it appears that Eckstorm had requested Flower to find out some information for her. Flower's return letter included: "Now this seems so clearly the class of information you are looking for, that it almost looks as if it were made to order. I never had any hint that his name had ever been connected with any drowning. But it is plain that after a summer's association with him, David thinks he is none too good. According to David he is a good man to work under when his jealousy is not aroused."

This correspondence between Flower and Eckstorm occurred prior to the 1904 publication of, "The Penobscot Man." The

---

of 1901, the summer Flower refers to, David Libbey had long since retired from river-driving and was living in Newport, Maine. The David referred to in the letters from Flower was another man, as noted in this text, a David Cremins.

hints Eckstorm gave of her interpretation of the conversations she had with John Ross of his version of the event, are at odds with all of her interviews and letters. Yet, she wrote the final publication story according to John Ross that Prouty was not to blame. The fact that Eckstorm left these letters with her papers, and her summary of Attean's death is proof that while she respected John Ross's version of the event for the book, she may have always suspected there was more behind the cause of the tragedy.

The following note from Flower was dated, January 3rd in the journal notes, but the exact year of 190x(?) is obscured. The letter mentioned the drives of 1902, indicating this was written that year, or later. Eckstorm likely had this information for the original publication of the book and chose not to use any of the details that were at odds with what John Ross had told her.

Flower writes: "I did the best I could with David on the Dingbat Prouty question. He says he never had much private conversation with Prouty, the most of it having been scattered over two half days that they worked together with no one else very near. In the boat "they had no time to burn on social repartee." And after work, Dingbat was generally surrounded by more sincere worshippers, for it is hard for David to bow down to strange gods .... First, as to Dingbat's place of birth, he says he has heard Maine and Shediac, New Brunswick, given the honor of producing him. He thinks his age would be about 55 - - it would be less rather than more.[50] He is a small, "chunky" built man, weighing about 140, slightly "sandy" complexioned face, a little of the hatchet order with a peculiar set of wrinkles about the base of the nose. To these he is indebted for a

---

[50] Cremins guessed right to Prouty's approximate age at the time, given Attean drowned in 1870 (age 40), that would put Prouty at about 21-24 years of age at the time of the accident.

considerable fraction of his facial expression. He wears a number-5 (size) shoe. He is not a married man but when not in the woods makes his home at a not very reputable place somewhere in the vicinity of Old Town - - or at least this was the gossip of the boat's crew. Prouty is quick as a cat on his feet, yet and reckless to a degree. They ran "Indian Falls" all except the last pitch that summer (1901) and several other places that no other batteau attempted. David got into this boat through the influence of Charles Graham of Springfield who had been a member of the crew for some time. Prouty worked for Con Murphy on the East Branch of the Penobscot in the summer of 1902 and David was on the West Branch.

"David had heard all about the drowning in which Prouty had figured and had seen the graves of the men. He had never heard Prouty blamed for it in any way. He had always understood that Dingbat saved his life by jumping as far as he could from the boat and letting her go. David says that it is the man in the bow that captains it and takes all orders from the foreman of the drive.[51]

"According to him, Dingbat is 'a devil of a feller,' and he says most emphatically that he thinks Prouty would 'play it unfair and low down' to get away with a rival who thought himself a better man than he and tried to show off with a view to giving others the same impression. Indeed, by his information it was not always necessary for the man to show off. He has heard that a young fellow from the Miramichi once cut the key log of a jam on the Penobscot, a feat that both Prouty and one

---

[51] Eckstorm, added the following caption when she filed the letter with her notes: *'Correct; but in this case, Prouty was new, perhaps his first day in the boat, and Joe Attean the best man on the river.'*

"Top" Campbell another bubble-rider[52] had hesitated to do. The spirit displayed by Prouty towards him was such that the foreman of the drive discharged the young fellow lest some harm should come to him. This may be legendary but it carried so far as David is concerned.

"Some idea of David's intimacy with Prouty may be gathered from the fact that he always called David, 'George' and the name was accepted without protest. He says Prouty was a good enough man to work under and had the ability, or rather faculty, to infuse some of his reckless spirit into his crew. He showed some evidence of excitement when he struck a very rough bit of water, but none of fear and he usually swore a little, perhaps to compose or reassure his men a little when they struck the roughest pitch....

"Questioned as to the possibility of there being a strain of Indian in Prouty, he said he did not think there could be enough of it to cut much figure."

The typed transcription of the letters end there; the editor has found no further correspondence between Eckstorm and Flower. It is very likely that Eckstorm came upon the acquaintance of Flower through her writing, or his. Flower had contributed, to such publications as *Forest and Stream* (1892), and in his article, "*About Hoodlums*," regarding game law violations he mentioned 'Miss Hardy.' He also contributed to the paper, *Turf, Field, and Farm* (1902). However the acquaintance between Eckstorm and Flower was made, it appears that Eckstorm trusted the knowledge of the Province man and felt comfortable

---

[52] In another section of Eckstorm's journal notes, she had written, "Jot says, 'foam-walker,' 'bubble-kicker', and 'bubble-walker,' were Province words for one who rides logs. Bubble-rider would fall to the same based on Flower's home of Central Cambridge, New Brunswick.

with him as a go-between to find out what Cremins knew about Charles "Dingbat" Prouty.

As to whether Prouty acted in any way, directly or from inexperience, to cause the accident on the river that day is certainly still an unknown. The notes and details from the Eckstorm letters are included in this edition for the reader to better understand what Eckstorm knew, and how others felt about Prouty.

Attean Pond

Annotated Edition Commentary

In this essay, Eckstorm referred to the tombstone of Joseph Attien, with the name being spelled as such. In her book, "*Old John Neptune and other Maine Indian Shamans*," Eckstorm wrote she copied the following from the gravestone of Joseph's father in 1911, "John Attian, Governor of the Penobscot." This name of French origin, derived from Étienne, translated as Stephen, has been spelled as Aitteon (Thoreau's spelling), Attien, Attian, and Attean. In most recent years, the usual spelling is now Attean. The current gravestone, on Indian Island of the Penobscot Territory is spelled Joseph Attean, as is his father's name on his marker. The various spellings of the surname may have contributed to the confusion of a name of a Maine pond being associated with the man, even at the level of the State of Maine Legislature.[53]

---

[53] For additional confusion on Maine place names in this region and legislative actions, see, *Katahdin, Pamola, & Whiskey Jack –*

Near Jackman, Maine, on Route 201, there is a turn-off overlook facing Attean Pond. Along the roadside there is a sign posted by the Bureau of Public Lands Maine Department of Conservation, with an abbreviated story of Joseph Attean.[54] The placement of the sign, with the scene of the pond, gives one the impression that the pond was named for Joseph Attean. It was not and the placement of the sign is misleading.

History tells us that Attean Pond near Jackman takes the name from Etienne Orson, a late 1700s settler. The pond was named on deeds and maps many decades before Joseph Attien was born. Attean Pond is in Attean Township, which had been on the maps before Maine was a State in the Union, the naming of the Township and Attean Pond occurred sometime around or after the Bingham Purchase. Attean Township (T5R1, NBKP) was quit-claimed from the commonwealth of Massachusetts to John Bradley, of Fryeburg for $3000 in 1833 (Book 32, pg 503). Much of it later was sold to the Coburn family, of Coburn Mountain fame in the same region of the state, then subsequently it was deeded to the State of Maine in a land exchange.

Readers of this book know that Joseph Attean, the guide and tribal governor, died on the West Branch of the Penobscot, and his body was found in Shad Pond, near current-day Millinocket. If the Maine Bureau of Public Lands and Conservation wants to honor Joseph Attean, this sign should reside over Shad Pond, not this pond, for it was on the shores of Shad Pond where his boots were hung in a tree for all to remember.

The sign may be cause of even further confusion. In 2019, Governor Janet Mills stated in her inaugural address of January 2nd, that this pond (she noted as Attean Lake) was named for

---

Stories & Legends from the Maine Woods, Burnt Jacket Publishing (2021).
[54] The sign is at this location as of the year 2021.

Joseph Attean. The pond, may have at times been referred to as Attean Lake, but not on the maps, and it was not originally named for Joseph Attean, the Penobscot Nation Governor.[55]

Not only is this pond not named for Joseph Attean, saying so is actually worse, than saying nothing at all. For those who know Penobscot Nation history, will know that in 1835 some Penobscot nation members disagreed with John Attean (father of Joseph) and John Neptune. In 1839, the opposition party presented Tomah Socalexis and Attean (Etienne) Orson to the Governor of Maine as two of the four persons making up their parties slate of delegates.

This began the old and new party system in the Penobscot nation. While this Etienne Orson would have the same name as the person noted as the settler and trapper of Attean township, the date of birth does not align to make that feasible. Etienne Orson, of the Penobscot nation, as of the 1858 census was born around 1803, so it is not likely that it was this Attean who was the hunter and trapper who had first settled in the area near Jackman, unless possibly an earlier relative. Given the naming of townships were often based on land purchases or lotteries, with deeds often not well documented, the actual origination may be lost. Research continues on the original settler and his

---

[55] The transcription of the Mills inaugural address reads: *"The Wabanaki people know this bond. Their wisdom was passed along by people like Joseph Attean, legendary Governor of the Penobscot nation, a brave, open-hearted and forbearing individual, who guided Henry David Thoreau in his first moose hunt, through the vast and primitive wilderness to Chesuncook Lake. The plaque that overlooks Attean Lake — named for him – reads, 'Rise free from care, before the dawn, and seek adventure.' "* and so on, available online.

history to determine the true naming of Attean Township and Attean Pond.

Joseph Attien was Thoreau's guide in 1853, he was a Penobscot Nation Chief and governor, and he was one heck of a Maine woodsman, lumberman, and river driver. While it would be a fitting tribute to name a pond after him, this Attean Pond was not.

Additional References:

1. Township Deeds and maps from the 1800s. (available online)
2. Indian Place Names of New England (Huden, 1962)
3. The Handicrafts of the Modern Indians of Maine, Fannie Hardy Eckstorm (1932).
4. Map of the Bingham Purchase. Image included.

The following is a crop of the image of the map used for the Bingham Purchase. Attean Pond is labeled as such, and was known by this name since the late 1700s. The labeling of the Moose River is also clearly shown. Likewise, the land office map from 1821 labels the entire Township, Attean.

The handwriting writing is, "This plan represents the Bingham Kennebec Purchase and is a copy of a plan sent from the State of Maine for the purpose of (*illegible – creating or correcting*) the map of that State. The scale is 160 chains to an inch." Boston Jan 12, 1844.

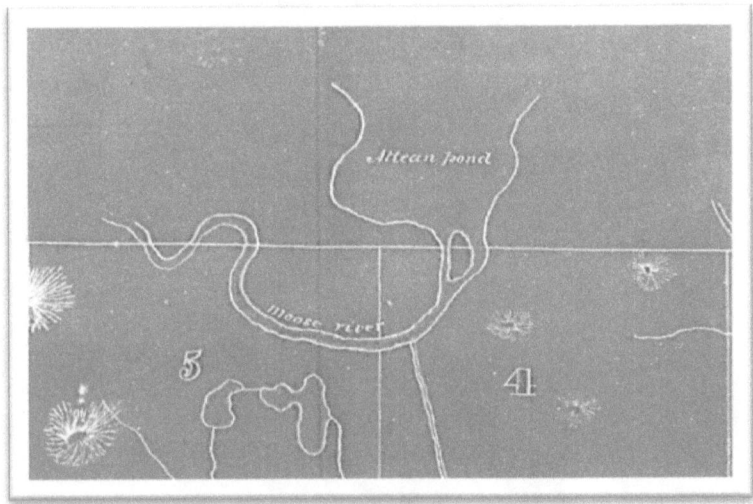

DAVID STONE LIBBEY

Maine River-Driver, Woodsman, Inventor, & Writer. Libbey corresponded with Eckstorm on the Attean death as well as other river stories. Eckstorm honored Libbey with a book based on his journal notes. An annotated edition of that text, with additional content, is available from Burnt Jacket Publishing.

IX — THE WEST BRANCH SONG

THE origin of this ballad was mentioned earlier, within the discussion of *The Drowning of John Roberts, 1852*. The words were given by a lumberman in 1916 to a student who subsequently provided them to Roland Palmer Gray for his book. Eckstorm noted that while Gray thought the ballad referred to the West Branch of the Penobscot, the facts and names did not line up when she researched it further. Nonetheless, we hear another story of a young river-driver who lost his life on a Maine River. This ballad refers to the West Branch of the Union River.

The West Branch Song

c. 1850s

Come fellowmen and lend an ear
A melancholy tale to hear

About one poor mortal, he
Who has sunk and gone to eternity

He hired out with William Brown
To help him drive his lumber down,

And up the West Branch quick did go
Which proved this young man's overthrow.

He started out to break a jam
That had formed upon a rolling dam;

And as he started for the shore,
He fell, alas! to rise no more.

He fell into the dashing spray,
Where wild the waters do make their way;

And within three minutes all was done,
When the work of eternity begun,

Three times he rose, all in our view,
As if to bid us all adieu.

Our boats they being all on the rear,
We could not reach our comrade dear.

We put a boat in at the dam,
We rowed three miles below the jam.

MacMann with grapple all in his hand
Raised this young man from his bed of sand.

X — THE GRAY ROCK OF ABOL

Transported we are, from the pretty maidens fair,
On the banks of Abol Stream,
Where the wolves, and the owls, with their terrifying howls,
Disturb our nightly dreams.

> *adapted from,*
> The Lumberman's Life

IN this story, Eckstorm connects the drowning that occurred at the gray rock of Abol, and a conversation between Henry David Thoreau and his guide, Joseph Polis, documented in Thoreau's journal of Sunday, July 26, 1857. While the interaction between the two men is not her main thesis for the essay, Eckstorm crafts a story with multiple themes for the reader to consider. However, this recounting of the tragedy is more than a telling of the lumbermen's superstitions on cursing at the river, especially in the shadow of Katahdin.[56] This story is history, and more so, an account of where history failed to be written when opportunity first presented itself.

---

[56] The Katahdin legends, documented by Eckstorm, are given in, *Katahdin, Pamola, & Whiskey Jack – Stories and Legends from The Maine Woods*, Burnt Jacket Publishing, (2021).

Eckstorm began this story with a poem, adapted for her purpose.

"The region of which I speak is a dreary region ... by the borders of the river . . . and there is no quiet there, nor silence . . . . The waters of the river . . . palpitate forever and forever beneath the red eye of the sun . . . . But there is a boundary to their realm — the boundary of the dark, horrible, lofty forest . . . .

"And mine eyes fell upon a huge gray rock which stood by the shore of the river . . . . And the rock was gray, and ghastly, and tall, — and the rock was gray . . . .

"And I looked, . . . and there stood a man upon the summit of the rock . . . .

"And mine eyes fell upon the countenance of the man, and his countenance was wan with terror . . . . And the man shuddered, and turned his face away, and fled afar off, in haste, so that I beheld him no more."

— Poe.[57]

---

[57] To introduce this tale, Eckstorm selectively used words from Edgar Allan Poe's *Silence – A Fable*, which was possibly written in 1837 or 1838 originally titled, *Siope – A Fable*. Poe had written the full story based on the river Zaire. Eckstorm applied the prose to the West Branch of the Penobscot. In the chapter Eckstorm added to the 1924 printing of the book, she referenced one uninformed book reviewer who stated to the effect that Poe wrote a story about the Gray Rock of Abol. Poe had died in 1849, some years before the tragedy on Abol Stream occurred.

This is the story of the man who was drowned at the Gray Rock of Abol. Here is the whole story — all sides of it: make of it what you will.

"The Indian thought that we should lie by on Sunday," writes Thoreau, and it is not the only instance where Thoreau naively chronicles some attempt on the part of Joe Polis to bring his manners up to the standards of woods etiquette. Thoreau continues with what Polis told him: "Said he, 'We come here lookum things, look all round; but come Sunday, lock up all that, and then Monday look again.' He spoke of an Indian of his acquaintance who had been with some ministers to Ktaadn, and had told him how they conducted. This he described in a low and solemn voice. 'They make a long prayer every morning and night, and at every meal. Come Sunday,' said he, 'they stop 'em, no go at all that day, — keep still, — preach all day, — first one, then another, just like church. Oh, ver good men.'"

Here evidently comes a gap in the conversation. It is plain that the hermit of Walden was not impressed by this improving example, or said something slighting, and Joe Polis, ever a stout debater, sought to strengthen his own argument for Sabbath-keeping by some unanswerable proof of the goodness of these men. Ordinarily, would Joe Polis have told the story that follows? He must have known many such, but he never told another to Thoreau. However, the proof of these men's piety being irrefutable, he brings it forth, telling Thoreau: "'One day.' said he, "going along a river, they came to the body of a man in the water, drowned good while, all ready fall to pieces. They go right ashore, — stop there, go no farther that day, — they have meeting there, preach and pray just like Sunday. Then they get poles and lift up the body, and they go back and carry the body with them. Oh, they ver good men.'" Not a very correct account of what happened, as we shall see, but what Joe Polis thought he had heard from John Franceway,[58] who was there. The two Indians had agreed that to give a Christian burial to this man was a sure proof of goodness.

But is the poet-naturalist impressed with the beauty of this act of piety to the unknown dead, the mere body of corruption now, but once a man, —

"Cut off even in the blossoms of his sin,
Unhousel'd, disappointed, unanel'd"?[59]

"I judged," wrote Thoreau, "from this account that their every camp was a camp-meeting, and they had mistaken their route, — they should have gone to Eastham; that they wanted an opportunity to preach more than to see Ktaadn. I read of a similar party that seem to have spent their time there singing the songs of Zion. I was glad that I did not go to that mountain with such slow coaches."

The reverse of the shield presents a very different picture.

The only one of this party whom I have known personally was, at the time of this little woods excursion in 1857, already something of a veteran in adventure. He had hunted big game on the coast of Africa and pirates in the China seas; he had been

---

[58] Francois, of course, but called Franceway when it was not made into Plassoway, Brassway, or Brassua. John Brassua, or Franceway, was well known to the Hardy family. In his essay, "A Fall Fur Hunt," Manly Hardy wrote of Franceway, whom he met near Caucomgomoc Lake as, "a man weighing over two hundred, a good hunter and one of the best boatmen on the river."

[59] From Shakespeare's Hamlet, Act 1, Scene 5, when the Ghost speaks those lines to Hamlet, to explain he was cut off from life with the meaning, 'To die, with no chance to repent his sins or receive last rites.'

harried and almost annihilated by such a typhoon as comes but twice in a century, and he was one of those who, with Commodore Perry, turned a leaf of destiny by ranging Japan with the nations of the West.[60]

By his friendly courtesy, I have under my hand an unpublished autograph account of this trip, written before Mr. Thoreau had ever set pen to paper upon his own record. Such a vivacious little narrative as it is, effervescing with puns and bright word-play, turning all the hardships of a toilsome cruise into the most laughable of adventures. Not even Theodore Winthrop's boyish account of his trip down the West Branch touches the fun and frolic of these psalm-singing ministers.[61]

There were eighteen in the party, — ten theological students, two friends of theirs, and six boatmen, with three batteaus. They made the trip from Bangor to the top of Katahdin and back in ten days, coming from the summit of Katahdin into Bangor in just three days, which must be very near a record, there being no railroad then above Old Town. It was an uncommonly rainy year, and they suffered tortures from black flies and mosquitoes. The bulk of their food was hard-tack and dried herring. They made forced marches, and had totally insufficient tent-room. But there is not the suspicion of a complaint all through this little history, not even that first night in a rainstorm, when eighteen men are trying to decide how they are all to sleep in a shelter tent but twenty feet long, and the problems of stowage are so great that one of the boatmen inquires whether "the long ones

---

[60] Professor John S. Sewall (1830-1911) of the Bangor Theological Seminary. Sewall was a sailor, Congregational minister, professor at Bowdoin College, and he certainly was a veteran of adventure. His experiences sailing the China seas were recounted in his book, *The Ship's Log of the Captain's Clerk: Adventures in the China Seas*. Eckstorm knew Sewell, and of his adventures of the 1850s on the U.S.S. Saratoga. His book was published in 1905.

[61] Theodore Winthrop wrote of his West Branch trip in 1863.

will take the tent lengthwise or crawl in twice." The meagreness of their outfit they made up for by the mock splendor of their titles, being officially known as the Grand Mufti, the Bivalvular Purveyor, the Drum Major, Esculapius, and the Bashaw of Two Tails, "who was no tale-bearer in spite of his slanderous title, whose duty it was to keep the stragglers up, to preserve the caudal extremity of the line in due proportions, and bring the tour at last to a successful termination." Upon the top of Katahdin the Grand Mufti fell to calculating "how large a constabulary would be required to put down such a rising of the mass," and the shivering Drum Major "broke out into demi-semi-quavers all over; in fact, his music only made to achieve alternately a 'shake' and a 'rest.'" Thus it is all, excellent fooling, not a bit like the "road to Eastham." Mr. Thoreau need have had no fears that he would not have been put quite upon his mettle to keep up with either the wit or the paces of this party.[62]

In due place mention is made of that Sunday spent in a camp of green boughs just below the timber-line of Katahdin, — "a Sabbath among the clouds, long to be remembered as most like to the Sabbath above the clouds. There were songs of Zion — and meetings — even a sermon in our gypsy camp. Had we climbed so far toward heaven, yet not to get a glimpse of the pearly gates? . . . Katahdin was to us as were the Delectable Mountains to Christian and Hopeful, whence could be seen with

---

[62] Thoreau is not without his critics, and Eckstorm certainly wasn't the first to mention his shortfalls when it came to the Maine woods, no matter how much she praised his work. However, Thomas W. Higginson, a personal friend of Thoreau, wrote to Eckstorm and said of her essay titled *Thoreau's Maine Woods*, "I knew Thoreau well and was one of the most devoted readers, but have never seen his limitations so skillfully analyzed." (See appendix in, *Exploring the Maine Woods – The Hardy Family Expedition to the Machias Lakes*, Burnt Jacket Publishing, (2021).)

telescopic faith some of the glory of the Celestial City." (One has the right to meditate upon what one wills; the curious may compare Mr. Thoreau's profitable cogitations, when on the same spot, upon Titans, Chaos, Vulcan, and Prometheus.)[63]

Forty-seven years after that was written, another member of the same party recalls the day: —

"You remember the Sabbath we spent upon Katahdin, the glorious outlook from the mountain, the serious, but grotesque appearance of our company as we joined in the Sabbath services, Parker in his shirt-sleeves and gloves, with mosquito netting over his head, preaching the sermon, while the rest of us, a number of whom have gone to worship in a grander temple, were reclining in positions which we would hardly commend to the congregations whom we have ministered to since in the House of God.

"One of my pleasantest memories of that Sabbath is of our boatmen, who seemed the most interested participants in that service, two of whom, I was told, not long after were converted and took a manly stand for Christ, one of them joining the church in Old Town, and both dating the beginning of their religious interest from that Sabbath and the way we kept it, so different from any they had ever witnessed in that region. All of our party on that trip have seemed very near and dear to me, and not the least precious to my memory are the men who so kindly, and in such a brotherly way, guided and cared for us. How faithfully and nobly our Indian guide led us! Those rivermen are

---

[63] In reference to the contrast in Thoreau's writing in *Ktaadn*, as he attempted towards the summit of Katahdin, "Occasionally, when the windy columns broke in to me, I caught sight of a dark, damp crag to the right or left; ... it reminded me of the creations of the old epic and dramatic poets, of Atlas (one of the Titans), Vulcan, the Cyclops, and Prometheus." Prometheus was sentenced for his crime by Zeus, chained to a rock on Mount Caucasus, where a great eagle gnawed at his liver.

more serious and thoughtful than they usually have credit for. They are sharp and quick to read character, especially to know who is interested in them, and no men, I believe, are more faithful to a trust which has been committed to them in confidence."

The records are full, but upon one point there is not a word, and that is how they found and buried the body of that dead river-driver. Had not Thoreau recorded it, I, who have inquired somewhat closely into woods history and for many years have known the chronicler of the expedition, though hearing often enough of the man who was drowned at the Gray Rock of Abol, might never have heard the sequel to the story. The only public mention any of the twelve seems ever to have made of the incident was some time after Thoreau's thrust was published, when one of the party printed a brief statement of the facts in the "Congregationalist" for August 17, 1866.[64] He says: — "The body which we found near the head of Lake Pockwockamus was that of a poor lumberman, drowned some four or five weeks before, in driving logs. The spot was so near the ground where we had determined to halt for dinner, that we kept on, dined, and then a party of volunteers went back to perform the last rites of sepulture. A rudely carved fragment of slate was nailed to a tree at the head of the grave, and served to tell the occasional hunter in these trackless wilds of the disaster which had befallen the sleeper beneath. A brief prayer at the grave, with a few passages

---

[64] Thoreau died in 1862, and thus would not have seen the 1866 rebuttal to his classification of these events. Although, his essays for *Ktaadn* and *The Maine Woods*, were first published as magazine installments in 1848, the book, *The Maine Woods*, was published posthumously in 1864 from his journal notes and the earlier articles. The book was likely wider read than the original articles, thus explaining the delay to the "Congregationalist" letter in response to Thoreau, and his position on what Joe Polis had tried to convey to him.

from the Book of Books, was the simple service which committed dust to dust.

"It was not because we were a party of 'slow coaches' that we halted for this act of respect to the remains of a brother man. The incident was certainly a sobering one; and yet there was a degree of satisfaction in being able to carry back to the friends the tidings that the body of him whom they mourned, and for whom they had twice sent parties in search, had been found and had received Christian burial."

These are the documents on both sides, for whose discrepancies in fact and feeling the two Indians, Polis and Franceway, are accountable. They are more than the mere papers in a case. Here, on either side, drawn up as if in review, are the two parties to the difference, men with the best that culture, learning, and philosophy could give, yet neither seeing in the incident anything deeply significant; and between them files this little column of woods-bred men who read in it so much more, who are so struck by its rarity and beauty that they listen gladly to sermons and change the current of their lives. They speak of it to each other and, as it flies, the story grows until what seems truth to Joseph Polis is quite unlike the facts.

Deep impressions imply adequate causes: what was sufficient so to impress Joe Polis? For he did not get his version of the story from John Franceway. John knew that only a part of his company went back to bury this man. The chronicler, cross-examined, says that he was washing dishes for eighteen men; others also were absent. John knew that they made no unnecessary delay, for on that day, the twenty-sixth of June, they covered the whole distance from the foot of Ambajejus Carry to the mouth of Abol Stream. Doubtless he told Joe Polis this, and Joe, knowing the country well, could not forget it. Only twenty-four days elapsed between the date of John Franceway's return and the day upon which Thoreau wrote in his journal, not time enough for a woodsman to forget anything which had been told him; yet here is Joseph Polis, fully convinced of its truth, telling Thoreau, "in a low and solemn voice," that the whole party stopped a full half day on Pockwockamus Carry, about midway of their actual day's journey, in order to do honor to the grave of an unknown man, and the implication is strong that the most of this time was filled with religious services on his behalf. No wonder that to Thoreau it touched on the grotesque!

How is this to be accounted for? Fraud it is not; it cannot be forgetfulness; lack of information is hardly possible; it cannot be from a pious reverence for masses for the dead — for Joe Polis was a Protestant Indian.[65] It is sheer artistic instinct, the human trait of wishing to inclose what is uniquely excellent in the rarest and costliest setting. Joseph Polis had improved the story unconsciously.[66]

Thoreau, who had come into the Maine woods to study the Indian, might well have taken time to probe this subtle matter, for here is something truly strange. However, with his luckless knack of blundering when he came in contact with men, in his own phrase, he "improved his opportunity to be ignorant." The most significant incident that ever came under his observation while he was in the Maine woods he bungled utterly. Once,

---

[65] FHE: So he told Thoreau; but he died a Catholic.
[66] Here is the not so remarkable, but the driving for accuracy that Eckstorm always seemed to strive for, where she is literally examining the written words, which she often did. When Polis told Thoreau, "They go right ashore, — stop there, go no farther that day," is there really anything to analyze when compared to what the minister wrote: "The spot was so near the ground where we had determined to halt for dinner, that we kept on, dined, and then a party of volunteers went back to perform the last rites of sepulture." These are minor details and are really of the same story. Eckstorm's point is the comparison in the reactions between Thoreau and the minister.

indeed, he had been hot on the trail of a solution. In camp at Kineo he had seen for the first time a bit of phosphorescent wood, and kindled by its cold fire, he writes four pages about the phenomenon. "It suggested to me that there was something to be seen if one had eyes. It made a believer of me more than before. I believed that the woods were not tenantless, but chokefull of honest spirits as good as myself any day."[67] But in just two days from that time Thoreau was shutting the mouth of the man who could have told him all he wanted to know. Joe Polis knew all about the man who was drowned on the Gray Rock of Abol; Joe Polis could have shown him all the spirits he wanted to see![68]

Ah, the graves in the woods that one who knows can tell of, lying singly, by twos, by threes, by half-dozens! This One, That One, The Other, — then, as recollection must travel back of the limits of one man's life. Some One, Nobody-Knows-Who, but

---

[67] FHE: Pp. 244-248, *The Maine Woods*, New Riverside Edition. The context is well worth looking up. (This is a reference to a page number in an old edition, but the same can be found in any copy.)
[68] This interaction is reminiscent of when, in 1857, Joe Polis had begun to tell Thoreau about the legend of Glusgehbeh and Mt. Kineo (See, *Katahdin, Pamola, & Whiskey Jack – Stories & Legends from The Maine Woods*). Thoreau, in *The Maine Woods – The Allegash and East Branch*, wrote, (*in part*), "Kineo rose dark before us, the Indian repeated the tradition respecting this mountain's having anciently been a cow moose,—how a mighty Indian hunter, *whose name I forget*, . ., He told this at some length, though *it did not amount to much*, . ., An Indian tells such a story as if he thought it deserved to have a good deal said about it, only he has not got it to say, and so he makes up for the deficiency by a drawling tone, long-windedness, and *a dumb wonder* which he hopes will be contagious." The same stories, told by these same Indians, to a listener such as Fannie Hardy Eckstorm, or E. Oakes Smith, are fascinating tales of Native American culture, with lessons in geography and navigation.

it must have been a grave, for the ground is springy and hollowed, and about there is a line of mould as if long back, a fence of logs had guarded a little space. So many of them! and every one doomed to be obliterated within the lifetime of the men who knew all about them. That is what gets upon a man's mind and gnaws it like a bone, the knowing that where he falls he will lie, like a log in the forest, unburied or lost to recollection. The quiet cemetery with white palings and neat headstones; the narrow, orderly streets; the heaped-up mounds grown with grass; the society of kindred and acquaintance although in perpetual silence, and the undisturbed possession of even a narrow plot of earth come to him in his visions with a desire as strong as the longing for life itself. He knows how it will be with him, — to be jammed in the rapids under rocks, to float in some dark eddy, to be cast out under the tossing, creaking flowage of some lake, never to be found, or to be buried by the pathway, even so near that the passing will soon go on over his head, and the men who come after and curse the hollow in the road that fills up with water will not know that it is his grave.

It was so with those three buried at Howe Falls on Nahmakanta, where supplies were hauled over the graves on purpose that the men might not know and lose their courage. He remembers at Pollywog Pond the eight graves in one place, and one in another, of those drowned on Nigger Pitch;[69] two at the mouth of Bean Brook; seven at Howe Falls Deadwater, of those who died of smallpox, and six more at Logan Joe Mary, dead of the same scourge.[70] There are all those who have died at Ripogenus, and those down by Grand Falls, where their names

---

[69] The use of this word has been removed from place names in Maine.
[70] This was told to Eckstorm by Lewey Ketchum and was likely a logon place near the Jo-Mary Lakes given the context.

are scratched upon the rocks, the only enduring memorial in all the woods. How many he knows of here and there, lying singly, unmarked, buried in silence to wait in awful solitude. Every grave is his own in possibility: he never thinks of it slightingly. Death is still Death in the woods, though outside now it may be nothing but death.

Yet not even the solemnity of a death in the wilderness explains why John Franceway and those other five, some of whom knew this man and were near at hand when he was drowned, regarded this incident as so deeply solemn. For it was not the prayers and preaching upon the mountain, it was something else that so impressed them. Behind the stage on which they were but players was the terrifying hell-fire of Calvinism, Methodism, Wesleyanism, mingling in contiguous incongruity with the Romanist's purging flames; and before that lurid background they were all playing in a drama of redemption and damnation, not knowing when any one of them was to leave the stage, nor what he was ordained to do upon it. But this man's part was clear: he had played it out to damnation, and made his exit, and no man might deny that the doom was warrantable. It was the tragic rightness of his fate, than which the greatest of the playwrights have conceived nothing more sternly just, that conquered their imaginations.

For they knew the whole story; they had witnessed the man's sin and his prompt, almost miraculous punishment; and they knew that his ghost cried unburied; yet now they saw him redeemed from the damned into purgatorial hope, and, by a special providence of God, given what no man buried in those woods had ever had before, the rites of Christian sepulture, — a man who died under the curse of God, by a just judgment; who was lost irrecoverably; who was found at the last possible moment, his grave consecrated, his spirit set at rest.

Moreover, because the Indian who saw it chanced to tell another within three weeks of his return, and because *that one,* by a still rarer chance, told it to a man who wrote everything down, even the things he did not understand, the man who died forsaken and alone has had the whole world come to his obsequies. So far from being placed obscurely in the wilderness, that Gray Rock of Abol stands in the eyes and sight of all.

These are strange stories, but they well up out of the hearts of men, and in them are the issues of life. Men do not perish alone, unknown, forsaken, forgotten. The constitution of the universe forbids. The truth about them must leap out some time, and be written on the skies like the flashes of the midnight Aurora; somewhere it is to be known what they were, where they failed, wherein they made their conquests, — their treachery, their faithfulness — their cowardice, their courage — their shamelessness, their honor — but most of all and longest enduring, their better parts.

We come now to the story, no more the facts about the story, but the story itself.

There are many gray rocks on Abol: Mount Katahdin put them there. Katahdin rules over all that West Branch country, a calm despot. Mute, massive, immense, hard-featured, broad-shouldered, nowhere can you get in that country where the broad forehead of Katahdin is not turned upon you. Snow and rain it sends to that region; it floods the river from its flanks; its back cuts off the north wind, making the valley hot; the road of the farmer it has closed, and the way of the lumberman it makes unduly difficult, by sowing the whole country with millions of tons of granite chipped from its sides. From Abol all the way down those many falls, Pockwockamus, Katepskonhegan, called more often Debsconeag, Pescongamoc, which we now call Passangamet, and Ambajejus, the river in half a dozen places is choked with these great granite boulders, quarried by the frost from the sides of Katahdin, and by the ice transported all over the country. Katahdin makes all that region what it is; it made the falls, and, indirectly, the back-breaking carries around them; it made the sand on Abol, the first place on the way downstream where you notice clear sand above freshet level; it turned the course of the glaciers and so directed the horsebacks of the glacial drift; it made the Norway pines[71] that grow on the horsebacks, with their hearse-like plumes switching in the breeze like stiff, rustling silk; and it made all the gray rocks. In this region a "gray rock," or a "great gray," is the accepted synonym for a boulder of Katahdin granite.

Abol is the first fall upon which Katahdin has laid a heavy finger[72] being the nearest to the mountain. It goes by many names, according as the Indian has been twisted into forms more or less easy for the lumberman's tongue, — Aboljecarmeguscook, Aboljecarmegus, Aboljacknege-sic, Aboljackomegus, Aboljackarnegassic, — but it means just the same to say simply Abol. The signification is not "smooth ledge falls," as Thoreau gives it — that is Sowadabscook, a hundred miles farther down. The name means "place where the water laughs in coming down," and belongs to two streams of crystal water, blue as ice, that spring from the side of Katahdin and enter the river just above the falls, which by Indian custom take their name from the stream.

---

[71] FHE: *Pinus resinosa*, the red pine, "wrongly called Norway pine," says Gray, but here always so misnamed.
[72] FHE: Not to be construed as meaning that there is no granite above this point. Loose granite appears on the lower end of Ripogenus, and ledge granite not far below, but the drift boulders are not aggressively conspicuous till near to Abol.

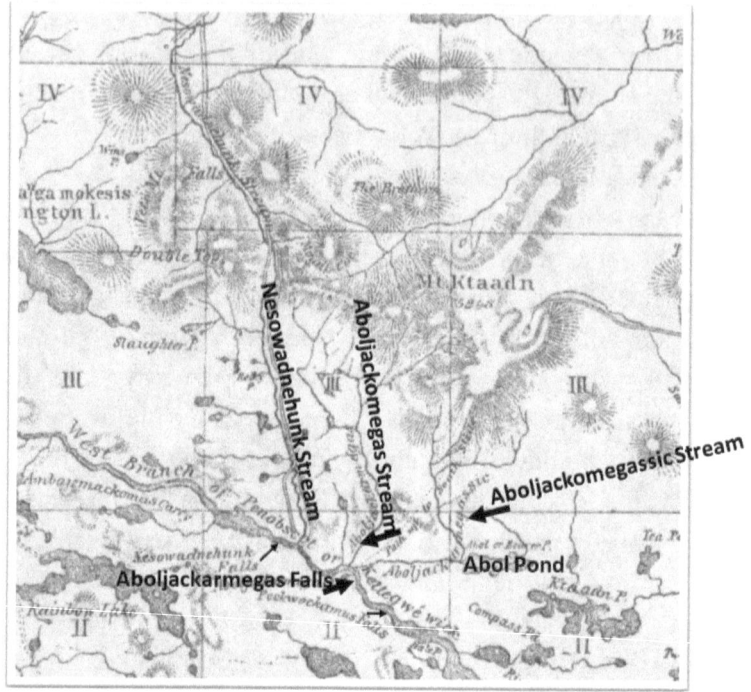

From Hubbard's 1899 Map.

- Aboljackamegas Stream is now Katahadin Stream.
- Aboljackamegassic Stream is now Abol Stream.
- These are the streams Eckstorm mentions "of crystal water, blue as ice, that spring from the side of Katahdin and enter the river just above the falls."
- Abol Falls was labeled, Aboljackarmegas Falls and is between Nesowadnehunk Falls and Pockwockamus Falls. (Not to be confused with what is labeled on current maps as Little Abol Falls, upstream, nearer Abol Mountain.)

- - - - -

The fall at Abol is nothing stupendous. There is half a mile of very rough water, but no sharp pitch. At the head, on the right, lies a low, sandy island overgrown with inferior brushwood, and, like the rest of the carry, bearing a few scattered Norway pines. The passage behind it is closed by a wing dam, making a dry way; one might go upon the island without thinking that it had ever been parted from the shore.

Here by the head of the island are the gray rocks of Abol. They lie close to the water, at some stages under it, great slabs of granite, as true as if split out by the hand of man. Most of them are from fifteen to eighteen feet long, about four and a half feet deep, and of a thickness varying from that of a thin slab of nine or ten inches, to one of two and a half feet mean width. Several lie parallel, their fractures curving coincidently, showing that they have been split since they arrived. All are large, but one ranks all the others. It is thirty-six and a half feet long, five feet and ten inches at its widest point, and four feet and nine inches at its greatest thickness, with mean dimensions not very considerably less, perfect in shape, the most tremendous natural obelisk anywhere to be found. These are the gray rocks of Abol, rifted out of the side of old Katahdin, which crouches lion-like only six miles off, watching them as the Sphinx watches the little shrine between his paws, looking out over the desolation of the wilderness.

When the water is at its height, most of these slabs are submerged, but there is one rock that is always above the surface. This is the one that has a name. Old men sometimes call it the Goodwin Rock, but those who are younger and those who came before, for fifty, sixty, perhaps almost a hundred years, have known it as the Gray Rock of Abol. Standing where it does, within the suck of the current, though so near inshore, — for the current draws upon the head of the island, — a man is always stationed upon it when the logs are running, to prevent jams from forming. There is not the slightest danger in working upon the Gray Rock. It is about three feet out of water at driving-pitch, dry always; it is close inshore; the water is not yet rough, only strong; and it is the coarse granite from Katahdin, upon which a man's foot cannot slip. There is no danger at all upon the Gray Rock, no more than upon a ballroom floor.

But now it is almost fifty years since Goodwin of Stetson found that rock his doom. Of a May morning, too, when the little wintergreen sprouts, tender and red, were coming up on the cradle-knolls, and the bees were in the blueberry blooms, and here and there a wild woods-strawberry, blossoming white, made the drivers think of home. There was such a bright stillness on the morning, and Katahdin, the old giant, still snow-capped, looked down benignly, as if he had waked up good-natured, and, throwing off his blanket of clouds, had put up his head before doffing his nightcap. "Good-morning to you!" he called out to the river-drivers working on the foaming river a full mile below his crown. They waved him back a salute. They yelled as they worked. It was great fun to work on such a clean, crisp morning, and as they felt the strength of the current and rode down to the head of the falls, balancing on a single log, they yelled at Goodwin on the Gray Rock.

That was not Goodwin's day to be merry. Something had gone wrong with him, and he stood on that gray granite from the mist-time of early morning till luncheon-time, when they lost him, a sombre figure wrapped in sullen thoughts, lunging spitefully with his pick-pole at every log, however innocent of evil intentions of jamming, that ran out a blunt nose by his rock just to have a look at him. Whenever they came near him, the poor dumb logs, he prodded them viciously with his pick-pole, and drove them off into the slick of the current and cursed them for their stupidity. Not even the brightness of the morning beguiled him from his evil humor. No man knew what the matter was. He did not have a bad name, his mates spoke well of him; it might have been homesickness; it might have been the toothache; it might have been the wave of world-woe that surges over a man now and then from depths he cannot sound; but there he stood, all alone on the gray granite, stretching out his fist in wanton perversity of spirit, and with blackening oaths cursed God Almighty, damning God to God's own face in the wilderness all alone.

"There ain't no sense in talkin' that way," said one man to another in disapproval as they rode down past on their logs.

"It's darin' too much, even in a safe place like he's in, it is," replied the other, riding his log right into the white of the rapid; "I wouldn't do it, not here, not for no money."

Still the man on the shore station cursed, swore, damned with imprecations everything that came near him, and no one knew, no one ever knew, what was the trouble with him.

For he disappeared. He was in a safe place, and he fell off. He was in quiet water, strong, not bad, and he did not reach the shore. He was a good swimmer, but he never struck out. One man saw above the slope of the current downstream of the rock, a pair of hands reaching up toward heaven, — just a pair of hands, never anything more.

The man who had seen this told the others. "I seen him stand there like he was on a barn floor, and I seen him lift up his fist an' shake it right straight in the face of old Katahdin, an' I heard him holler like his voice would rattle lead inside him, "To hell with God!" And then when I looked the Gray Rock was all empty, and in the water I seen only his two sets of fingers movin' slow-like in the mist that sticks close to the black slick of the falls. I seen 'em open once, an' then they shut an' was gone."

"That was a judgment," said the men one to another.

"That was sure a judgment for swear-in'," they answered solemnly, continuing their search for his body.

But the body was not to be found.

"And it ain't to be expected it ever will be. It ain't often that you do find 'em when they dies so by a judgment," said one of the wise ones who could remember much that had happened on the river. "Lucky for you fellows if everything keeps quiet around here. I'm glad I'm goin' right along with the head of the drive and shan't have to camp none on this carry."

The man next to him — who was to stay — looked at him a little startled — and kept silent.

It was as they had predicted, nothing was ever found of the man, though two parties were sent up on purpose to search after the drive had passed down. "He left a mother," as the phrase is, which means in woods talk that he was the only son of a widow, and for his mother's sake all was done that could be done. But the search was fruitless.

"I knew it would be just that way," said the wise one; "it's always so with judgments; that's a part of it — they can't never be quiet till they are buried, and they don't never get buried, not that kind, when they die damning God that way."

What of the weeks that followed in the desolation of the wilderness?

The little flowers sprouted leaves and buds, and the buds grew to blossoms; the pine pollen drifted down in golden showers, and the tree swallow built her nest. Everything alive was happy and moving.

There was no foot of man, however, on those carries. Showers fell and the damp they left dried up, and never a human foot-track was imprinted upon the softened soil.

But round about the rocks of Abol, under the pines on the carry, those tall and funereal Norways, what was it that wailed and cried?

"Crushed by the waves upon the crag was I,
  Who still must hear these waves among the dead,
Breaking and brawling on the promontory.
  Sleepless; and sleepless is my weary head!
            *   *   *   *   *   *
Nor Death that lulleth all, can lull my ghost.
  One sleepless soul among the souls that sleep!"[73]

"And I wouldn't not want to camp on that carry, not now," says the hunter; "for mebbe I should be for seein' things."

Your guide is not superstitious. Ask him if he believes in ghosts, and he will look straight through and beyond you.

"No," says he, as short and sharp as a rifle-crack.

But then your guide knows many things which it is not to be expected that he will impart to you. When the wind sobs outside and the rain is on the roof, the fall rain that brings down the withered leaves, and you sit by the fire listening to the wailing wind, then will be the time you choose to talk to him of things you know yourself.

It was your father's cousin who had warning when his friend's ship went down in the China seas; the day and the hour he knew. Did his friend not appear at his bedside at the edge of dawn, his hat crushed down over his eyes and a gray ship's blanket drawn around his shoulders, just as he had sprung up the companionway when the ship reeled under her last blow and foundered? It was two days after they had cleared from Hong Kong, and he always knew what he saw. Your uncle, he had seen things too. Once, when he was sitting in his cabin in mid-

---

[73] From Greek Anthology written by Archias of Byzantium. The verse tells of when death comes to the body in a foreign land, the spirit is condemned to have no rest.

ocean, in the calm of evening, a woman passed through the room wringing her hands, and she passed through again and wrung her hands, and a third time, still wringing her hands, and he never knew what it meant, only he saw it.

"And it's lucky he didn't ask her no questions," says the guide, speaking up promptly;" for anyone that talks to a ghost, they don't live the year out, they don't live long mostly. I knew a man — and it was my father — he was followed by a ghost, and she spoke. She asked him for a cup of salt he had borrowed, and he said he'd pay it back, and he did, but he didn't live long after that."

Your guide is not superstitious, but he has seen some strange things. He knows, for one, that murdered men, and suicides, and men who have died under a judgment are never easy till something is done for them. "If a man kills himself, his ghost is bound to stay around the place he did it as long as the house is there; there was Frank Black killed himself in a camp up by Grant Farm, year the war broke out, and they didn't have no peace nor quiet long as them camps stayed. And if a man is murdered, he will stay round till his body is found; if you want to know for sure, there's the way Dudley Maxfield's ghost haunts round that poke-logan[74] hole up to Ayers's Rips. But if a man dies under a judgment, then they don't never find his body, not at all, and that was how it was with Larry Connors."[75]

Up and down that carry at Abol all that month and the next ranged the spirit of the man who was drowned at the Gray Rock. That is the name he has come to be known by, not his own, but as "the man who was drowned at the Gray Rock of Abol."[76]

---

[74] Poke-logan, same as logon.
[75] Larry Connors from chapter IV.
[76] Because these superstitions of the woods are known to guides, like Franceway and Polis, a man *dead by judgement* wasn't

In the rain beneath the Norways, in the moonlight by the sandy carry-end, he paced till cock-crow. The nights were short then, but he paced till daybreak. In the cloud of the falls-mist he wandered, more impalpable than that, searching among the rocks for his former habitation. When he had found it, down along the tangled shores of the deadwater below Abol, he traveled, slowly, each night a trifling journey, following what he must not lose sight of, desiring infinitely the burial which was to be denied him.

"To have no peace in the grave, is that not sad?"

Shorter still grew the nights, yet longer grew his journeyings, for the stream became stronger and talked louder, and threw up spray and beat among the rocks of the ragged Pockwockamus. It is a rough and terrible journey down among those rocks, and the lost soul might well have shuddered as he saw what happened to the tenantless and battered body, useless, yet still so precious, which he was following. On the shortest night of the year, it came safely out of the current of the deadwater into an eddy some distance below the fall.

It was, and doubtless still is, a pretty spot, with tall trees overarching and a sandy shore, so quiet and beautiful, and yet not far above are the great gray rocks and the thunder of the falls. There by the moonlight, upon the sandy shore, all night long and many nights paced the tortured spirit. The current does not move that eddy, — and the sun beats down upon it, — and the days of grace are numbered, — and no one comes.

Then the woods resound with singing. All up and down the river the shores reverberate, and Katahdin smiles grimly, his

---

expected to be found. When his body was found by a roving band of ministers – well then, that was to be regarded as important.

head bare and bald now to the summer sun, to see the joyous troop that comes along. What jokes they make, what merriment on the hot, hard carries, what a pace they travel at! The woods at that day had never seen such a throng of pleasure-seekers. Eighteen men of them, and all singing!

But the guides were thoughtful at times, and sometimes they looked at one another or passed a quiet word. It had begun at Ambajejus that morning, when one boatman slyly nudged another and asked privately, "Where we be campin' down tonight?"

"Head of Pockwockamus most likely," was the answer. "It's a strong pull from there to the top of the mountain in one day, but seein' they want to camp on top, that's the easiest thing to do. We'd better save our backs on these carries what we can today, and take it out of our legs tomorrow."

"You can count me out on that Pockwockamus boughdown," said the first, and he made a pretext of looking at the pitch on the boats to draw the other away with him out of earshot of the rest. "Think a minute," he said; "where do you suspect that that Goodwin has got to? You can just bet your money that it's no bone to camp downstream of *him*."

"It ought to be all right with ten ministers along to keep the boogers off," demurred the first; "and it's too hard a trip to try to make all these carries in one day, with three boats and only six of us fit to lug boat. It's two miles of solid carry, and that makes almost six miles of lugging boats, too much for one day, and it's most as hard poling up over them rocky hell-holes; and then that dratted old mountain tomorrow. Tell you, flesh and blood has some rights, I guess, as well as dead folks!"

"You'll find me campin' just upstream of Abol when you come to hunt me up tomorrow mornin'," said the first quietly.

"Oh, they don't do folks no hurt that ever I heard of," remarked the other.

"Well, I seen him alive mebbe last of anyone, and I ain't a-goin' to take no risks. I ain't lost no ghosts, and I don't want nobody else's huntin' me up and being sociable. What's to hinder droppin' some of our boats along? We can leave the little wangan-boat right here at the foot of Ambajejus, and drop one of the big ones at the foot of Pockwockamus, and let them fellers farm it from there up. That makes only one boat on the last two carries, and two on Debsconeag and this, and saves a whole barrel of backaches. Tip the wink to John an' we'll do it."

"Think them fellers will be suspicious of anything?" asked the other.

"Them?" retorted the other. "They'll be blind as bats that has lost their spectacles; lots of things left for *them* to learn after they get 'em all booked up down to the Institution! This ain't no place for us to be stoppin' to educate them unless we show 'em how to ride shank's mare[77] on these blasted carries."

The plan was adopted; the boatmen breathed more freely. It was just at dinnertime, a quarter of a mile below the foot of Pockwockamus Carry, where the beach is sandy and the water shoals inshore, that they came upon the body of the man who for five weeks had been missing.

There they gave him Christian burial, close by the water, very close, as it had to be, and yet above the line of the freshets. "Two of our boatmen knew him," writes he who headed the burial party,[78] "and spoke very kindly and feelingly of him. The body was much swollen, and so decomposed that we could only dig a shallow grave in the sand close beside it, which the boatmen made with their paddles. The men gently and reverently lifted the body into its resting-place; we had a funeral service; one of the men covered the remains with sheets of birch bark which he

---

[77] Shanks' mare, or shank's mare, means, by one's own legs in going from one place to another.
[78] FHE: The Rev. F. P. Chapin of Hudson, N. H.

cut from a tree, and we all seemed to be brothers united by more than any earthly tie, as we proceeded on in our journey."

For the first time ever known within these woods, a man had received Christian burial.

The boatmen did not talk much about it then. It was not till they were camped by the mouth of the lower Abol, the fire blazing and supper eaten, that two of them, by a common inclination, wandered off to the shore of the clear stream and sat there in the sunset afterglow, which turned Katahdin to a purple amethyst and flushed the water pink beyond the dark reflection of the further bank.

They sat silent. One had a bit of hard-tack, and he crumbled it slowly to toss to the fishes, watching the lunges that the white chevin, ever active at twilight, made for the flakes as they settled.

"Them's awful spry fish, them chubs," said he, as if natural history were all that weighed upon his mind; "I've seen 'em before now peel a raw potato all white just jumpin' at it that way, so sharp in their jaws. And the eels, too, they're all for — they're bad," said he, suddenly checking himself. "You seen how it was today? *You* understood?"

The other shook his shoulders, but did not reply.

The one who found a relief in words went on. "One minister is enough to do the job for most of us; he oughtn't to be so very bad off with *ten* of 'em — think so?"

"Guess he *needed* most of 'em," responded the other, not too hopeful.

"But don't ye think that 'mongst 'em they could manage to get him his 'Come-all-yer'?"

It was a free woods rendering of the Scripture invitation, *"Come unto me, all ye that labor, and are heavy laden, and I will give you rest."*

"Well," he went on, not insisting on an answer, "it was an awful lucky thing for him that they chanced to come along just now, for he couldn't have fleeted much longer. No one can't say that Friday wasn't no lucky day for him."

The other did not speak. The silence suited him. He sat with his hands around his knees, looking at the red glow of the evening sky and the twinkling evening star. "Say," said he at length, "how hot do you suppose hell is anyhow?"

The next day was Saturday and they climbed the mountain. By the next this man was ripe to listen to sermons, and it is reported that they did him no harm.

The next day they all came flying down and pushed far along on their road to the settlements. On the way they paused. It was by the grave of the man whom they had buried. One of them — it was Chapin, who had headed the burial party — brought forth a piece of slate that he had with him and nailed it to the tree at the head of the grave. It said only: —

George Goodwin, June 26, 1857.[79]

More they did not know, neither age, nor home, nor the day he died.

---

[79] This date of June 26, 1857 (a Friday) was likely the burial date, for Eckstorm signified the ministers did not know the exact date of death. Thoreau began his trip on Monday, July 20, 1857, and the discussion with Polis noted six days later. This was some twenty-four days after Franceway returned from guiding the minister's party. The written records show the drowning occurred some four or five weeks prior to the body being discovered. Another mention of John Smith Sewell and this event is given in, *The Maine Woods – a fully annotated edition*, by Jeffrey S. Cramer. That text includes a footnote related to the day in Thoreau's journal stating, "John Smith Sewell, one of the party at the time, later related in a talk before the Bangor Rhetorical Society on 12 April 1858: 'On the bank we made him a grave – and there he rests beneath a tree, which is fixed with a rude carving of his name and age on a fragment of slate.'"

It was almost certainly Sunday labor by which that rude inscription was scratched with a jack-knife upon the bit of slate, — found upon the granite side of Katahdin where slate is rare, and carefully treasured under many difficulties against this use, — but it was labor to be justified by the strictest Pharisee. Never again would they have opportunity to mark that lonely grave with any sign that it was consecrated ground. So they nailed it to the tree at the head of the sleeper, who did not stir, nor moan, nor attempt to talk to them, and they left him there to sleep until the Judgment.

Tree and tablet are both gone now, I am told; a simple post marks the place, just opposite the head of the second island in Pockwockamus Deadwater, on the right shore, directly across from Ben Harris's camp. An Indian guide tells me that he now and then clears out about it to keep the forest from encroaching, and after his day someone else will take up the task. It is consecrated ground, the only hallowed spot in all that limitless forest. There, two rods from the water, three at most, close by the place where they found him, still rest the bones of the man who was drowned on the Gray Rock of Abol and, by a miracle of God, after death found mercy.

MT. KATAHDIN, FROM NEAR ABOL STREAM
(Editor's Collection)

XI — THE LUMBERMAN'S ALPHABET

A is for Axes, you very well know, and
B is for Boys that use them so;
C is for Chopping, which they do begin, and
D is the Danger they oft times get in.

Chorus:
So merry, so merry, so merry are we,
No mortals on earth more contented could be,
With a Hi! Dera! Ho! Dera! Down!
At the woodsman's shanty there's nothing goes wrong.

E is for Echo that through the woods rang, and
F is for Foreman, the head of the gang;
G is the Grindstone that swiftly goes round, and
H is for the Handle so smooth and so round.

Chorus.

I is for Iron, with which they do mark pine, and
J is for Jolly Boys, all in a line.
K is for the Keen-edge our axes we keep, and
L is for the Lice to keep us from sleep.

Chorus.

M is for the Moss that we chink into our camps,
N is for the Needle with which we mend our pants,
O is for Owls that hoot by night, and
P is for the Pines that always fall right.

Chorus.

Q is for Quarreling, which we don't have round, and
R is for River, which we drive our logs down;
S is for Sled, so stout and so strong, and
T is for the Team to draw it along.

Chorus.

U is for Use, which we put our teams to, and
V is the Valley which we draw our sleds through, and
W is for Woods that we leave in the spring
And now I have sung all that I'm going to sing.

Now there are three letters I can't bring in rhyme,
So will leave them off now, but will bring them next time;
For the train it is ready, the whistle doth blow,
So it's Good-by to my darling, I'll to the woods go.

XII — A CLUMP OF POSIES

Now Katahdin is a pretty place
And pretty girls are in;
You'd think it was some nightingale
When they begin to sing,

And as we gently glide along
We'll make them taverns roar,
And we'll drink a health to old Katahdin
And the girls which we adore.

from, Katahdin Green
– A Lumberman's Ballad

THIS chapter is a story of a trip to the Ripogenus Dam, which took place in June of 1891 when Fannie Hardy was just shy of turning twenty-seven. Her purpose in traveling to the West Branch of the Penobscot River that year was specifically to document the men and the working methods of Maine's best-known river log drive. Earlier that year, before the Hardys embarked on this excursion to the Maine woods, *Forest and Stream* published no less than ten essays from Fannie Hardy on the subject of Maine Game Laws, poachers, and out-of-state sportsmen. In her account, she detailed offenses, and named certain offenders; names she was given by a reputable acquaintance. In one particular accusation she offended known poacher Jack Russell, of whom she wrote (*in summary*), "(*I have a letter from*) a perfectly trustworthy man who tells of thirteen moose which he has known to be wasted (*near Duck Pond,*

Cusabexis Lake, Mud Pond and Harrington Lake) ... (*It*) may be said that, since no particulars are given, a large part, if not all these, might have been killed by Jack Russell, the Nova Scotian renegade, who killed so many last year for the skins." Eckstorm's informant was the man who was to guide for her, and her father, on the excursion described in this chapter. With the ink still nearly wet on the articles, she took to the woods in the exact area where the rough character Jack Russell was known to hunt.

The guide Manly Hardy employed for this trip was Wilbur Webster, who played a prominent part in this story. Not only was Webster a *terribly able guide* and woodsman, he may very well be credited with protecting the lives of the father and daughter.

June 1891

I NEVER met the lady face to face, and none of the men ever told me whether they thought her plain or pretty, though they gave out that she was "all right," and that they were *Amici usque ad aras*,[80] or its woods equivalent. However, there can be no question about the truth of the story: for we were in the woods that year and had the same guide, Wilbur Webster, who was drowned that winter in the lake behind Kineo. Were he alive, he would vouch for all I say; but I heard enough of it from others. On the whole it is a pretty story.

Down on Ripogenus, where the little knoll springs in the road to give you a view over the treetops of that rounded mountain

---

[80] Latin for, a friend to the very end, a friend as far as to the altars, or a friend whose only higher allegiance is to religion.

with the shining patches of ledge near its summit, from which all hunters long have called it the Squaw's Bosom,[81] — just about halfway across the carry, a natural resting-place, and delightful withal because it is so cosy and yet so open, is the Putting-in Place, where in spring the river-drivers launch their boats for the adventurous passage of the other mile and a half of Ripogenus. It is delightful there in springtime, hedged with birches, carpeted with bracken, murmuring with the hum of bees and of the rushing river many rods below.

RIPOGENUS GORGE – LOOKING WEST
Image from, Hubbard's Guide to Moosehead Lake (1893).

---

[81] Squaw Bosom Mountain is now named, Moose Bosom Mountain. It is located just south westerly of Double Top Mountain in the Baxter Park Range. The new name is based on Maine Legislative action where all places with the word "Squaw" were replaced with "Moose." For the linguistic derivation of the word *squaw* the interested reader is referred to, *Hubbard's Guide to Moosehead Lake and Northern Maine, Annotated Edition, (2020)*.

There the batteaus are laid out bottom up; there the fire smokes under the searing-irons and the keg of pitch is kept hot, while the old batteau-pitcher, deft and wise at his trade, goes over the sides and bottom of each one, and daubs and smears and sears with his irons until he has made ready each boat for her ordeal by water, soon to be undergone. Here he sings to himself and smokes, runs his left hand lightly but searchingly over the smooth surface, scanning it with close-bent head, before he lifts himself with hands on hips to straighten his bowed back. He is an old man, used to the River; he likes his calling, but he does not meddle much with young and little things, either to notice or to molest. The brown hare thumps up and sniffs at him and thumps off again; the vireos and red-starts carol to him without his hearing; and the little flowers grow bravely, unpicked and perhaps unseen. Even the coy lady's slipper, that wanton, wayward flower, who spreads her skirts and flutters her ribbons, curtsying and coquetting, playing fast-and-loose with all her lovers; who hides herself in the forest and turns invisible and every year seeks a new home, — even she did not try to fascinate the old man by her capriciousness, but grew boldly out in the sunshine, in a great clump, as thickset as a garden plant, and almost within the cart-track of the carry road.[82] These, however, were the demurest little flowers, not blushing pinkish like their coquettish sisters, but immaculately white and as staid as Quakeresses; they raised their eleven little heads — a very large family for their tribe — and lifted their great waxen lips and spread their fluttering pennons in purest innocence and childlikeness. There was never a prettier bunch of lady's-slippers, and yet of the almost two hundred men who passed there several times a day, not one seemed to have any

---

[82] FHE: Cypripedium acaule, the stemless lady's-slipper, our only common species here. (Also known as moccasin flower. Of the orchid family *Orchidaceae*.)

more eyes than the old batteau-pitcher, not one had ever given them the compliment of a glance. It took something very like a miracle to make those men see what one would have supposed that they could not help seeing; for the little clump of posies is the <u>beginning</u> and the <u>middle</u> and the <u>ending</u> of this story.

A CLUMP OF POSIES
(Editor's Collection)

A miracle is, literally, something which excites astonishment. The cause may be decried as commonplace, but there was certainly no deficiency in the effect when the men came dragging in at dusk from their outposts to the camp at the upper end of Ripogenus, and found a new tent there pitched right among their own, and in it a Woman.

"Well, that does beat all hell!" was their frank comment, and there followed interrogations very much to the point, in satisfaction of which those who were lucky enough to have been at the upper end of the carry that afternoon, and therefore possessed of the news, announced that though she wasn't quite a pullet, she wasn't no old hen neither.

"Schoolma'am?"

"Naw! Not a bittee!"

"Glasses an' short hair?"

"Naw!" (more viciously). "All right, I tell ye, all right, an' Wilbur Webster backs the deal. Friends of Joe Francis's an' Steve's,[83] an' come up the Lake[84] with the Old Man,[85] who's comin' down tomorrow. Stands to the West Branch Drive to do the pretty thing by 'em."

Up in the carpenter shop, which was built on an extravagant scale, with the sky for a roof and the whole earth for a floor, and nothing else in it but a litter of shavings and a tall horse for making poles and peavey handles, some of the older men discussed the incident without approval.

The grumbler, who was not young, swore about the folly of bringing a woman on the drive where men had to work and didn't want to be side-stepping, and where they maybe might like to talk some to their blame[86] selves all on the quiet when the blank logs was contrairy,[87] without having to stop and think who was by.

One of the others suggested that at the worst she couldn't be everywhere to once, — which was axiomatic, — and as there was a hundred and seventy-five of them against her alone, they

---

[83] Joe Francis and Steve Stanislaus were friends of Manly Hardy. Stanislaus was the cousin of Joe Attien (or Attean).

[84] FHE: "The Lake" always meant Moosehead.

[85] The reference to Old Man, was to the boss, or foreman, of the river drive. At this date, on this stretch of the river, the foreman was Cornelius (Con) Murphy.

[86] Used here as informal, to blast or damn, as mild curse, as in talking to themselves while riding a log.

[87] Old spelling, opposite to what is logical or expected, as when the logs were at a right angle or locked in a jam.

could gamble on at least a hundred and seventy-four chances in their favor, which was long odds.

Still the grumbler allowed that it was rank inconsiderate to come their way at all; that the drive wasn't no place for a woman anyways, and folks that were well off stayed at home and let men work; and if the women took to coming there so thick, they'd be just obliged to leave the logs in the woods to rot all by their blank selves. He was right, too. Tourists have no more business on the drive than Sunday-school picnics have between firing-lines, and if anything unpleasant happens, they may blame themselves.

There was no rejoicing among the old men over the advent of a woman. Down the hill, in the two long rows of open-fronted tents, with the fires between, the younger fellows also sat in gloom. It did seem a little homey, perhaps, to have a girl around, especially to know that there was a nice girl around, whom one could look at without speaking to, and who would be as much above the reek of their daily life as if living on the top of Katahdin.

She had on a red dress? – Well, just like a red-bird in a glass case, to be looked at respectfully without touching.

Ripogenus was hard enough to get logs and boats over; and the life was monotonous in spite of its dangers. This would be something different, something like going to church, thought one or two. Maybe she might speak to some of them, to a few of them, to one or two of them anyway.

Then they looked across the fire at the fellows on the other side of it. And they saw themselves! Such a set of tatterdemalions[88] never graced a corn-field. They looked from man to man and saw hardly a whole garment apiece. They saw rags, and they saw holes, and they saw scriptural patches of new

---

[88] Tatterdemalions: a person dressed in ragged clothing, a.k.a., ragamuffin, or scarecrow.

cloth upon old garments, producing the prophesied rents. There were men with trousers abbreviated to a sort of trunks, or cut off, just below the knee to prevent "calking,"[89] and some sensitive souls, who abhorred setness of design, wore their nether garments with one leg cut below and the other above the knee. There were some without coat, vest, or trousers, or any part of them, but attired in full suits of underwear. This economical and attractive costume, sometimes white, but oftener originally a vivid scarlet, reduced by rains and perspiration to a whitish red, once whole perhaps, but now pinned together with huge horse safety-pins and variously adorned with patches of old mittens, was an ultra style which would have attracted attention in the most exclusive circles. There were men in rigs in which they would not have let their own mothers see them, and men who, tired and hungry as they were, would not have come down the carry-path till after dark, had they known beforehand that there was a woman on the carry. Oh, the dovecote[90] of the West Branch Drive got fluttered that time!

But what cause had they to look for such a calamity? It was thunder out of a clear sky, — everything all right in the morning when they left, and then the thunderbolt! No human foresight could have warded off the stroke, for never within the memory of the oldest man, not of the log-marker, nor the carpenter, nor

---

[89] Calks being the steel points on the bottom of a logger's boot, pronounced *corks*, sometimes spelled *caulk*. Pants were cut short so the spikes would not catch in the pant leg. Later, loggers began wearing heavier duty pants, coated thickly with paraffin to a point they became known as 'tin pants' due to the stiffness and they could nearly stand up on their own when set in the corner for the evening.

[90] Dovecote, a settled or harmonious group or organization.

the batteau-pitcher, not of the men who had almost outlived their usefulness, had there ever been a woman on the drive.

"And to have my broadcloth suit to home!" lamented one of the most out at elbows, breaking the gloom.

"And that Chinyman ain't sent back my shiny collars yet this week," said another, the joke being that there was not a Celestial within a hundred miles as the crow flew, nor a starched collar within two days' woods journey.

"Well, you'd ought to see me in my patent leathers and high dickey and ram-beaver," put in a third. "I reckon I'm just scrum when I *do* get fixed up; but it ain't no use; this here toney underwear that I'm a-sportin' is too far ahead of the spring styles for this northern climate; makes me look like a last year's bird's nest."

"I count an old swamp robin's nest[91] a heap tidier lookin' set o' tatters 'n them clothes what you have on, Bill. It don't look quite so all fallin' to pieces; but the wangan bills on this drive's goin' to be somethin' hijjus.[92] I was hopesin' to come out with a dollar or two to the good, time we got into boom, but I guess I shall blow it all in for wangan, and come out in the Company's debt same's as usual."[93]

The man next to him was looking at his feet stretched out to the fire. There were neither heels nor toes to the socks he had on, but still he accounted them presentable; anything is that has an inch or two of the top left. "Guess I shall have to give 'em their time, boys; they'll do for patches anyhow. If there was

---

[91] FHE: "Swamp robin" is the vernacular name for the hermit thrush and also for the olive-backed, the two not being distinguished by woodsmen; but as the former nests on the ground, this man must have meant the olive-backed thrush's or even the catbird's nest.

[92] Hijjus – having the implication of tremendous, or high.

[93] Wangan was the general term for supplies. The wangan store accompanied the men on their journey down the river.

more pairs of 'em, it would be easier to shingle 'em on over the worst o' the holes. Say, can't I swap my jackknife for a pair of old mittens?"

Thereupon the price of old mittens and stockings went up by jumps, till the market in worn-out socks was the firmest ever known on the drive. No danger of its being suddenly beared by someone with a reserve of foot and hand gear. That year there wasn't a cast-off garment left upon the end of the carry, and everyone knows that usually the path of the drive is littered with old clothes and old shoes. The demand for thread and needles was lively also, and had anyone been playing Peeping Polly that night, long after their usual hour for turning in, the West Branch Drive might have been seen bending over their work, patching by firelight, in weariness of soul, but with the honest intention of being presentable on the morrow.

But when they got a chance at the wangan chest and could endow themselves in its glories, what a brave array of aniline[94] they did present! Even Solomon might have studied their attire to the profitable neglect of the lily of the field.[95] To attempt to describe the styles at Ripogenus that year would beggar the describer. Full suits of underwear went out of fashion with a bound, and a kaleidoscope of cut and color followed, — red, blue, green, yellow, stripes, plaids, patches. The Girl had known a little of the rainbow attractions of Epstein's and of Pretto's, but such cheerful combinations of color were wholly new; she

---

[94] Aniline – in reference to the compound used in manufacture of multi-color dyes.
[95] A reference to the Gospel of Matthew, 6.28 – 6:29: "And why do you worry about clothes? See how the flowers of the field grow. They do not labor or spin. Yet I tell you that not even Solomon in all his splendor was dressed like one of these."

wondered where is the Zeitgeist's shop[96] and the roaring loom which wove such clothes. Some no doubt they brought into the woods with them; some they purchased from the wangan chest; but some must have come straight from Tom a Bedlam's.[97] It would have turned the head of any girl who thought that so much was done on her account. This one never dreamed of that, — I have thought since then that she was rather stupid, for a girl. She was pleased with the fantastic costumes and with their picturesqueness against the green background. She found O'Connor[98] a good comrade, and she forgot that she was either part of the show herself — or the sole spectator. Least of all did she imagine that she and the gentlemen of the extraordinary clothes were taking parts in a little comedy of courtesy, chivalry, and sentiment as pretty as it was light. Something of it she perceived while she was with them; a part she did not learn till after she had left them; and the prettiest part of all she would never have known anything about, had not the clump of posies at the Putting-in Place stopped her to tell a dolorous tale. (But that is yet to be told.)

When the Girl went up to visit O'Connor on the drive, it was in the face of some friendly expostulation. O'Connor is known to be a noisy lad, and quiet folk are sometimes aghast at his performances.

---

[96] Zeitgeist – capturing the time and meaning of the era, the place and the period of time.
[97] "Tom o' Bedlam" is the title of an anonymous poem dated from early in the 17th century. It is written in the voice of a homeless beggar. The term was also used to describe beggars.
[98] On this drive, there surely was a man named O'Connor; probably several. The author's reference is general, and while her sentiment applied to a good number of the men, the stereotype in the poem that follows in no way can be applied to most rivermen; named O'Connor or otherwise.

O'Connor of the Drive:

"You could hear him when he started from the Rapogenus Chutes,
You could hear the cronching-cranching of his swashing, spike-sole boots,
You could even hear the colors in the flannel shirt he wore,
And the forest fairly shivered at the way O'Connor swore.
'Twas averred that in the city, full a hundred miles away,
They felt a little tremor when O'Connor drew his pay.

"O'Connor reached the city and he reached it with a jar.
He had piled up all the cushions in the centre of the car.
— Had set them all on fire, and around the blazing pile
He was dancing 'dingle breakdowns' in a very jovial style.
And before they got him cornered, they had rung in three alarms,
And it took the whole department to tie his legs and arms."[99]

---

[99] FHE: O'Connor from the Drive, in Mr. Holman F. Day's, Pine Tree Ballads.

Of course, the drive is not all O'Connor; no one estimates, at the highest figure, that it will yield more than nine hundred and twenty-five one thousandths pure O'Connor, the remainder being an alloy of the virtues. Even Bangor is philistine to this extent; for the wisdom of Bangor about woodsmen is largely the fruit plucked from the tree of police-court knowledge.

So Bangor had said, and said seriously:

"Why do you take your daughter up there?"

"How *dare* you do it — among all those rough men?"

"Do you really think it is —?"

But he thought it *was*.

Bangor does not realize that, next to his courage, what most distinguishes O'Connor is his respectful behavior to women. He may be drunk, but he is never insolent to a lady, never affronts her by look or comment, never makes it unpleasant for her to pass through the streets that he frequents.

When in the woods and lacking all the temptations which make city life so briefly but uproariously happy, O'Connor shows his more attractive side, and the Girl was pleased to see how charming it was. The men on that drive were probably not selected for their good clothes or their superior morals, but with an eye solely to their ability to get the logs along. They were officially classified as "white men, Irishmen, Province men, Bluenoses, Prince Edward Islanders,[100] Canadian French, St. Francis, Micmac, Penobscot, and Passamaquoddy Indians;" but among all this mixed crew, in almost a week of familiar intercourse, not a man failed to be honest, orderly, and civil. Not a man was heard to swear, and the only impropriety of any sort

---

[100] FHE: The last three (Province men, bluenoses, and P.E.I.) were called P. I.'s, though, strictly speaking, a P. I. is a Prince Edward Islander. (Bluenose was a nickname for Nova Scotians, dating back to 1785; also the name of a famous Nova Scotian fishing and racing vessel of the 1920s and 1930s.)

was unwitting, and was promptly rebuked by several who could see, what the speaker did not, that it must be overheard. Boxes of camera plates, which would have been unbribable tell-tales to any meddling with the tent during long hours of absence, showed that not even an innocent curiosity ever went so far as to look at what was left in their keeping. In all ways they proved their good-will.

The Girl was charmed with other evidences of their kindliness. They were kind always to their great horses, which that year for the first time were used to draw the boats across the carry. The squirrels frisked about the wangan tents almost within arm's length of the cook. The little birds were tame and numerous. The wild hares seemed to know no fear. One day the men found a fawn too young to walk. They petted and talked to it, brought it out to be seen, and then carefully left it where the mother would find it again.[101] A hermit thrush had built a nest close beside the carry road, within the campground limits. She had selected that spot before she knew that men and horses and dynamite and millions of logs, thundering down over the falls, were to shake the earth itself and break the sylvan stillness. She had not dreamed that twenty-six great boats, drawn by heavy-footed horses, clanking stout harness and straining at the sledge whose runners clung to the bare earth, were to be dragged past her little house under the broken cherry-sprout overarched with last year's bracken. Yet she stoutly held her ground and stayed

---

[101] There is a common myth that if a human touches a fawn, the human scent will cause the doe to abandon its young. While it is best to leave the fawn alone, for the doe is usually close by and will return, the doe is not likely to leave the young due to the scent. Fawns are born with almost no scent, a mechanism to help minimize detection by predators. If a human scent is left on, or near the fawn, a curious predator or a domestic dog, may follow the human scent, which would lead directly to the fawn.

upon her eggs, though only a rod away passed the bustle of the drive. The nest was pointed out to the men that they might not accidentally crush it, and often they would stand in the road and watch the little bright-eyed mother, but not one of them ever startled her in order to see the eggs. When they were all gone and the carry was quiet again, she was still there under her little house, bright-eyed and confident.

The men were fond of flowers, too. Later in the season, when flowers are more abundant, the drivers will often be seen picking the harebells that grow upon the ledges, or a sprig of cardinal flower from the water's edge. If there is a pond lily to be had, it will be found twined into some driver's hat-band, or looped about his neck by its twisted stem. For some reason they had not noticed that clump of lady's- slippers at the Putting-in Place. There they lifted their heads in brave array, thickset and green as to leaf, waxen and pure white as to petal. Perhaps the men avoided trampling on them, possibly they admired and left them on their stalks, but for some reason, neglect or conservation, no one disturbed them.

Up, down, and across that carry for almost a week flitted the Girl and her attendants, chatting, observing, photographing, fishing, idling in unalloyed delight through the longest and brightest of summer days, the guests of everybody. At any moment and at any point between Chesuncook Pond and Ambajemackomas, they were likely to appear, she with her camera, Wilbur with his rifle, and there was always someone right there ready to be of service. Big Oliver, the cook, had beans and biscuit to spare in any quantity, — and they were good. The men wanted to give her a chance to see how a jam is picked, and twenty of them picking off on the Little Arches insisted on standing still, that she might have a good chance to take their picture, while she as unweariedly waited for them to get into action.

BREAKING A JAM AT THE ARCHES, RIPOGENUS, 1891
'Now, all together!'
Photo by Fannie Hardy Eckstorm.
Image courtesy of Special Collections, Raymond H. Fogler Library, University of Maine.

The men on the stations were always ready for a visit. There was an Indian boy, tribe and name unknown, who had plenty of time to spend hunting for a partridge's nest, which they never found, though they had some fun in hunting. There was a Province lad watching on the Little Arches when she came to wait there for the men to come down and pick a jam. He was on an island, to be reached only by walking a log across to the shore; but he must go ashore and hunt up the butt end of a log to make her a seat. Then because there was a cold wind drawing down the gorge, in spite of the warm June sunshine, he must go ashore several times to get wood to build a fire for her, by which they sat and chatted until she saw just what is that homesickness which takes a man engaged at dangerous work far off from home.

Evenings, Joe Francis and Steve Stanislaus would come dragging wearily up the hill to eat a little supper at the tent, or to drink tea out of tin dippers as they lay about the fire and told stories, such stories that the echoes of their laughter may be heard yet hanging about the bluffs on Ripogenus.

The morning after their arrival the Old Man[102] came down, — he was not at all old, being the youngest of the three contractors of the drive that year; the name was a mere courtesy title. Out of his short time with his men he took almost half a day showing points of interest, explaining the technicalities of the work, telling old stories, acting as guide himself all the way across to the Big Eddy, three miles below, that nothing worth seeing should be missed.

Such a perfect excursion in the woods never was, and yet, although it did not trouble her, the Girl had noticed something strange. Wherever she appeared, the men, if not too busy, seemed to be a little watchful; they were very careful of her; they treated her regardfully. She had the strictest orders never to go out of sight of her companions, and Wilbur always carried his heavy Winchester, which she knew was loaded. Is there danger in the house of one's friends? What possible harm could threaten a girl so protected by a universal good-will? She knew that she did not even need attendants on that carry, much less a rifle to defend her. There was nothing to shoot at that season. If there had been, they did not wish to shoot it. Moreover, it had been specially arranged not to bring a gun on the excursion. The girl was puzzled by this little cloud of apprehension which

---

[102] Cornelius (Con) Murphy, an Old Town lumberman and a foreman of the drive. Eckstorm described him in her journal as, "a big, stout man, with a beard on his chin, florid and kindly."

everyone seemed to see except herself. It is the custom in the woods to obey orders and ask no questions: one who is keen arrives at conclusions in other ways, and "other ways" is precisely the woman's way.

The afternoon was hot, and it is a long trip down to Ambajemackomas and back to Ripogenus Lake. "What's the use, Wilbur, to carry that big forty-four seventy?" said she. "The camera and plates are load enough; it's six miles down there and not a step less back again, and we've been down to the Big Eddy and back this morning. Better leave the rifle behind, hadn't we?"

There is no wile feminine so hard to fend against as a little friendly interest; Wilbur was caught unprepared.

"There's nothing to shoot anyway at this season," said she, helping him out, as one does a trout with a landing-net.

"There's bears," said he rather desperately; "you know June's just the season for bears to be running about."

She was entirely satisfied that it was not bears. She was not afraid of bears anyway; yet she did not know what was the real reason for carrying the rifle, not knowing as much as everybody else did.

For Wilbur Webster, when he arrived at the carry, had brought down news; Mr. Murphy had verified it, and rumor therewith picked up the report and ran with it as only rumor can run, spreading everywhere that the Sunday before, this being Thursday, one Jack Russell had sworn openly in the 'Suncook House[103] that if certain people came into the country where he was, he would shoot them on sight. Two days after that they appeared on the very spot where he uttered his threat, and it remained to be seen whether he would back down. The situation was not without interest at any time, but with a woman figuring in the title role, it was unique; certainly it appealed to the West

---

[103] Chesuncook House.

Branch Drive. To have a scoundrel like Jack Russell threaten to shoot a lady who was their guest passed the limit. They were no longer critical spectators; the game was their own, and they played it with zeal.

Thereafter Wilbur became the centre of innumerable conferences, all semi-private.

"Do they know it?" was always the first question.

"I told *him* first off," was Wilbur's stereotyped answer. "We didn't want to spoil *her* good time, so *he* said to take my rifle, and we'd see whether the woods was a free country." [104]

"S'pose she suspects anything?"

"Shouldn't be so much surprised," replied Wilbur. "When she asked me why I lugged that big forty-four, I just floundered around in my mind for a minute; you can't lie to her quite as easy as you can to a sport, so I struck bears. 'Yes, there's bears,' says she, kind of cool and twinkling. She knows as well as I do about how much bears are going to be bothering around this whole West Branch Drive."

"What's he got against her?" was another question.

Then Wilbur explained the origin of the grudge.[105]

"Say, that so? Can she prove it on him?"

"I rather guess she holds a full house on facts," modestly responded Wilbur, not stating that he was the man who had supplied most of them, at some personal risk.

"Oh, it will stand law all right," said Wilbur.

---

[104] Possibly meaning Manly Hardy, but more likely Con Murphy. If Murphy had first required no weapons be brought along for Fannie's documentary, this news had changed his position.

[105] Mentioned in the introductory remarks for this chapter. At the time, Eckstorm hadn't been made aware of Jack Russell's threat. Additional, never before published journal notes are included in the Appendix.

They were waiting at the Putting-in Place among the men gathered to meet the luncheon boy. That was why so many men had leisure to stand and talk. It is one of the sights to see the luncheon boy come trotting along with his firkin of salt beef and baking-powder biscuit in one hand, and in the other an immense coffeepot, carried by a bail, while down his back hang a double row of pint dippers strung together by the handles, reminding one of Jack Mann's saying that, *'the worst load he ever carried was five-hundred-pint dippers without handles against a head wind.'*[106] The Girl could very easily amuse herself questing about after birds and flowers, while she waited for a chance to get a photograph of the luncheon boy.

"The law," went on Wilbur, the Girl just now being out of range, "is just the thing Jack Russell got too much of out in the States; it's more for his health to stay up here to 'Suncook where he ain't reminded of jails. Your Old Man[107] has got a warrant out against him for assault, and the sheriff could have both hands full of papers if the complaints all came in to once. Jack Russell takes his settlements out of court, now you'd better believe. Maybe what he said to me wasn't nothing but guff, but maybe I ain't going to keep my eyes peeled for things moving in the bushes the other side the river!"

"Oh, he ain't looking for trouble; don't you worry, Wilbur," said one.

"No, I ain't worrying any; I'm keeping my sights up for eighty yards *and* a few extra cartridges in my right-hand pocket."

A hunter's voice is always high-pitched, and a little excitement, which makes him forget his usual caution, will

---

[106] A chapter has been added to this annotated edition on Jack Mann, river driver legend.

[107] Could have meant the drive foreman, Con Murphy, or John Ross himself.

cause it to carry far. The Girl heard this last remark. She was some distance off one side, looking at some flowers.

"Oh, come here, Wilbur," she called, "just look at this bunch of lady's-slippers! Aren't they the prettiest ones you ever saw?"

So Wilbur had to come and admire. It seemed to the Girl that there had been enough of a conversation which carried a man's voice up so high and made him forget his proper caution. What he was saying was very likely only "talk for P. I.'s" (which is a sort of buncombe), but that remark about the rifle-sights she bore in mind. She sat down and thought it all out at the next opportunity. She knew the butt end from the muzzle of a rifle, and knew that a hunter would not be likely to have the slide of his sights up for any such range; but what he had said seemed to have the ring of substantial truth about it, that he was prepared for a long shot. There are no long shots in the woods in June; one cannot see eighty yards then, unless there is open ground; here there was no open except along the river. One doesn't go prepared to shoot bears across a raging river with inaccessible bluffs and no means of crossing. Besides, bears would never account for that stringent order never to get out of sight. She was beginning to perceive that here was some mystery.

What was it which Wilbur had told, and Mr. Murphy had corroborated? That the Sunday before at the 'Suncook House, Jack Russell, "as mad as Mike," had spit forth his spite against certain people.

What was it about? Oh, about his killing rising twenty moose last summer for their hides; she had written something about it, and had sent him one of the papers with it in, so as to be fair.

"And if either of them ever puts foot into this country again I'm going to shoot 'em!" said Jack Russell.

"Well," spoke up Wilbur, who was among the crowd, "guess you won't have to wait long for your chance. Jack."

"How's that?" asked several.

"Oh, I hear," went on Wilbur as nonchalantly as if the letter announcing it were not in his pocket, "that they are coming up the Lake tomorrow, both of 'em."

"Where to?" asked Jack, wavering.

"Right down here, Jack." And the steel in Wilbur's voice must have rung clear.

"Who's goin' guide for 'em?" inquired Russell.

"I be, Jack!" retorted Wilbur.

Blades were out then. Wilbur was a proved man, and there was no mistaking what he meant.

This was too much for Jack Russell. He found it was just the right time to set some bear-traps up Harrington Lake way, which was miles out of the road of all tourists, far back in the woods. The whole of Chesuncook rippled with laughter at the performance, and then all subsided to a calm. What disturbed Wilbur was that Harrington lies on the further side of Ripogenus, quite a convenient distance for anyone who wanted to stroll down for the day and, in some warm and mossy nook, to lie across an impassable chasm and take pot-shots at photographing tourists scrambling over the rocks on the other side.

Meantime the Girl knew next to nothing of what was going on. Here and there she caught some shred of conversation which, when raveled out, always gave the name of Jack Russell, and she wondered into what sort of stuff it had been woven, and especially what kind of goods could bear Jack Russell's name on every yard; it was considered no guarantee of quality at that time and place, for he came as near being a desperado as anyone there in the woods. She did not think anything about Jack Russell, least of all would she have suspected that the drive was taking his threat seriously. It was enough that everybody was so kind, and that no one except once ever did anything which displeased her. That time she was angry — and then she wasn't.

"RIPOGENUS, 1891."
Photo by Fannie Hardy Eckstorm.
Image courtesy of Special Collections, Raymond H. Fogler Library, University of Maine.

- - - - -

It was one noon coming back from the Big Eddy;[108] it was hot, and to save time they were returning by the carry road instead of by the river-bank. At the Putting-in Place she looked for her clump of posies. They were missing. Not one was left.

A flame of anger burst forth at seeing them so despoiled. "It's a shame!" she cried. "I wouldn't touch one of them, they were so pretty, the prettiest moccasin-flowers that ever were, and now

---

[108] A place on the river found east of the Ripogenus Dam and West of where the Nesowadnehunk Stream enters the West Branch.

someone has gone and picked all that great bunch! Can't people ever learn to leave a pretty thing alone!"

Her anger had not cooled before there came the dappled dawn of a new idea, and she ceased to blame the spoilers until she should be sure.

Men are fickle creatures, and those she had seen here were about to be fed. If they had picked the flowers to look at, they would gaze at the waxy blooms a moment, then roll them in their fingers and, when the flowers hung limp, and their hands were full of meat and drink, they would drop them where they stood. There she would find the wilted, yellowing blossoms, with flabby, hanging pouch and draggled, twisted pennons, telling the world-old story of thoughtless ravage. She looked all about. There were no flowers there.

Then she looked at the plants again, more carefully. Their poor little denuded stems stood up tall and stiff, full length; every flower must have been nipped off just beneath its little chin; it was not done hastily, nor ruthlessly with the whole hand, but deliberately, with thumb and finger.

Then she blushed, neck and ears, redder than her hat. The doubtful dawn of her idea was full day now; she knew what had happened. For there came to her some chaffer on the way up from the Big Eddy. She had stepped in a muddy spot in the road, and they had told her, Wilbur and her father, that of the men who saw that track not one would ever efface it with his own; that sentiment still was dear to woodsmen. She had laughed and thereafter avoided the muddy places; one would not wish to put too great a strain upon sentiment. But now she remembered that when she had called to Wilbur, she had touched the flowers, lifting their heavy heads as she praised their beauty. That had sealed their doom. In eleven different pockets, pressed in the folds of a home letter or crumpled in the corner of a greasy pocketbook, the eleven little lady's slippers were carried as keep-sakes.

It is many years since that occurred, and yet she can never help feeling guilty for compassing the destruction of those pretty flowers; though glad that she can give to them a more enduring life.

That was not all, though she did not know it till long afterwards, when the clerk of the drive told the story. Wilbur's rifle was really not of the slightest consequence; it might just as well have been left in camp. For the West Branch Drive had taken upon itself to settle everything in its own thoroughgoing way. It decided — that is, enough of it decided, and there was no call for contrary-minded — that it objected to having Jack Russell interfering with its company. Then they discussed the matter of ways and means.

"Send him word," said one, and who so apt to be the man as the very one who had grumbled loudest about having women on the drive, "send him word to leave our company alone. If he don't, tell him we've got men enough and we've got rope enough." —

The message was somewhat pointed. It is quite a distance from Ripogenus up to Harrington, all woods, and P. L. D. runs no post-office department; but it was delivered with dispatch. On our way home, when Jack Russell ran into us on the upper end of Chesuncook Carry, a sort of head-on collision, before the Smiths of Chesuncook as outside witnesses, and it was fight, run, or be friends, he was entirely civil. Although too much must not be inferred from such a statement, we parted quite as cordial as when we met. However, Chesuncook shook with inextinguishable laughter; its merriment was both loud and long-continued, and it became so disturbing to Jack Russell's ears that by the time the leaves were falling, he turned his canoe prow northward, and was last seen going down the Allegash in search of a climate more congenial to his health.

The Penobscot Man was originally published in 1904, a mere thirteen years following the essay in *Forest and Stream* where Eckstorm called out Jack Russell for not only poaching, but for hide poaching. Not only did Eckstorm never shy away from controversy, she took it head on, as this story shows. The trip may have been to document the mechanics and detail work done on the drive, but it is not known if Eckstorm ever published something with those specifics. Her essay about the drive was rather about the character of the Penobscot man. Instead of an essay on the woodsmen terms, river-driving operations, or the tools the men used – all notes she wrote in her journal – she instead utilized the Russell controversy to focus on the kindness of the men. In particular, she weaved a story about the clump of posies to illustrate the character of the lumbermen.

Later in her life, Eckstorm would again spend time with the lumbermen and river-drivers to record the words of the ballads the men would sing of their woods-life experiences. She diligently documented those verses with added historical commentary on the origins, possible locations of places mentioned in the songs, and lyric variations in her book, *Minstrelsy of Maine*.[109]

Of Wilbur Webster, he was more than a guide to Manly and Fannie Hardy. It was Fannie, who wrote the obituary notice for Webster that was published in *Forest and Stream* on January 28,

---

[109] *Minstrelsy of Maine – Folk-Songs and Ballads of the Woods and Coast*, Fannie Hardy Eckstorm and Mary Winslow Smyth, Houghton Mifflin Company, Boston and New York, (1927).

1892. Her words were a tribute to the guide. The eulogy demonstrates the Girl was smart, compassionate, and a good friend to Wilbur Webster.

WILBUR WEBSTER
Drowned in crossing Moosehead Lake, Jan. 4, 1892.
Wilbur R. Webster, of Northeast Carry, guide and woodsman, aged 30 years.

A photograph with a handwritten caption by Eckstorm that reads, "Wilbur Webster. This is the guide mentioned in the story called 'A Clump of Posies' -- a typical Maine Woodsman of the best sort."
Photo by the Lewis Studio in Kineo, Maine.
Image courtesy of Special Collections, Raymond H. Fogler Library, University of Maine

- - - - -

HAD he lived the whole **FOREST AND STREAM** family would have known him, for it was the editor's intention to introduce him to that goodly company and to add from his fund of woods observation and experience to the store already amassed. Of this loss I do not speak, but of the man: we were friends.

In the first place he was very much a man, prompt, decided, quick, outspoken, meaning what he said, ready to defend it. He had a fine, manly way of standing by himself and accounting to himself for what he said and did, which is the semblance of independence and well became him.

Some people have an atmosphere about them; others do not. Wilbur Webster was decidedly of the former sort. If you knew anything about men you knew the instant you faced him that here was a positive character. His letters, too, had a breezy rustle in them that made them charming even to one who did not know the writer. He spoke of things with a knack that nature gave him, just as she gave him his taste for tools and handicraft; for he was a man of many professions and perhaps better able to take care of himself in the woods by comfortable expedients than any man we have had since Hiram L. Leonard, the fly-rod maker, left our woods some thirty years ago. Aside from his inventive turn he had all the trades of the Indian; he could build his own canoe, make his own snowshoes in every part, make his own moccasins and not only kill the moose but tan the hides he made them of. In hunting and trapping he was well skilled for a man of his years. He could, without shame, take his place among cooks, lumbermen and river-drivers and do the work of any of them. He had also been a special warden at one time.

Nor was this all. He had knocked about the world somewhat in his more restless days and had had experiences. The eight days that we were together last spring were an Arabian tale; for, first it was when he had been a sailor, and, lying out on the bowsprit, had watched the porpoises play round the vessel's bows; then he was loading cotton in the South, commenting on Southern life as it appears to a Yankee stevedore; the third day we were alligator hunting with him in the bayous, at which trade he had spent some weeks or months; or we learned to ride a Texan broncho,[110] or we hunted moose in the woods of Maine. Always there was life, and light and shadow in his stories. Who can tell, until the whole story of that stay last spring with the West Branch drive at Ripogenus can be written down, how evenings when the dusk was gathering, Joe Francis and Steve Stanislaus would come dragging wearily up hill to our tent after their day's work, and we would all lie round the fire on our blankets, drinking clear tea from tin dippers, and either telling stories or comparing woods notes? — evenings when the inimitable Joe told us his "Old Non Comprend's Dead," when Wilbur always came in a good second, and Steve beamed silent but appreciative in the fire glow.

Those were days to be framed in silver! "The pictures," wrote Wilbur of some photographs I sent him, "bring back many pleasant recollections of the scrambles over logs and rocks, our search for the oven bird's nest, and above all, the moose stories that used to take my attention and spoil my cooking." He should have added that no small part of these were his own. "He hit out pretty straight at us guides," he wrote me this fall of a man he had been off with, "for telling big stories; but all the same, I don't believe he doubted any of them."

This last is highly characteristic of Webster. He was proud of the fact that what he said couldn't be doubted. He spoke straight out at you with blunt directness, and you must abide and believe it. That Saxon frankness was as marked a feature as his Saxon blue eyes and ruddy beard. Flinching and double-speaking were

---

[110] Broncho (or more typical, bronco), an unbroken horse, broadly a mustang.

not taught in the school where he was brought up. And yet he was always more than willing to substantiate what he said. I remember one day a question came up about the nesting place of sheldrakes. Father and I said, "in old stubs;" Webster said, "on the ground." We knew that we were right, and did not doubt that he was also, but still he was anxious to have us see for ourselves. If we went back by way of Caribou Lake and the Grant Farm, said he not once nor twice, but many times, he would agree to show us all the sheldrakes' nests we wanted to see, and all on the ground. And so he did. We scudded about in Caribou Lake, making from one rocky islet to another between the flaws — "If it hain't on this one, it certainly would be on the next"— until we saw under the little spruce bushes, as he had said, the big nest full of eggs wreathed with down and feathers; and that noon, on the last high ledge toward Ragged, we dined on sheldrakes' eggs, with the June sun blistering our noses and a blue-backed swallow twittering to her mate from the door of the old woodpecker's hole in the islet's solitary stub, where she had her nest.

One could not see Wilbur Webster long without observing that he had nerve and coolness and no small measure of that more brilliant courage which attracts more attention even if it be not so useful. He, indeed, never boasted, either what he could do or had done; he spoke of times when he had been overventuresome — he wouldn't do that now, he said — and of times when he had been afraid; but when I urged the dangers of a course of action from which I would dissuade him, the smile in his beard said that these were the chief attractions. Prudent he doubtless could be, for a hunter must have that good grace, and yet his natural bent was to rashness, of which I may, perhaps, cite an instance. When I was working on the game laws there was a certain delicate matter which I desired to investigate. It was, in fact, so delicate that I thought not even those who knew me best would wish to put their knowledge on paper for me. Then the question was, who could tell me best. On account of his clear understanding and ability to write definitely and coherently, I chose to ask Wilbur Webster.

At this time our entire acquaintance consisted of passing each other without speaking two years before on Mud Pond Carry and two letters on game matters — nothing besides this except slight business acquaintance with my father. Now it happened that in choosing him I had selected the very person who knew more about the matter in question than anyone else. The result was that he sent me promptly full particulars, with no guarantee of my good faith, although he registered the letter for fear of its falling into the wrong hands and requested me to burn it immediately. The information thus given was of great service to me, although for himself discovery of what he had done would have been dangerous if not fatal.

Wilbur Webster was educated, but not in the schools. He left school at twelve, which he deeply regretted, as also that he had spoiled his mind by reading too much trash. For my own part, I see no cause to complain of a mind no more spoiled. It was strong and penetrating, naturally inclined to ask questions for its own solution. It was alert and inquisitive rather than heavy, but it was logical, and always kept well to the point. This indeed was particularly noticeable in his letters. The minds of woodsmen are generally clear, but their letters resemble rabbit tracks in their lack of continuity. Here, however, was one who wrote with ease and felicity. His observation of nature was true and good, minute in details with which a woodsman does not often burden himself. He had a fine taste in books and a reading wider than common. Dickens and Scott he spoke of, I remember; and he talked of Disraeli and Adam Badeau, to me unfamiliar ground; he said also that he liked Emerson. And in current events he was well posted; on undecided issues, fair minded. I remember that we were talking on prohibition that last evening at the Grant Farm and that I noticed with pleasure the points he made. He hid behind no conventionalities of phrase. If you wanted to argue, he left his intrenchments and came out single-handed; so was conversation with him refreshing and profitable.

I think it no more creditable to misrepresent a man for the better at his death than to do him this injustice for the worse in his lifetime. No one was freer to own that this man had faults than himself. He was a man of quick, hot temper, less steadfast than resolute, with less forethought than afterthought, of many faults and failures if he were judged by his own report; for, whether because he liked us as we liked him, or because we were all Penobscot born and therefore inclined to be clannish, he spoke to us without reserve. But at worst his faults were those of a nature inclined to be noble, while his virtues were sterling. Yet it was not to everyone that he showed the side which he uncovered to us, "I despised that party," he said, speaking of one that he had guided; "I was hateful as I could be. Why, I swore enough to have kicked me out of two parties, let alone the rest." Because he disliked a man, he seemed to think it good cause for making that man dislike him. It was part of his impetuous promptness. Yet he was most generous wherever he found anything to praise. On occasions he was enthusiastic. I remember his saying of one New York man with whom he had been guiding, and of whose respect for the game laws he had the highest admiration, "That man was the straightest man that ever came into these woods." And of others now and then he said, "Oh, they were straight, they weren't sports."

But his chief attraction to me was his power of growth. Bit by bit he told us his life and we put the bits together. It was wonderful how from so troubled a life, a brain seething with thoughts and an almost fevered energy driving to action and change, he was working his way to clearer views and settled convictions, to an understanding of all-pervading order. He had an innate clearness and brightness of soul — that drove away fogs and clouds — a health of soul that needed no tonic and yielded to no odds; for it was noteworthy that with him habits which commonly take stronger grip with years were losing hold — not trampled under but outgrown. He was superior to these things; they dropped away. To us this growth in poise and candor of spirit, with the ripening thoughtfulness that attended, promised much. It was the promise as much as the achieve that was so refreshing and made our friendship.

I do not mean to preach, but one never has too many friends. There is left alone the young wife who had lived much with him in the woods, sharing many of his adventures, and of whom he always spoke with tenderness.

- Fannie P. Hardy.

Never before published information from Eckstorm's journal notes and additional research on this story is included in the appendix of this new edition.

GREENVILLE WHARF AT HIGH WATER, 1891

Photo by Fannie Hardy Eckstorm, taken June 1891 on the Ripogenus Trip when they arrived in Greenville, prior to heading to Northeast Carry. It was then that she first met and spoke with Mrs. Wilbur Webster.
Caption: "Looking east from Eveleth's Wharf."
Image courtesy of Special Collections, Raymond H. Fogler Library, University of Maine

XIII — THE BURNING OF HENRY K. ROBINSON'S CAMP

THIS ballad takes us once again to the north woods near Moosehead Lake. Here we travel in January of 1873 with the loggers many miles up the winter road past the Katahdin Iron Works, past Kokadjo, to Grant Farm, and then to Robinson's camp on Ripogenus Stream, near the outlet of Harrington Lake. The Robinson, of whose camp is noted in the ballad, was a respected lumberman from Brewer. The camp burned while the cook was out hunting up a deer to cook for supper. The distance in miles these men walked, in the dead of winter, will be fully appreciated following the reading of the Appendix on the Clump of Posies story.

The Burning of Henry K. Robinson's Camp in 1873

by

Henry Thompson, *logger at Robinson's Camp in 1873.*

Come all you rambling young men and listen onto me,
While I relate a story that happened in seventy-three.
We hired with Henry K. Robinson into the woods to go,
For to pass away the winter, through stormy sleet and snow.

It was early in December, on Wednesday the third day,
That myself and Jimmy Grady we started on our way;
We hoped that night, if all was right, the Iron Works to gain,
And the next day to Roach River go, through stormy sleet and rain.

And early the next morning, before it was quite light,
We started for the Grant Farm unto Weymouth's camp that night.
Our legs being tired and weary, the fourth day on the road,
It was our delight when we hove in sight of the place of our abode.

The next day being Sunday, which God has given to us
That we might love and worship him and his mercy trust,
All things he has prepared for us, no doubt was he thought best,
When he gave us six days to labor and the seventh we might rest.

And early the next morning, before it was quite light,
Mr. Robinson looked around the camp to see if all was right.
He called the boss up to him and unto him did say:
'Come, George, you are my leading man, come show the boys the way.'

There was Grady and Deplissey and likewise George and Al,
They were chosen out of our number the timber for to fall;
They started for the forest to find the trees that's sound,
And soon they brought their lofty tops all tumbling to the ground.

All names I will not mention, as you may understand,
There were twenty-five or thirty, all good and able men,
All working with good courage while scattered to and fro,
And it was their delight, coming home at night, to see the landings grow.

But soon misfortune came to us, as you will all soon hear,
It was in the month of January, just twelve days from New Year,
When Charlie came and told us that our camp had burned down,
That our clothing and our bedding laid in ashes on the ground.

And when the boys all heard the news, they all looked very sad,
Saying, 'We've lost our place of shelter and all the clothes we had.'
A cold night coming on and nowhere for to go,
The sky was our covering and our bed was in the snow.

But all that night by good moonlight, for cold we did not fear,
We hovered there, with watchful care, till daylight did appear.
And when the daylight came at last, like ravens we were fed,
When Georgie stepped out in the yard and unto us he said:
'Come, boys, at last this night is past, with many a chill and pain,
Let us all take hold like heroes bold, and build our camp again.'

Three days of hard labor, each man he done his best,
For to have his camp built up again and have a chance to rest,
And the third night, by good moonlight, we moved into our camp once more,
We settled down, both safe and sound, as we were once before.

And now that camp is finished and we have settled down again,
I will give you the initials that you may guess my name,
There is 'H' for hard, and 'N' for none, and 'R' for royal role,
Just add 'YE' and you will see my Christian name is told.

Then there is 'T' to take each letter and place it where it belongs,
And then to proceed to 'OMP' for 'H' will not go wrong;
Then spell the sun that rules the day, gives forth its silvery light,
Those letters told, my name unfold, if you will just place them right.

And to conclude and finish, this winter's nearly gone,
And springtime is a-coming when we will all return home,
For to greet our wives and sweethearts, how happy it will seem,
And we'll go no more on the rapid shore of Rapogenus Stream.

XIV — WORKING NIGHTS

John Ross from off the drive has fled,
He has left the molasses and the bread,
He's eaten bean-swagan till he's nearly dead,
All on the banks of Schoodic.

from, Driving Logs on Schoodic

IN THIS chapter we fast forward ten years following Eckstorm's Ripogenus trip to this reporting of the changes taking place on the West Branch log drive. While some log driving on Maine's rivers would exist until the early 1970s, the building of north woods roads, especially The Golden Road, cut through the forest and drastically changed the methods of logging. However, to those who knew the old lumbering ways, they saw changes happening decades before trucks, chainsaws, skidders, and feller-bunchers hit the north woods. By the turn of the century there was a noticeable shift in how work was getting done, and how men worked. People had changed, methods had changed, and the ownership went from a dispersed group of lumbermen, to the big paper companies.

IT WAS almost September, time for the logs to have been down in Argyle and Nebraska[111] and sorted, and here was North Twin Thoroughfare with two big booms choked in it. The little steamer that runs to the head of the lake was forced to lie by and wait for them, and aboard of her two old river-drivers, leaning against the pilot-house, were pouring contempt on all they saw. It was not conversation, but a series of snorts and snarls of disapproval, which, by study, could be disentangled into condemnation of — first, any company that could be so behindhand with their logs (for no such late drive as that of 1901 was ever heard of); second, any crew of men who would allow two booms to choke each other in a narrow thoroughfare; and third, all men so imbecile as not to see the way to unsnarl the tangle.

The men upon the logs ran around aimlessly, like bewildered ants; they got a piece of spare boom, much too short, and with it lengthened one of the main booms; when it failed to relieve the congestion in the narrows, they did not know what to do; they tugged and pried and poked and hauled, they went sloshing and spattering and bouncing around on the logs, and nothing

---

[111] Argyle, Nebraska, and Pea Cove were names for Maine booms, the holding places for logs down river closer to Old Town. There the logs were held and often sorted by the log-marks of the owners. A wonderful way to experience the history of a Maine log drive is a visit to an old boomhouse. The Ambajejus Boomhouse is on the National Register of Historic Places and under the care of the West Branch Historical Preservation Committee. As of 2021 the boomhouse, accessible only by boat, was still open for visits.

came of their labors. For four hours the little steamer lay there, and still the problem of those two booms was as great as in the beginning.

The veterans on the steamboat were entirely free in giving their opinions about the whole performance to everyone but the men at work. To them they offered no suggestions. A calm aloofness characterized their demeanor.

"Any ten-year-old child could tell 'em what they'd ought to do," said one of the old men to the other. "All they've got to do is just to cut both booms and jine the ends of 'em, and they'd slip those logs through them narrows like a cat goin' through a hole. Makes a heap of difference if there's two cats both bent on gittin' through at the same time!"

"Of Course!" agreed the other. "Any fool could tell 'em that, only half tryin'; but what do you expect of 'em this year, when there ain't a single man on the drive that knows the river?"

I took the phrase home with me — not a single man on the West Branch Drive who "knew the river!" It was sheer impossibility, for there were always twenty men at least, any one of whom could have carried the whole drive down from Chesuncook to the boom. It had always been the glory of the West Branch Drive that it had so many men who had driven the river for a score, for thirty, some for almost forty years. The men love that river as they love no other; it is the most difficult, the most dangerous, the most honorable post to be found, and the pride and boast of the West Branch Drive has always been, not its supple young foam-walkers, who could traverse the froth of those white rapids without wetting a shoe-tap, but its battle-scarred boatmen, who "knew the river." For one who survived, many, it is true, had died young, but these older ones had all been lions in their day.

"Billy," said I, when I got home, speaking confidentially to one who had served his three and thirty years on the West Branch Drive, "where were you this spring — West Branch as usual?"

"Oh, no," said he slowly, "I didn't drive this spring; I'm gettin' most too old for that." He began river-driving at the ripe age of thirteen, though it was some years before he qualified as a West Brancher; and he probably would know how to handle a boat even yet.

"Where was Joe? Where was Steve? Where was Joe Solomon? Where was Prouty? Where was this one, that one, the other?"

These were a dozen names that spelled West Branch in large letters. He shook his head at every name. — Where were they all? Oh, at home; all getting old like himself, or at some easier trade than river- driving, or off on the East Branch working for Con Murphy, who was a lumberman from the peavey up.[112]

My sky had fallen. Never had I heard of anything more astonishing. Then light broke through a rift, but it was the light of a gray day. Times had changed. It was P. L. D. no longer; no longer the old "Company" for which our men had slaved so willingly; no longer Ross, Murphy, and Smart contracting for the drive; no longer any of the old neighborly names that we had always known; no longer men above who had been the messmates and bunk-mates of those below; no longer men below who obeyed orders only when they did not see a better way, who worked with all the strength there was in them, and

---

[112] Con Murphy, mentioned in the earlier story, a lumberman foreman, had moved from the commercial West Branch, now being choked by large commercial entities, to the East Branch of the Penobscot.

on day wages were partners in interest and responsibility in as fine a piece of cooperative labor as any man can instance. The loudest grumbling I ever heard from river-drivers was not about their food, or their wages, or their long hours, but about being ordered to leave certain small parcels of logs which it would cost unduly to save; they wanted to "leave the river all neat and clean;" they were anxious to do their work well.

The times had changed indeed. That year the great stranger company had taken the drive to show us how much better Millions of Money can manage those things. There was a railroad to its own doors; there were steamboats at its service on all the lakes; it had a telephone the length of the river; it had unlimited capital, — and all these our own leaders lacked, fighting the wilderness bare-handed. Besides, the Great Company very nearly owned the state: it owned the water-power; it owned the forest land; it guided legislation; it had made enormous improvements and was contemplating others which will end God knows where, if they do not improve us all out of existence. It was supreme, the incarnation of the Money Power, the eidolon of the Juggernaut Capital which is pictured as ready to crush all who will not bow down — and some who do. Never before had we seen anything which quite so boldly flaunted the legend, *Money is Power*. It could do what it pleased. It could buy what it pleased. It could buy everything.

Everything but men!

So not a single man of the old West Branch guard had bowed down to it, not a single man who knew the river had bent to its magnificence, but every man of them had shouldered his cant-dog and marched off to work for one who was "a lumberman from the peavey up."

It was superb.

It was epically large.

The Millions of Money had it all their own way that year. The Great Company showed us many things about log-driving, chiefly by way of bad example. It has just had an opportunity given it in the courts to make partial reparation for its sins of ignorance. However these other damages fall out, that to its own reputation is quite beyond repair. It has been demonstrated that Money cannot drive logs, nor buy the men who can do it. The splendor of the Dollar, in public imagination at least, has suffered an eclipse.

But still the cost! Comrades of the peavey, that was your swan-song.

> *Nevermore* will you gather in the springtime, as you used to do, to fight the furious river for the logs committed to your care, raging like wild Achilles over his fallen friend;
> *Nevermore* will you work eighteen hours a day and call it fun;
> Nevermore toil for ninety days or a hundred without a break;
> *Nevermore* (and here's the test) will you be called on to work nights.

And I, never again shall I behold men looking like those I used to see when they came off the drive — white and Indian crisped almost to a blackness by the sun, baked with the heat, bitten by black flies, haggard, gaunt, sore-footed, so that, once their driving-boots were off, their parboiled feet could endure none but the softest kid or congress cloth, and even those I have seen them remove whenever they could; and above all sleepy, falling asleep while they talked to you, gaping from unutterable weariness, dropping into a dead slumber if left alone for a moment, and waking with a jump when anything stirred. In those days they worked both day and night.

Lewey Ketchum was talking with me about it. "They don't know how to work now, and they never will work again the way they used to. In those days we had breakfast and everything packed into the boats before it was daylight. You could hear them clinking things about in the boats before you could see the boats, if the morning wasn't clear, and we were out on the logs before daybreak." One hardly needs to be reminded that in these northern latitudes dawn comes early in June.

"And then we used to work nights." That other, mark you, was just the day's work, even though it began not much after midnight. "We could do more work nights. Logs run faster then, can't tell why, but they do; so we used to sluice nights, and booming down the lakes was mostly done at night, — that is, we got along faster nights. If we had stopped to do it all by day, we would never have finished it, with the winds springing up. You see, we didn't have any steamers in those days, and the logs all had to be towed by hand.[113] Now they've got steamers on all the lakes, and the men think they can't do anything without them. They'll wait half a day to save an hour's paddling. But in the old times — well, you know it was hard and dangerous, but we did it because we liked it. It's a whole lot of fun to go into a bad place where you just know you can come out all right if something don't happen. You get to liking it. You get to wanting it when the year comes round. We always went on the drive just because we liked to be there, such a lot of men on the logs and all trying to get them along and beat each other, and all having a good time at it. It wasn't the pay" — (and no one ever supposed it was the pay, West Branchers, good though it was in

---

[113] Here, Ketchum is making a reference to a head-works raft, the operation of which will be explained shortly.

those days)¹¹⁴ — "we didn't work just our money's worth. There was all those logs to be taken care of, and it kind of seemed as if a man ought to do the best he could. Everybody in those days did the best he could."

It is the testimony of an English Indian, Tobique bred; and I would that I might show you how, in placing the stress upon a question of duty where our own French-descended Indians would have laid it upon necessity, — a relic of the days of *il faut* and *il doit*, what they "had got to do" not what they "ought to do," — I catch the glow in Lewey's quarters of the red coat of Her Majesty's colonel, and hear the echo, a hundred years and half the world removed, of the cheers that answered Nelson's signal at Trafalgar.¹¹⁵ So fine a thing as this that Lewey said must be unconscious. It shows clearly enough what their work has done for these men's ideals. Hire an old riverman to work for you, and there will be little cause for complaint.

---

[114] The evaluation of "good" is relative, even if they worked for more than money. In her journal notes from the 1891 Ripogenus trip, Eckstorm documented the pay rate of the general worker on the drive was $1.85 - $2.00 per day. Head boatmen made up to $4 per day. This rate is equivalent to about $60 (U.S.) in 2021. Considering the men worked much more than a twelve-hour day on average, even if their meals were included, the hourly pay was certainly low considering the conditions and dangerous employment. However, as a point of reference, tradesman such as top bricklayers in 1891 made on average $3 per day; laborers such as coal heavers made $1.85 a day; and engineers (unspecified type) up to $3.00 per day. So certainly, the wage rate was comparable for the time, and those attracted to river-driving and logging did that type of work partly for the atmosphere of the location. (Source for wages: *Wholesale Prices, Wages, and Transportation, Committee on Finance Report 1893*, Washington, U.S.A.)

[115] The Battle of Trafalgar when the British Navy fought the combined forces of the French and the Spanish.

Two hundred and fifty men,[116] all doing the best they could! That was high endeavor, and it made manly worth. I know that in their own words the West Branch Drive "wasn't no holy Sunday-school," and with them the fireside moralities were often lacking; but over against their most shocking breaches of morals balance the magnificent morale of more than two hundred men (not to mention the many hundreds being educated on all the other drives) who were living sternly up to this high ideal of duty. When they died, they died doing their duty; when they lived, they carried back to field and forge and camp and trade the habit of doing the best they could; and the leaven of their example permeated the whole class till they tolerated no shirking, no "sogering," no unfaithfulness to a trust. The Penobscot man is a willing worker, capable in emergencies, true to his trust, knowing well the difference between "ought" and "ought not." And the drive was the college where he learned all this.

How much does a man working at day wages think he ought to do to earn his hire?

Here is the story Lewey Ketchum told me: it was rather a funny story, he said, — at least he told it for such, omitting much which I am bound to supply, and not suggesting that there was anything meritorious in what he did, because of course "a man ought to do the best he can." So many ellipses of information and explanation have to be filled in by me that I cannot reproduce his soft, cadenced English, wholly unlike our knotty Yankee idiom.

---

[116] FHE: The West Branch Drive numbered from 150 to 200 men at the start, and 250 or 300 men later when the logs cut lower down had been received.

He was on Chesuncook — Gazungook, as he softened it, Indian fashion — in charge of a boom. It was the last boom of the rear, and he must not keep the crews waiting. There was no steamer there then, — there was none till 1891, — and all booms had to be towed by hand. Now Chesuncook is a lake eighteen miles long, and a boom comprised from two to five million feet of logs. To tow by hand such a heavy, unwieldy float of logs, many acres in extent, for so great a distance was always a work of magnitude. If the wind was contrary, it became by so much the harder; great loss of time might result from having to anchor under the shore; or of labor, from being carried back even to the starting-point; or of money, from logs rolling out from under the boom, or the boom itself parting and all its contents being spread abroad, a great portion of them never to be recovered. Delays were costly, the risks great, the labor terribly severe. Three days and nights it took, under favorable conditions, to warp a boom down Chesuncook, and it was heaving anchor all the way. Ask any sailor about work at the capstan bars, and then ask him what he would think of taking three days and nights of it without change of watches; probably he would tell you that it cannot be done. And yet it always was done in warping booms across our lakes, and one crew of men had to do it. Their meals were brought to them from the shore, and what little sleep they got they took upon the head-works; but there was very little sleep for anyone unless they had to anchor under the lee of the land.

To make all clear, the great boom, made of logs linked end to end, having been stretched about all the loose logs it can safely hold, is made fast by a short warp to the head-works.[117] The head-works is a raft of triply cross-piled logs, one log long

---

[117] The *boom* are the logs chained together around the millions of feet of logs within the loop to be towed. The *warp* is the rope from the anchor. The *head-works* is the raft the men worked on, *warping the boom*.

by about fourteen wide, all hewed to fit and stoutly tree-nailed together. Up to a recent date iron was too scarce in these remote outposts of the woods for any common use, and wood had to take its place; even at Chesuncook the booms were always double thorough-shotted with stout wooden pins instead of being linked with chains.

Upon the head-works raft was set the capstan, a great spool made of a single log, revolving about a central shaft, and pierced around the top for eight capstan bars. There were no pawls at the bottom, as on ship capstans, to prevent its surging back, but a number of small sticks slanting upward toward the barrel kept the warp from fouling under the spool. An anchor, seldom weighing over three hundred pounds (but usually 200 to 300 pounds), and about a thousand feet of inch and a half rigging are used in a warping boom. To judge of the weight of the warp, it is enough to say that, laid in coils with slack between, it takes twelve men, — the drivers at Ripogenus told me it would take fifteen men, — each carrying a coil upon his shoulder, to lug such a warp across a carry. These long warps are left behind, but I saw them carrying the shorter but heavier hawsers for sweeping the eddies, and as the undulating line crawled slowly up the hill, it looked like the folds of a great serpent. The anchor, the long booming-warp, the stout snubbing-hawsers, and a boat are the chief equipment of a booming crew. The anchor is boated out ahead and dropped; then all hands man the capstan bars, two men to a bar, and begin to spool up the warp. When the anchor is under-foot, the boom is left to drift with the headway already gained; twelve of the men boat out the anchor while the other four feed off the warp from the spool. Then the boat comes back, the men tumble out upon the head-works, and throw themselves upon the capstan bars, to begin their tramping around and around and around, as they wind up the straining warp. Thus, inch by inch, the boom is drawn across the lake, two or three miles in a day of twelve hours being all that a full crew at the bars can accomplish.

MEN TURNING A CAPSTAN ON A HEAD-WORKS RAFT
Photo Courtesy Maine State Library

Lewey Ketchum's crew took their logs at Umbazooksus, the very head of the lake. It was about dusk when they tied their boat to the stern snubbing-post of the head-works and wound the first turns of the warp upon the windlass. They worked well, boating out, warping up, heaving anchor, inch by inch, foot by foot, by the main strength of their arms hauling along that great unwieldy float of logs. They made a path around the capstan where their spiked shoes tore out the splinters, — all within bright and new, all without new and bright, and that circle fouled with the wear of many spike-shod feet. That was the first night. Then the hawser began to bite into the barrel of the capstan, and left ridges where the heavy rope had jammed the fibres of the wood. That was the first day. Then the hawser began to show the fray of running over the front of the raft, and little pick-ends of hemp stood out from it. That was the second night. Then the men began to show it, men being tougher than wood and hemp, and able to stand more strain. They began to fall asleep at their work; they began to drink strong tea to keep themselves awake, and, in spite of that, they nodded as they paced round and round and round the capstan, and fell fast asleep, still working, never forgetting to step a little higher as the warp rose with each revolution, but moving more slowly because they were asleep. That was the second day. Yet their work was but two thirds completed. The third night was coming.

HORSE POWERING THE CAPSTAN.
The use of horse-power to turn the capstan on a head-works raft.
Photo Courtesy of West Branch Historical Preservation Committee

Not that Lewey Ketchum let his men work thus continuously without rest or change. He knew too well how to get work done to make that mistake. There came sometimes a little breeze favoring them, and then Lewey had some spreads laid down and made his men turn in. They lay down like a basket of kittens, curled up all sorts of ways, but kept from rolling off by the bulwark around the headworks. Glad enough were they for the rest and sleep, yet before they took it they made a sail out of another of the great woods spreads, ample enough to cover twenty men, stretching it upon light poles put up before the capstan. Sometimes the breeze would last an hour or two, and the raft would sail as far as if they had been manning the capstan bars all the time. Then the breeze would die away, or it would draw down Cuxabexis,[118] or it would be openly unfavorable, and then once more it was "Turn out, boys!" and the anchor was laid out ahead and the capstan groaned again. But the men had been refreshed, and came to their task as good as new.

But not so Lewey. He never shut his eyes. While the others slept, he watched. They might get refreshment; he must go to the end of his task without it. The men offered to take his place and give him a chance to sleep. He knew their goodwill, and also how, having had a little sleep, they would fall back into it all the more readily. No man could take his responsibility, and he would let no man take his place. That was the last boom of the rear; if that were carried back, the whole drive must wait for it, and he would risk nothing. So there he sat watching while the rest slumbered.

It may have been that they had a lantern on the corner of the raft to guide the boat in boating out; it may have been, as in old times, that upon a graveled space they had built a little fire, and that there as formerly they kept a kettle of tea, which boiled day

---

[118] The lake and stream, north of Chesuncook.

after day, the grounds never emptied, but a new handful and a fresh supply of lake water added whenever the supply ran low. By the third night this would have tanned sole leather: it was very nearly strong enough to keep a man awake. One can see that Lewey must have gone to it often, not for the tea, nor that it should keep him awake, but just to make an errand. It is so still and quiet broad off in a lake at night that if one sits, making no movement, although not asleep at all, he falls into a moon-gaze and, being quite conscious, is yet unable to move; he sits rigid, and his soul wanders off upon the waters and cannot get back again into his body. That is just as bad as being asleep.

There was little enough to see. The stars were out in northern clearness, and, as the night lagged on, he saw the Virgin pace across the sky, following the sickle of Leo and the Twins, and down the lake he saw the Scorpion rise, with upraised sting and red Antares in his head.[119] But the stars are a silent folk, indifferent company to one who does not know them well. Of sounds which he did know there were few enough. There was the wash of the ripple along the logs, the creak of the thorough-shots, groaning occasionally, the slacking of the big quilt if it spilled a little of the breeze. A horned owl hooted twice from the shore; a fish jumped once; a night-flying wild duck steamed past at full speed, whippering his wings just over the water, and once, off the mouth of Caribou, a loon lifted his voice in a long and desolate cry. Yet the sounds came so seldom. All that made it seem that he was not floating midway between the stars burning above him in the sky and those twinkling below him in the glassy lake, was the fire on the corner of the raft and the stertorous breathing of fifteen tired men asleep behind him. The loon called again. He wondered if it betokened a change of

---

[119] Antares, a red supergiant, is in the range of the fifteenth-brightest star in the night sky, and the brightest in the constellation of Scorpius.

wind. He dipped his finger in the lake and held it up to catch the breeze. The wind had died away. "Turn out, boys!" came the word. Already the morning star was paling all her sisters; it was almost time for breakfast on the drive, and the crew was ready to go to work with new spirit.

Perhaps Lewey could rest now, for they were getting well along toward the piers. But Lewey could not rest. It was his boom to see safe in, and until he had given up the charge of it, accidents might happen. The crew were waiting for that last boom of logs, and he must not fail them. Lewey must work, and work as hard as any of his men, for the boss of a driving crew never wears kid gloves; all his authority comes to him from going where no one else dares go, from beginning first and quitting last, from doing the most work in the best manner.

So Lewey braced to the handspikes and began to heave on the anchor. He did not even doze while he walked round and round the capstan. He was too far gone for that. There was a little fever no doubt, and some twitching of the nerves, but he was very strong, and he moved on springs; people feel that way when they have gone without sleep long enough. He did not always answer quickly to the men; he did not hear them, — the veins in his temples sang too loud for clear hearing; but there was no man who could do more work. When he got his boom down where it was to be turned out for sluicing, he had been three full days and nights without sleep, and most of the time working at the hardest sort of labor.

It was getting along toward supper-time when they went up to the carry. Lewey saw that his men had something to eat, and told them to turn in. It did not matter if it was not dark; they could sleep anywhere now, and had earned an extra allowance. They turned in, and in two minutes were as sound asleep as rabbits.

Now comes what Lewey called the funny part of his story. A good deal of the above he did not tell me. He spoke as to a comrade who could supply all the details, which accordingly I have supplied, because I know what must have been true. He himself sped straight to the point that after three days and nights he could not sleep. It was all so noisy on the carry. Men came and went, and they shook the ground so. He did not hear them much, but he felt the ground shake. And the little birds made such a cheeping and bother about going to bed; their small voices were pitched high, so that he could not help hearing. As the dusk fell and the evening star grew golden, the frogs peeped and piped, and an old bull-paddock[120] off somewhere bellowed like a moose in October. After that the men were restless, lying in a long line under their shelter tent. It sounded like the bellows and the forges of an anchor factory to hear them. His wrists throbbed and he could hear his heart and the pulse in his temples, and he could not close his eyes because he could see so many things. It was like looking under the ocean through a water-glass, he could see so many things which no one else could see. Not a wink of sleep did he get, and that the fourth night.

His men turned out fresh and bright.

"Had a good sleep; makes a man feel fit," said they, stretching their arms.

Lewey felt weak in his arms, and he had no appetite for beans. His men looked solicitous, — offered rude kindnesses, bade him loaf for the day and see if idleness could not unstring his nerves. After some hours of hanging about the wangan and the carry-end, it seemed to him that, if he could get off somewhere where it was quiet, he might perhaps go to sleep. Indian-fashion, he said nothing about his intentions, but took a

---

[120] FHE: A local and ancient name for the bullfrog.

little spread, his own private property, for he never liked to use the bedding common to the crew, and along in the morning he started off into the woods. He went perhaps a quarter of a mile, till he could hear neither the logs, the lake, nor the men, and found a smooth, dry spot among the trees. The birds did not cheep so loudly as they had done earlier in the morning, and it was quiet and calm there. Lewey wrapped himself up head and ears, — anyone who has ever camped with him knows how like a great gray chrysalis he can make himself appear, a human *Cecropia*,[121] covered with dew, dead twigs, and dry leaves, which, in a night of sleeping out, adhered to his blanket cocoon; one would never think there was a man inside, but expect it to hatch a mammoth butterfly. Even after he got all rolled up, he kept on seeing things as before; but in a quarter of an hour he ceased to realize that he was living in a glass case a mile above the earth, a kind oblivion stole over him, and he slept.

That was the last Lewey knew. There is no means of measuring time in sleep, and when we wake, even from the sleep of death, it will always be the next morning. When he waked it was because an unexplained hunger gnawed him. He felt quite himself, not very strong perhaps, but fresh and bright and able to hear things properly. The sun was getting near meridian; he calculated that he had had four hours sleep. He had not eaten any breakfast, he remembered, and that quite accounted for his friendly feeling toward the cook. So he took his spread upon his shoulder and went back to the carry.

But there he was Rip Van Winkle: there was not a man there; there was not a log there; there was not a boat; there was no one at the dam; every single thing was gone; the ashes of the fire were cold, the blackened embers lay dispersed, the cross-bills were pecking around the empty pork barrels for the salt, and the

---

[121] In reference to the cocoon of the cecropia moth.

red squirrels stretched their necks from behind old camp-wood, wondering if they dared come near enough to snatch a coveted morsel of stale bread. Lewey was dumfounded. He had left a large crew here when he went to sleep, and now the rear had cleaned up everything; they had hidden the anchors and carried off the warp and gotten the last barrel of wangan out of the way, and no one had been across the carry that day. He could not tell how long he had been asleep, — a day, two days, a week, — nor whether he should come up with the crew at all before the logs were all in boom.[122]

He took his spread by the centre, and holding it with the corners dragging down his back, he set off down the carry. It is half a mile across; when he got to the lower end he could see, almost down to the outlet of Ripogenus Lake, the first signs of human life, two head-works, one on either side, warping down the rear. It is quite a cry across that lake, and as there was no boat awaiting his convenience, Lewey took the path along the right-hand shore. It was almost noon, and he was faint and dizzy, but there was nothing else to do. It was not till he was well down toward the carry that anyone discovered him. Then a shout went up.

"There's Lewey!"

"See there! That's Lewey now!"

"Say, Lewey's found himself all right."

"Hello, Lewey! Been padouksi?" — which is to say, sleepy.

"Well, sleepy-head, tell us, is it today or tomorrow?"

They made him the butt of all sorts of jokes, but seemed uncommonly glad to see him. Lewey did not say it, of course, but he was always a prime favorite on the drive, and it seems that they had become alarmed on his account.

---

[122] Meaning a boom, well down river, maybe as far as Old Town.

They had been worried when he did not appear after a reasonable time; they had become most anxious when he delayed unreasonably, for there in the dew and the dead leaves and the silvery spiders' webs, the bright sunshine and the green leaves blotched with yellow light, Lewey Ketchum had slept a whole day and a night and a half of a day again. The drivers had done some nine hours' work on their second day before he showed himself. Meanwhile some accident was feared, and they had hunted for him everywhere. Dazed with loss of sleep, he might have tumbled into the lake, and they searched the water round the dam. Or he might have wandered off into the woods, and half the crew had been out whooping and hallooing to call him in.

Then they thought that, crazed with sleeplessness, he might be in such condition that he could not understand their uproar even if he heard it, and might wander hopelessly and perish in the wilderness. So they had sent men all the way through to the Grant Farm to spread the news of a man lost.[123]

And all that time Lewey was quietly sleeping within rifle-shot of the camp. Being an Indian and a hunter, he had known how to hide himself, and being enveloped head and ears in his spread, the trump of Gabriel would not have roused him, even if all the lesser angels had joined in the fanfare.

"It was," so Lewey told me, laughing, "very funny." But about a man's working three days and nights without sleep, because he was a day laborer on other men's property and thought it was his duty to do the best he could, Lewey had nothing to say: that was all part of the day's work. It was customary in those days for a man to do the best he could.

---

[123] A walk from the upper end of Ripogenus Lake to Grant Farm to deliver this news would be no small undertaking, although all in a day's work for the woodsmen. This distance was detailed in the appendix, *Clump of Posies*.

The Great Company can train all that out of our men: we are quick to learn. We heard the evidence in the big log case which for four days was a school of the woods to the people of Bangor, and it was plain enough that there was a difference.

The Great Company was, in polite legal terms, requested to answer to a question of tort for the loss of logs committed to its care in the year 1901, the same being due to willful neglect or to gross incompetence.[124] A lawyer could put it much less candidly, but that was the popular impression from the evidence. Actions for tort for log-cases were such a novelty that this proved a sensational attraction; nearly everybody was there to

---

[124] The P. L. D. (Penobscot Log Driving Company) was formed in the middle of the 1800s, a legal entity made up of individual lumbermen and land owners. This arrangement provided them a way of sharing the river highways in a method of cooperation. Logs were marked and sorted at the booms according to ownership, but driven together at the time of best water conditions. The drive was then run by able men on the logs, under the management of terribly able men, such as John Ross. Up until 1901, The Penobscot Log Driving Company, by charter of the Maine Legislative, had the exclusive right of driving all logs on the West Branch of the Penobscot. In 1901, P.L.D. legally contracted, with State approval, for the Great Northern Paper Company to drive the logs. This was not an unusual occurrence, for P. L. D. yearly called for bids to do this work. The weather – drought and then an early freeze - along with negligence in the year of 1901 caused a great deal of trouble for the Drive. A hint at the claims against Great Northern Paper is given by Eckstorm in this story. The case eventually made it all the way to the Maine Supreme Court, (Marsh v. Great Northern Paper Co., 101 Me. 489, July 24, 1906 · Maine Supreme Judicial Court), where the decision was in favor of the plaintiff with judgment for the sum of $9871.31 (about $300,000 in 2021 U.S. dollars). However, that lawsuit did not end the battle, and the big money of the Company wasn't about to go away quietly. By 1903, the P. L.D. signed over all control of the West Branch to Great Northern Paper.

hear and to form an opinion. The fourth day of the trial, the interest growing rather than abating, they had upon the stand a witness who was a lumberman "from the peavey up."[125] He was an expert; almost forty years he had put in on the river as master and man. When he used to go on the drive, he testified, the crews did their best work sluicing at night, but "nowadays they don't seem to work much nights." The spectators laughed, — so many of them had worked on the logs themselves; they felt so strongly for the old times and burned so hot against the new. The counsel for the defense fluttered at the phrase and objected, — he, too, understood, — and the offensive clause was stricken out.

They do not work much at night now, it is true. Whose fault? There is no need of it, — and that is well. But in the old time, when they did it because a man ought to do the best he can, the example of faithfulness to a trust was set them by their leaders, and they made a fair copy of it. They were quick to imitate, — and they had never heard about actions of tort, — and they were silly enough never to weigh their labor over against their duty.

It was the requiem of the West Branch Drive that Con Murphy sang when he said that "nowadays they don't seem to work much nights." Great Corporations get only what they pay for, or a little less; what men slave for, die for, work nights for, is an Ideal, an Example, and a Man.

---

[125] The earlier hint from Eckstorm meant the person testifying was Cornelius 'Con' Murphy, the lumber boss who gave her the tour along the West Branch during her Ripogenus trip back in 1891.

THE STEAMSHIP KATAHDIN
The Katahdin sits at berth under a full moon.
(Editor's Collection)

The Katahdin is the only steamship still running on Moosehead Lake. The boat now runs by diesel engine and takes visitors on cruises. This technically is the Katahdin II, as the boat was built in 1914 to replace a prior vessel of the same name that caught fire. The steamer was transported in sections from Bath Iron Works by rail. While the loggers Eckstorm mentions in this book never rode on this particular ship, many of them rode the various steamers that worked the lake. The Katahdin last hauled a log boom on the lake in the 1970s.

RIPOGENUS RAPIDS

A photo showing the rushing water just after the current-day Ripogenus Dam. During the time of the West Branch Drive, logs were sluiced through this narrow canyon.
Photo courtesy of Mary Louise Osborne.

XV — LAKE CHEMO

THE BALLAD *Lake Chemo* was a most popular song around Bangor for Lake Chemo, or Chemo Pond. This was a day-trip get-away location for many who resided between Bangor and Old Town. The reader will recall from the chapter on Jack Mann that he lived in the vicinity of Chemo Pond. Eckstorm noted that 'Chemo' was a corruption of the Indian word K'chimehgwaak, meaning 'the big bog.' To the northwest of Chemo Pond, there is a large bog that runs into what is today Blackman Stream.

The pond, when approached by area residents from the south or east, was called Leonard's Pond, and they referred to the bog distinctly as Chemo. Over the years, the pond became Chemo and has been referred to ever since, with Mr. Leonard and his namesake pond long forgotten.

Lake Chemo

A Lumberman's Ballad, origin and author is unknown.

I left old Lake Chemo a long way behind me,
With many a tear back to Oldtown I came,
And if I but live till one year from this August,
I'll pack up my traps for old Chemo again.

CHORUS:
There pickerel are plenty and perch in abundance,
The Whiskey and new milk they both flow like rain,
And if I but live till one year from this August,
I'll pack up my traps for old Chemo again.

'Tis pleasant to think of the shed-tent we slept in,
Tho' the walls were thin cloth and the roof was a pole;
How familiar the chirp of the birds in the morning
And the Doctor digging the beans from the hole.
CHORUS

I think of fish-chowder red-hot from the kettle,
And pork that we frizzled so nice on the fire,
With big, roaring Crawford raising the Devil
Till three in the morning before he'd retire.
CHORUS

As the sun was setting in most royal splendor,
And the birds were singing their songs in the trees,
Then one of our party was seen without clothing,
Promenading the beach and enjoying the breeze.
CHORUS

The name of this poor and unfortunate fellow
Is kept from the public just merely to show
The respect that we have for each one of our party;
The names of the most are here given below.
CHORUS

There was Rowe, Cushman and Baker, and Douglass and
   Skinner,
With their wives and their sweethearts and others a score,
And last, but not least, came Miss Scott and Miss Nichols,
Two gushing young damsels from over the shore.
CHORUS

Now all you old fogies who want recreation,
Just go out to Chemo, if you want some fun,
There you'll find all our names engraved on a shingle,
Outshining in brilliance the rays of the sun.
CHORUS

Another story about Jack Mann of Chemo Pond

The Northern, in 1924 included a series of articles on an excursion through the Maine woods that was said to have taken place before 1870. The writers met Jack Mann at North East Carry, close to the West Branch. On departing, one said, "Good-by, Jack. Keep on dreaming."

Jack replied. "Yes, I will, and when you turn in nights, and are watchin' the sparks go up into the tree tops, and the shapes the smoke takes on; think of Jack Mann and you'll see me amongst the shapes there, and I'll tell you things that'll happen right there years from now. Good-by. Good luck."

The men gifted Jack Mann a clasp hunting knife for his courtesy in providing them with information for their trip. It is unknown if those travelers knew how William Mann became known as Jack, as explained in the earlier chapter.

THE SOCIAL HOUR

Time around the fire in the evening was for telling stories, and singing ballads.

from, Lucuis L. Hubbard's – *Woods and Lakes of Maine – Annotated Edition*
Burnt Jacket Publishing (2020).

XVI — THE NAUGHTY PRIDE OF BLACK SEBAT AND OTHERS

> I'll eat when I get hungry,
> I'll drink when I get dry,
> I'll get drunk when I am ready,
> And get sober by and by;
> And if my Molly don't like it,
> I'll leave this land and roam,
> For I'm a river driver
> And far away from home.
>
> *from*, The River-Driver

ECKSTORM now brings the reader to 1876, the Centennial Celebration year of the Declaration of Independence. But that is not what made it a famous year as far as the Penobscot men would be concerned. Robert E. Pike wrote, "1876 was a famous year because the Connecticut (River) had both the highest and the lowest water ever recorded." And only John Ross could be counted on to get the lumber down that river, against all odds and popular opinion. So Ross bid on the job, won, and took his "Bangor Tigers" south to do what no other group of men organized under a company name could do. Pike continued,

"But they did it; they brought the drive in, using dynamite to blast water out of the very rock."[126]

It has been said, by those who are never satisfied with a good story of the underdog, that not every log was floated down the river, some froze in the low water and waited out the winter. Yet, in what drive anywhere did every log make it through? And if not every log that year made it down the Connecticut, did not Ross and the men of the West Branch Drive achieve more than any other river-drivers possibly could have? Not that the logs mattered. This book is not about the logs. Nor are the stories about the lumber owners, or the board-feet of pine that reached a mill. Eckstorm wrote about the men. The famous Connecticut log drive was simply the conduit of water for which another story of Penobscot character is given.

In 1876, Eckstorm was eleven, much too young to be concerned about log-drives, or what would be her later calling to document this era of Maine's history. The story of the accident on the Connecticut River was told to her by her father; he himself heard it from the rivermen who were there. Eckstorm added details to the broth on why the West Branch Drive had traveled south, creating this story full of details on Penobscot men pride and their skills driving logs.

I WAS more than a little angry with the man. He lived in such a nice and finicking world, where every virtue was scrubbed and dusted to the last degree and then set on a shelf marked "Please

---

[126] Robert E. Pike, "Tall Trees, Tough Men," W.W. Norton & Co. (1967), Ch. 22, River Driving in Maine.

do not handle," — real Dresden shepherdesses of virtues, of no use to anyone. Of the rough and tumble of qualities, good and bad, in a mucky world, and the way in which some of the best of them become besmeared with vices and yet all the while are big, living, breathing, life-engendering virtues, he had no comprehension. A diamond in the rough was no diamond at all to him.

I told him frankly that he lacked eyes. He could not see it so, — the blind never can; yet here he was, in his blindness, complaining of our lacking sentiment.

"You know nothing whatever about it," I returned rather hotly.

His looks said, *"You are very rude, but I am too much a gentleman to say so."*

(One who was a little less a gentleman and a little more a *man* would have come up gladly to that challenge, I thought; either he did know or else he did not — why evade the point?)

"What has brought our logs in for the last fifty years has been very nearly one third pure sentiment," said I, challenging again.

"That's nonsense," he objected.

"Their ideals," said I.

"The-ir i-*de*-als," he drawled, and the repetition was cynicism rouged and powdered; "and what, pray, leads you to suppose that they have any i-*de*-als?"

I had a choice of evils — to retire in anger, nominally defeated, or to argue down one who could never see the point.

"I can prove it," I asserted.

"And *I doubt* it," he returned suavely. "I-*de*-als! My eye and Betty Martin![127] What do such rough fellows know about ideals? They know nothing but rum and fighting and sickening

---

[127] The saying, '*All my eye and Betty Martin,*' may have originated as a sailors' slang in the 18th Century. The phrase was used to express disbelief or to mean nonsense.

displays of silly bravado! Haven't they any faults, these rivermen of yours?"

I saw my opening. "Ye-es," said I, remembering Sam Weller and looking metaphorically at the skylight;[128] "there is no doubt but they are proud."

"Which undoubtedly, like all the rest, is pardonable?" He was ironical.

"Which may be left to others to judge whether it is pardonable or not; there is no question of its being black pride. While you are about it, you may as well prepare to modify your opinionated doubts" — *that was rather good, "opinionated doubts," almost an epigram* — "concerning sentiment in log-driving and the ideals of log-drivers. It will be no harder to admit one of my points than all."

"No, no harder," said he, blandly irritating. "Go on with your story."

By the way that he slipped down into his chair and made himself comfortable with a palm-leaf fan before his eyes, I wondered whether he was not preparing to be bored. But then, how could anyone help enjoying Black Sebat? To think of him is to have a little warmer feeling toward the world, and to forgive some of its shortcomings.

Can anyone who is old enough to remember so far back ever forget that hot, dry summer of the Centennial year? A hot July, and a hot and rainless August, and a September hotter than either. It was beautiful, but one drooped under the merciless pelting of the sun. Even the last of September, train-loads of sight-seers, returning from the great exposition, full of pride,

---

[128] Sam Weller, the character in *The Pickwick Papers* (1836), by Charles Dickens. In court, he is asked by the judge if he sees his own father. Sam looks up at the roof and answers, "No, I don't, my Lord."

patriotism, and enthusiasm, anxious to talk to fellow-travelers of the wonders they had seen, gasped mute in the cars, and with every door and window open, coatless and collarless, regardless of all proprieties, hung limp upon the arms of their own car seat, or the back of the one in front.[129]

Such a train-load was crossing the Connecticut River at Springfield; it was not a river, merely a gravel-bed with a few pools of water here and there.

"Ma! Ma!" shrilled a boy, no more pervious to the heat than a cicada, "what's the matter with that river?"

"The only trouble with that river," said a passenger, willing to relieve the tired mother, "is that the bottom is too near the top; otherwise that is a very good river."

That was the year, and the river was in that condition, when John Ross made his great Connecticut River Drive. Only two days before that train-load of tourists crossed, he had gotten it out safe, past all the hazards of drought and heat. The men talk about that drive yet.

"And they made a song about that drive," says your guide, squatting before the frying-pan with his uplifted fork raised like a tuning-fork; "I disremembers the whole of it, but there was something in it about,

> 'Old Burke he gave a whoop,
> Harrigan gave a swagan,
> And Black Jack gave a soup.'

That's all I can think to tell you about that song now, but that drive of John Ross's it was a great drive, and that about the song

---

[129] The Centennial International Exhibition of 1876, was held in Philadelphia, Pennsylvania, from May 10 to November 10, 1876, to celebrate the 100th anniversary of the signing of the Declaration of Independence.

is all so; you needn't not doubt a word of it, for Black Jack did make a soup just the same way that song says." He spears the bacon in the frying-pan and drives it around a little, as if he were handling big pine. "But that drive was a great drive all the same," says he.

Why John Ross and the West Branch Drive were off on the Connecticut River that year; how they got the logs through on a river of such length, with no storage of water, in the face of such a drought; how they beat out fearful friends and taunting foes and strangers who were betting high on its being an impossibility, and all for the honor of the Penobscot name, is a story too large to be pictured on this little page. They all toiled terribly from early spring till mid-September, the longest drive ever heard of up to that date; and had the men been forced to come home beaten, there is no telling what they would have done, but it would near have broken their hearts. If they had not had child's faith and man's faith in John Ross, and if he had not known just the stuff that was behind him and what they would do for him, — if, in short, there had not been a general at the head and a miniature army behind, they never could have taken that drive through. It was a great drive.

My father was with that train-load of people that hot day when the boy asked what was the matter with the river. He was the one who explained the difficulty. Such a day as that he thought he had never experienced in all his life, the most of it spent out of doors. It was the heat of a strange country, the drought of a foreign land, among people who, though charmingly kind, were not quite of kin; it was all unlike the home country, and in two weeks — he took particular notice — he never heard a man swear.

He arrived in Boston, and in half an hour he was home again. A chill sea-wind was blowing, which made him reach for his overcoat. There was a tonic smell of salt in the air. On board the steamer, crowding about the bows, were thirty or more Penobscot river-drivers, the first to arrive or the last to get through celebrating, just off from Ross's Connecticut River Drive. He chronicled the fact that all he had lost in the way of swearing in those last two weeks was made up to him within fifteen minutes, with a considerable surplus to put out at interest. However, he was right at home, and he had need to be an octopus, or a polypus, or Briareus the hundred-handed, to take all the hands that were stretched out to him. So they got him in the centre of the circle, and those who knew him crowded round where they could clap him on the shoulder when a hand was lacking, while those who did not know him stood one side and very politely looked at the toes of their boots. Everybody talked at once.

"Hullo, *Man*ry!" That was an Indian, with a big slap on the shoulder.

"Say, glad to see you. Manly,'" — crisp and clear, and that was a white man, with a handshake.

"My soul, but we ben berry much blessed for seen you," — from an Indian again, holding out both hands.

"Well, by jings! where did they rain *you* down from, Manly?" — the hearty greeting of a white man.

Then little Sebattis Solomon pushed up for his turn. "By jolly, but we just so glad seen our own brudder!" That was Black Sebat, who never had a brother that anyone ever heard of.

There is no lack of heartiness in a river-driver if he is a friend of yours, and these were typical of their class, newly fledged from the slop-shop most likely, but still wearing their spike-soled boots, and not asking the officers of the steamer whether or no it was agreeable to the management. (All boat and train officials coming into Bangor had long since learned not to offer advice upon that subject unasked.) They were cheerful, if not actually inebriate, but orderly enough, and they were proud and very happy; there was no keeping to themselves their satisfaction at getting that drive in.

"She got it his drive in all right – John Ross did; I tell you *we done him!*" announced little Sebat, grinning and shining all over his dark face. They called him Black Sebat and Old Black. He was a short, small man, as black as Sambo,[130] hardly more than a feather-weight, but incredibly strong and wiry. He could tend sled all alone, the only man, an old lumberman said, that he ever saw who could do it, for that is two men's work. And he was devoted to the West Branch Drive and John Ross. That was the first thing he wanted to talk about.

"Dem logs she been all hung up, if ain't for us," he declared. There was more evidently on his mind; one who knew Sebat could tell when he was preparing to make known some feat of his.

"What did I hear about running Canaan Falls?" asked my father, making a good guess at it.

"Ah, ya-as, dem Sappiel Orson an' Sebat Clossian she ben gone over Canaan Falls," beamed Sebattis, trying to be nonchalant. "Dem Mitch Soc Francis she been drowned in it herself," he went on earnestly, drawing a step nearer to his theme.

"Whose boat was it that went over?" asked my father, perceiving that but one man more needed to be accounted for, and that Sebattis had not mentioned the bowman; he could make a shrewd guess who was bowman from the way Sebat acted.

Sebattis's face shone, beamed, was wreathed in smiles; he just stood and radiated good nature. "You heard it 'boutdat? Well, by jolly!"

---

[130] In "Uncle Tom's Cabin," (1852) Harriet Beecher Stowe has a character named Sambo. The origin of the use reaches back into the 1700s, with etymology that was not always considered derogatory.

But Sebattis had been too much the centre of attention. In some ways a crew of woodsmen reminds one of a pack of hounds, good-natured and peaceable fellows, each willing for the others to have some praise, but wanting his own share, too, and crowding up to get it. The individual feat of running Canaan Falls was suddenly side-tracked, and that other more general one of getting the Connecticut River logs into boom was brought to the fore.

"If that drive hadn't' a' got in, I — I — I donno!" said a tall white man with a pale yellow mustache bristling from a brick-red countenance, as he gazed out over the bay and thoughtfully bit off a large chew from his plug. "And my fare back all paid — but I — I donno!"

"Oh, I tell you, when we t'ought we was goin' been beat we swear jus' lak hell, sac-er-r-ré-*damn!*" said a Frenchman, a stranger, who had interestedly worked himself into the inner circle. "But I tell you, dat John Ross he's great old boy; she's ben all hung up good, down b'low — b'low what you call it Hollowyoke; she's all done for, high' n' dry, an' then she jus' blas' it out channel and took hees whole drive t'rough!"[131]

That was the fact. At the very time when, down in Hartford, the loiterers and gamblers were laying heavy bets that the drive was a dead failure, John Ross was blasting out a channel in the waterless river, and he took his logs through all right. The men were jubilant. It was their success. It was a Penobscot triumph. It meant to them all that a great victory means to an army, and though they stood in Boston, on foreign ground, were they not still the West Branch Drive, the greatest drive that ever was, the

---

[131] Referring to Holyoke, Massachusetts. "But I tell you, that John Ross he's a great old boy. The drive was all hung up good, down below — below what you call it Holyoke; she's all done for, high' n' dry, an' then Ross, he just blasted out a channel and took his whole drive through!"

drive that couldn't be beaten? Pride, pride, pride! They might try to look stupid, they might deceive one who did not know them, but no exultant college crew ever failed more signally to appear meek before the eyes of its friends.

It happened later, when my father had gone inside for his overcoat and was upstairs in the main saloon, that carved and gilded and Corinthian-columned saloon of the old Cambridge,[132] that one of the Indians came strolling through to find him, not quite steady in his mind nor on his feet, and yet following as a dog follows a trail that is familiar. There were ladies and there were children about, and to the unaccustomed eye Joe looked a little wild; he was, moreover, — that is, he could hardly be called half-seas over, for he was fully two thirds of the way across the bay;[133] but when he caught sight of my father, he grinned with contentment and came up like a smiling, wagging dog who loves his friends and can't begin to tell them how much. Joe Orson wanted to talk. He wanted to talk confidentially. So when he was persuaded to sit in one of the upholstered chairs, Joe put an arm about my father's neck and began in stage whispers which could be heard all over the saloon. The ladies looked a trifle perturbed at first, not being used to anything less decorous than a cigar-store Indian, but seeing that no harm came to the deacon, they soon settled their plumage and turned observers. Joe talked on, telling a long story, and hugging my father tighter and tighter. He was telling the story of the boat's crew that ran Canaan Falls. It was a reckless, unheard of, inexplicable folly. In time he gave a

---

[132] The Cambridge was a ship of the Boston and Bangor Steamship Company, formerly Sanford's Independent Line.

[133] The saying, 'Half seas over,' is a term for *fairly drunk*, so if Joe was 'fully two thirds of the way across the bay,' he was beyond *fairly*, at least in Manly's estimation.

reason, good and sufficient, but his first reply was also memorable.

"What made them do it, Joe?"

And Joe, eyes shining, beaming wide, trumpeted in his sepulchral whisper, "Well, you see, Oldtown Injun she's damn proud!"

Just so. There's no group of slouching rivermen idling about a corner, with their hats pulled down over their eyes, but among them, wherever you find a man good at his profession, you will find also, if all his faults were written on his forehead, as the proverb says, that he is "damn proud."

THE CAMBRIDGE STEAMSHIP
Image source: *History of the Boston and Bangor Steamship Company, Formerly Known as Sanford's Independent Line (1823-1882)*, published by the Boston and Bangor Steamship Co., 1882. The pamphlet states this steamer arrived at Penobscot Bay on September 1, 1867. The ship was 250 long with a 38-foot beam, and weighed 1500 tons and was capable of sleeping 450 passengers.

Joe said more. Just because he said it that afternoon in the saloon of the old Cambridge, steaming along toward home, and because it fell into the ear of one who for eight and twenty years has remembered it word for word, his comrades, whom every one condemned for an act of drunken rashness, shall be justified. A man must be in some way beside himself to be a pure idealist, just enough the fool or madman to be above the more immediate tug of self-interest. Even though that release came to these men by the way of a vice, their virtue was none the less a virtue. In due place I shall tell what Joe Orson said.

How came the West Branch Drive off on the Connecticut River? Because John Ross had contracted that year to take down all the logs on the river, from headwaters to Hartford. But if there were logs on the West Branch to be run, why were not the men who did that, the West Branch Drive? Which is a sensible enough question. Nominally they were; every drive takes its name from the river it is made on. Yet in a peculiar way, shared by no other river, the West Branch Drive was an entity, the product of the genius of John Ross. The other drives were made up of good men, who worked by the day; but the West Branch Drive was a little army, drilled and commanded by a military genius, and its virtues were preeminently the virtues of fighting men. For fifty years John Ross worked on the river, for about thirty he was one of the heads, when he was not sole head, of the West Branch Drive, and he trained his men to a degree of efficiency never known before. They came to believe that there was no place on the earth or under it that the West Branch Drive could not take logs out of, if John Ross gave the word.

Consequently, the Penobscot man fell into the sin of pride. He had no dealings with the Kennebecker; he scorned the Machias man; he made life a burden to the P. I.[134] Deep down in all of us, like the ineradicable wildness of a cage-bred wild beast, lies this fierce, intractable pride of the River. That is why I have called this book "The Penobscot Man," because I know that wheresoever he may be, he is not going to forget his river. On my first train journey, as a little child, when we were riding up the Kennebec, I remember making friends with the lady across the aisle, and explaining to her that I lived on a river, too, "a great deal bigger and a great deal nicer river than that river (pointing out the window); mine was the Penobscot River" — and she, poor woman, was a Kennebecker! It is a very naughty pride, yet how strong it is in the men who are rivermen! The poor Kennebecker, years ago, when he used to come here to work, was the butt of all sorts of contumelious jokes. In the days when our men carried their gear in an old meal-sack, his enameled cloth or flowery carpet-bag was dubbed in ridicule a "Kennebecker;"[135] and everything awkward was laid at the door of the stranger as a "Kennebec swing." In his wake the P. I. has suffered all sorts of reviling, and well for him when he is either an exceptionally able man or a very meek one. [136]

"I'd like to know what there is about that name 'P. I.,'" said a Western college man to me. "We had a fellow from down your way, and we always called him 'P. I.' — 'P. I. Murchison' —

---

[134] P.I. – short for Prince Edward Islander; or in general one from the provinces north of Maine.
[135] The Kennebecker luggage was often made from or covered in carpet fabric.
[136] Meaning once the Kennebecker ceased to drive on the Penobscot, the locals chose someone else to poke fun at in his wake.

or something else. It didn't mean a thing to us, but when we found it vexed him, we kept it up; but what was there in that to get roiled about?"

"Why didn't you," I asked, "call him Irish, or a Dago, or some soothing term? Why needlessly enrage a Penobscot man by calling him a P. I.?"

Yet, once the men from away are broken in, there is no more of this rough-carding. If they are good enough men to belong to the West Branch Drive, the real meat and marrow of it, then all distinctions of race and place are forgotten. There never was a more democratic organization on earth: all our head lumbermen have been bossed first or last by Indian boatmen, and have started at the foot of the ladder without favors. All the good men are Penobscot men. The name stands for something! Let there be trouble on the other rivers, let the logs be given up by the local crews, when that happened, then they would send over for a hundred or two hundred Penobscot men. Then all the old West Branchers would enlist, and march off and clear out that drive — and everything else they met on the road. Oh, the men have told me all about those old days!

Therefore, when John Ross contracted for the Connecticut River Drive, he took over all his Maynard boats and a hundred and fifty of his old men. Plenty of other men could be had fit to step-and-fetch-it, plenty of boats good enough for some uses, but for the solid core of his drive he took men whom he had trained himself, Yankees, Frenchmen, Indians, Province men, but all Penobscot. They would follow John Ross anywhere; they would do for him what will never be believed when the traditions once have faded. He was that rare creature, the idol of his men. "The King of the River," I have heard him called by a college man who had worked on the logs in vacations and knew of what he spoke. Nor is his a purely local reputation. Today, off in the Northwest among the great logs of Puget Sound, or down in the Southwest in some mining-camp or on some cattle ranch, you shall some day overhear a man who speaks of "joining drives," or who talks of a "plant" as an "operation" or who promises "to tend out" on court or a church social. If you are blunt, you will say, "Hello, Maine!" and get a blank denial; but if you are subtle in your mind and know your native tongue, even when meeting it in unaccustomed places, when you recognize the Penobscot man, let fall casually to your companion something about John Ross and what old Jack Mann said to him, even if you have to make it up out of whole cloth.

"And where did *you* ever hear of John Ross?" says he, hooking himself at your first cast.

"Where did *you*?" you return, the back-question being the proper Yankee retort.

"*I'm* Penobscot" — not '*from the* Penobscot,' for that would brand you an impostor, but just the barest phrase, "*I'm* Penobscot."

"So 'm I!" he says, which you knew well enough before; "what was that you were saying about John Ross?" He ends by inviting you to his house, his mill, his ranch, his assay office, and the next time he sights you across a street, he comes over and begins just where he left off talking — about John Ross.

We never had but two men who took hold of the popular imagination in that way. The first was old General Veazie, who built one of the first railroads in New England. Forty years, perhaps, after he died, I heard a man get up in an orthodox prayer-meeting and say of some character (whether in the Bible or out of the Bible I shall not tell), that that man "felt so big that General Veazie's great-coat wouldn't make a vest for him." That was fame.

Concerning the second, perhaps today, if you are going along the streets of Old Town, you may see some small boy mount a pile of lumber and clap his arms and crow, "Hi-i-yi! John Ross on a clapboard!" or "John Ross on a shingle!" or he may look saucily up into your face and exclaim, "Say I'm John Ross, or I'll kill you!" That, too, is fame! There is no longer any West Branch Drive; the Great Company has seen to that and swept away the old organization where friendly rivalry and fraternal discipline held the men together in a Round Table of noble and unceasing adventures. But it will take more than the Great Company to stop the mouths of the little boys of Old Town. Fifty years from now, — just as today, under the name of Pope Night, the children of Portsmouth, New Hampshire, celebrate Guy Fawkes' Day,[137] the children being the great conservers of old tradition, — fifty years from now, and very likely more, you will hear the little boys of Old Town crying out, "Say I'm John Ross, or I'll kill you!" And that will be fame!

But, we must tell the story to answer Manly's question: *"What made them do it?"*

---

[137] The history of Pope Night, the parallel to England's Guy Fawkes' Day, is quite complicated, but the November 5th anti-Catholic affair generally featured fires, drinking and mockery of elites and authorities. It was common in New England coastal towns from the middle 1700s through the start of the revolution. By the 1880s, scattered bonfires were still happening in New England coastal towns on that date, although the original meaning had long been lost. In 1892, *John Albee wrote in an article titled, "Pope Night in Portsmouth, N. H." (The Journal of American Folklore),* "In this town, not only is the reason lost, but there the name also, - the boys call it Pork Night." He included articles from the Portsmouth papers that reported, *"The festivities included the ringing of door bells, the tooting of tin horns, and the carrying of pumpkin lanterns."* Thus was the nearly three-hundred year evolution of what started out in England as a plot to blow-up the House of Commons in 1605.

For it wasn't a *who* made them do it, but the *what* pertaining to Penobscot pride, of which Manly was fully aware, yet he had to hear it from Joe.

So much of exposition of how we came to have the sin of pride; by way of illustration we have Sebattis Solomon. Sebattis could well illustrate several other sins, though it will be by his virtues that he is remembered. In trying to make clear what Sebat was like, no illustration seems so apt as that of an old-fashioned home-made rubber ball, the centre of pure rubber, tough as gristle, wound hard with home-spun yarn, a thread of white and a thread of black, but so commingled that without unwinding the whole no man might tell how much of it was black and how much was white, and so endowed with resilience that the harder it was hit the higher it bounced. You could no more keep Sebattis Solomon down than you could keep down one of those round-ended rubber dolls that bob up from all positions and balance anywhere.

What a quaint dignity he had, priding itself in all sorts of unexpected places! Once my father was remonstrating with him for being drunk. They were the best of friends, but Sebattis stiffened immediately. "Must n' you said dat, Manry!" he commanded. "Must n' you never said Sebattis Solomon she's drunk! 'Cause you see, she *can't be done!*"

Pride at times became a childlike vanity, as when he got his employer to write a letter which contained nothing but the news, four times repeated, that Sebattis Solomon was driving four white horses.

"You got it dat wrote down? Well, den you told him, 'Sebattis Solomon she's drive it four white horses.'"

Immediately came the question again, "You got it dat wrote down? Well, we want for tell it how Sebattis Solomon she's drivin' four white horses."

Yet for some notable feat of skill or endurance he would refuse both thanks and pay. Once when the drive was at Northeast Carry and some article of necessity was desired at once which could not be procured nearer than Greenville, Sebat took a heavy canoe upon his head and ran across the carry two miles and twenty rods, to Moosehead Lake. There he threw the canoe into the water and started out forthwith, late in the afternoon, to paddle against a heavy wind to Greenville, forty miles away. He arrived in the middle of the night, routed out whoever could get him what he came for, and set off at once to paddle back his forty miles, after which he again lugged his canoe across the carry, arriving early in the day. He was a small man, not weighing over a hundred and twenty, and he had lugged four miles and more, and paddled eighty. without rest and almost without food.

What was to pay? "Oh, she's 'bout day's work; s'pos'n' we call it t'ree dollar."

Hervé Riel's[138] half-holiday and leave to go and see his wife was princely compensation to what Sebattis asked.

Sebattis knew well the struggle of two natures. His notions of right and wrong were firmly implanted, and in his own way he tried to live up to them. Once he came bringing as a gift a crooked knife which he had made, the blade ground down from an old file, the handle most elaborately carved. "You see, she's 'gainst our principles," — (no one loves a long word better than an Indian,) — " 'gainst our principles hunt on Sunday; took us t'ree Sunday afternoons — made it dat knife-handle." We keep

---

[138] A reference to the poem, "Herve Riel" by Robert Browning. Riel was a simple sailor who led the French Fleet to safety through his knowledge of the rocky harbor. At besting the English, when asked what reward he would take, he answers, 'Leave to go and see my wife, whom I call the Belle Aurore!' and, 'That he asked, and that he got, — nothing more.'

it yet in memory of Sebattis. Alone, all alone in the woods, he was respecting his conscientious scruples about Sabbath-keeping.

It was when he was out among people that his moral nature was not equal to the strain. The sins of this world were so attractive to him. Once he was arguing seriously against paying his honest debts. He had planned a great and varied round of pleasures, the full circle of a white man's debauch, with all the buggy-riding he wanted. "We sorry we cahn' paid you; we owed it an' we ought paid it an' we got money, but we was goin' get drunk jus' like white man an' have hell of good time, an' you see dose t'ings she's berry'spensive." This time he squandered his money strictly according to the programme, but at other times he was not so successful. His love of fair play was a great disadvantage to him. After he had planned some sharp bit of knavishness, for fear he might not be quite fair about it, he would very likely go and explain to his unsuspecting victim his whole intentions and show just how and when he could best be outwitted. If his friendly offices against himself were accepted and his game was blocked, then apparently no one was so much pleased about it as Sebattis. "Well, you was smart! We didn't t'ought you'd got it your money; but you was smart!"

But one point he never failed in, and that was in fidelity to his work. I have known him to stay three weeks at the stupid task of watching a dam, though he had nothing to eat but spoiled pork and flour, and he knew that all the other boys were off having fun on the logs. He was with all his heart and soul wrapped up in the welfare of the West Branch Drive, and he would have broken all the commandments *seriatim* if that would have helped the logs along. Captain Hilton of Chesuncook, between laughter and vexation, was telling once how Sebat came along "playing big Injun," with a crowd of fellows tagging after to do his commands, and how he cleaned up the 'Suncook shores in the interest of P. L. D. "After he was gone along, you couldn't find a paddle nor a peavey anywhere, unless it was under lock and key. He couldn't read the marks on them, and he had to keep up his dignity, so he took no chances. 'She looks like P. L. D.; best way you took him, boys.' He even carried off my big boom anchor that weighed three hundred. 'Dat anchor, she look like P. L. D.; best way you took him.' P. L. D. never lost anything by Sebattis."

Nor could his other employers have been greatly dissatisfied. Mr. Dillingham, the Indian agent, said years ago that Sebat was trusted more than any other Indian that he ever knew. Lumbermen would let him go into the woods in the fall, explore his own berth of timber, locate his camp and hovels, build the same, take the whole charge of some thirty men and ten or a dozen horses, and bring his brook-drive down to the main drive, without having a white man go near him except to settle with the men. Judged by this, there must have been some ground for Sebat's sharp distinction between a man who is drunken and a competent man who drinks.

Sebat was quick to see a point. John Ross had a bad jam on at one time, too bad a jam to send men out upon against their wishes. "If you want to go out and break that jam, Sebat, there's a chance to get your name in the papers," said he.

Sebattis looked at him as sharp as a cock-sparrow. "What good do dead Injun get damn name in papers?" said he.

He knew very well that between the police-court records and the funeral notices, there was no room in the papers for an Indian.

"Sebat," said one of his many employers, willing to do a good deed for the world, "you oughtn't to swear so. Don't you know that you won't ever get to heaven if you swear like that?"

Sebat considered the proposition half a second, stopping his work to do so. "I tell you what, Jim; we goin' give him hard one!" Once more it was the Penobscot man, self-reliant and quite confident of arriving.

In this story of running Canaan Falls there is no sure evidence that Sebattis was the bowman of the boat; but another incident will show well enough that it could have been no other, — not while he was in the boat, as we know that he was. The story is delightfully Sebattis, too.

It was late in the Civil War, when men were in great demand, high bounties being offered to substitutes. One day a friend said, "Do you know a black little Indian who calls himself Sebattis Solomon?"

"I should think I might," was the reply. "He has worked in my haying crew for three years now; he enlisted only the other day and went straight off to war."[139]

The other laughed. "Where do you suppose he got to? Not to the war at all, for he didn't enlist. I was in the provost-marshal's office the other day, and this fellow came in, as drunk as an owl, with a lumberman who had been drafted, and who offered him eight hundred dollars bounty to go in his place. He was in his shirtsleeves, with a fig-drum on his head for a hat, and was marching around all ready to go to war; the job just suited him. He said his name was Sebattis Solomon."

"It certainly was; that is Black Sebat."

The friend said, "He marched up to the enlisting officer, and the first thing he said was, 'We want 'list. We want for 'list um colonel!' That was a pretty literal application of the principle of room near the top. They told him that they had no vacancies just then in that rank, but they could give him a good place a little lower down, with the rank of a full private. But he insisted on enlisting as a colonel. 'We want for 'list um colonel!' That was

---

[139] This reply came from Manly Hardy.

all that could be got out of him. He went off without enlisting at all."

Sebattis, it is plain, had a Penobscot man's opinion of his own capabilities. He knew that any man who could drive four white horses, or handle thirty Penobscot lumbermen, or take a drive down in the spring, was perfectly qualified to command a paltry thousand of counter-jumpers. No, sir! It was colonel or nothing! Not even that rank of full private and those eight hundred dollars — a large sum to a man who has holes in all his pockets — could break his determination to take nothing below his deserts. Therefore, one has no hesitancy in saying that he was the bowman of that boat which ran Canaan Falls, because there would have been trouble if he had not been; nor that, even if the intention did not originate with him, as was most likely, he was the one who sanctioned it. It was like Sebattis Solomon to have ideals which he held high and followed loyally, even though he got mired sometimes in the muck of his daily life.

And so, through the return of the river-drivers triumphant, their idealization of John Ross, because he always led them to victory, the dogged faithfulness and fantastic pride of Black Sebat, we come back to the Connecticut River again, to Canaan Falls in the blithe June weather, when a little farther down the river, however it may be there, the laurel is white as snow on the hillsides, and the thrasher sings and the wood-thrush, and the scarlet tanager flashes a living coal among the green of the chestnut-trees.

I never saw the place, know nothing of it, save as these men told the story, and repeat that only from the memory of many years back; but if it was as they said, Canaan Falls was a rapid which had never been run within the memory of man. All were agreed that it was impossible water. Just above the falls, where the full summer strength of the great river was rushing down, a bridge crossed, a bridge with stone piers. Behind each pier played an eddy, and on the lower side of one was a ring-bolt drilled into the rock. John Ross's drive was down as far as Hanover, and one boat's crew waited behind this pier while two of the men went uptown on an errand. There were four Indians in the boat, — Sebattis Solomon, Mitchell Soc Francis, Sappiel Orson, and Sebattis Clossian. Three out of the four had been drinking, though which was the fourth may be left to their intimate friends to determine; it could not have been Sebattis Solomon, because he would have resented the imputation of sobriety quite as quickly as he did its opposite.

It was snug and comfortable there, and they gathered in the middle of the boat and stretched out their big spike-boots; perhaps, if the errand was a long one and the boat dry, they curled down crosswise amidships, reclining against her flaring sides, smoking and whittling. There they sat, hats pulled down or pushed back, — for whoever saw a river-driver without his hat at one extreme or the other? — And laughed and chatted in Indian, gossiping, as Indians love to do, over the long-winded nothings which they spin out so attractively. It was fine June weather, the drive was all right; no thought now of those great meadows in Massachusetts where the current eats in under one bank, leaving the other high and dry, nor of the river's tortuous windings, nor the Ox-bow, nor the strong water at Titan's Pier, nor the falls at Holyoke, nor the shallows below the falls; they did not know the river and the "grief" ahead of them; they lay and chatted like the bobolinks that sang above them in the grassy banks. Every now and then a step sounded on the planking of the bridge; perhaps a shaking of dust came sifting down and was filtered in a band of sunlight, — men's steps, sharp and quick; women's steps, short and fussy; children's steps, uneven, joyously eager, or loitering by turns, as they paused or hastened, fancy-struck. Not all of the steps passed. Those who stopped to look over the rail saw beneath the queer sharp-ended boat and the four black, rough-looking men, talking a strange, soft language with liquid gutturals and pretty circumflexes; they saw them whittling in a strange way with a strange-looking knife, drawing it toward them with great precision, and they saw them also passing from hand to hand a flat black bottle. The men were drinking quietly, not enough to incapacitate them, — which, as Sebattis said, "can't be done." These men were doing nothing which they considered reprehensible, and one of them never drank. There was some joke on hand about the bottle just then. Sebattis Solomon had looked into it last, a little too long, perhaps, for the next man, holding it up to the light, shook it gently, as if to make more of what was in it. And he murmured ruefully in English, "Seems like them whiskey she's thunderin' few!" Then he passed the empty flask to the man who did not drink, who threw it into the river, and they all laughed softly. They were having as good a time as a family of muskrats before the white folks disturbed them.

For the feet up on the bridge kept up their rap-tap-tap. More and more of them came, and they kept stopping. Few passed, it would seem; for, looking up, one saw a line of faces looking down, straight down upon that boat.

The Indians talked to each other in Indian, commenting upon the number of people who were curious to look at an Indian, as if his place was in a show, and they chaffed Sebattis Solomon as being fit for the part of the monkey, turning an organ-crank in pantomime and pulling an imaginary string; Sebat was the butt of all sorts of witticisms.

Then a woman's high voice said, "Ask them, why don't you?" They heard that.

Then a man hailed them. "What time are you going to run these falls?"

"Ugh-hugh! said Black Sebat sharply, turning to the next man and repeating it in Indian as if the man could not understand

English. "He says, 'What time are you going to run these falls?' All these people are waiting to see us run these falls."

No direct answer did he make to his questioner on the bridge, which was an Indian trait; but there began an animated jabber among themselves in their own tongue. It was the first notion that any of them had of running Canaan Falls; for everybody who knew about water knew that the place could not be run. Some foolish loiterer, seeing the boat holding there, and perhaps not even knowing that an eddy is a good place to wait in, nor how many men make a boat's crew,[140] nor that watermen do not commonly risk their lives for the pleasure of people who know nothing about logs and water, not caring overmuch for their approval, had started the rumor that the Indians were going to run the falls. And already upon the end of the bridge fell the sharp pat of running feet coming to see the Indians act in the melodrama of running Canaan Falls.

It was not that which moved them to do it; there was nothing of the purely spectacular about it; Joe Orson, when he told the story, revealed that clearly enough, for, though at the time he told it he thought it was himself instead of his brother who was in the boat, all the more did what he say demonstrate, by its avowal of his willingness to have done the same, and his approval of what was done, that a perfectly pure and lofty motive impelled them to the act.

Perhaps the one sober man tried to dissuade them; for he would see that the foolish report of foolish idlers did not bind men to risk their lives. But the ideas of the others were just enough out of focus to make them loom grandly; prudence did not preach to them half so loud as it would have done an hour before. They saw larger relations, grander achievements, the ideal beckoning them; they felt the pressure of moral obligation.

---

[140] Only four waited in the boat, and to handle a boat of that size, the typical crew was six.

It is a stage that comes to an Indian in this condition with remarkable regularity of recurrence. He needs just that stimulus to bring all his powers out of a dual and antagonistic relation into harmonious working; for he is not one man, but two — a white man and an Indian, and only the finest and the strongest among them can bridge that gulf by their own wills.

So they talked rapidly, gesturing and arguing. Then Sebattis Solomon stood up in the stern and picked out a course. Then, while the others found their places, he ran forward to the bow, cast off the painter from the ring-bolt, and swung her to the stream. So they went down into the white of Canaan Falls.

How they fared I cannot even imagine, not knowing the place. What sort of water it was, too deep, too scanty, too rocky, too beset with heaving boils, they never told me. We had few watermen their equals, yet they could not make the run. The boat swamped and was wrecked. The men were thrown out into the swirl and rush of the water and carried down among rocks and white boils into the race of the rapids below. Three were saved, Sebattis Solomon being pulled in by a man who ran out and reached a pick-pole to him as he was being swept past; he grasped the extreme tip of it, but such was the grip of his horny fingers that he held with one hand in all that current and was drawn out safe. The man who had the best chance of all, who had won through to safety, and was resting in the eddy behind a pier of logs below the fall, in attempting to break through the current and swim ashore, was caught by the undertow and drowned.

Joe Orson told the story in the saloon of the old Cambridge, steaming home from their great Connecticut River Drive, his eyes very bright, his whisper most impressively aspirate. He was himself in just the condition to see things large, and no doubt he interpreted all more truly and even more dramatically for the slight mistake of not being able to tell whether he was himself or his brother. It held a noble pathos, too. This was no crack-brained, dare-devil feat, but an act of the highest devotion.

"You see we had to go. There was young man, old man, boy, gal, all sorts was lookin' right down on us. Oldtown Injun she got great name for ribber-drivin'. *We mus' go*. We knew it was die that time, but we must n' go back on our name!"

"Both sweet and becoming it is to lay down one's life for one's country," sings the stately Roman poet.[141] Four Penobscot Indians, men who have no country, in the face of dangers which they fully comprehend, cheerfully elect to die for the honor of the tribe; and the man who told it would have done the same; and all the others who were there approved it and would have done the same. The honor of the tribe, the fame of the West Branch Drive, the reputation of the Penobscot man, were the ideals that beckoned them.

Oh, the folly of all self-sacrifice, the vanity of all things beautiful, the lying promise of spiritual ends which the cynic preaches! "This might have been sold for much and given to the poor!" Verily. Yet when the poor had eaten and drunken it, what then? But the precious wastefulness, preserved within a book, — how many are fed from the ambrosia of such a fair and noble deed!

"But they were drunk when they did it," cry the modern disciples, indignant at seeing the virtue of sobriety infracted, "and that takes away the merit of the act." Yet remember that the thoughts which came then to them were but the reflexes and enlargements of the thoughts which filled their sober hours, not something new and unaccustomed, but what they commonly concealed, and perhaps could not act out with full volition. Prudence might have prevented the actual doing of the deed,

---

[141] In reference to the line, *Dulce et decorum est pro patria mori*, by the Roman poet Quintus Horatius Flaccus, born in Italy around 65 BC, and also known as Horace in the English speaking world.

dumbness might have tied Joe Orson's tongue in telling of it, had they been strictly temperate; but in all the thought would have been there, the impulse would have been there, the binding force of pride, the pure ideal of an honorable sacrifice, would still have been a motive working latently, even though we had never seen it as an active force.

What drives logs to market? Stout muscle; strong will; pure sentiment. Even here the Ideal has its place.

The gamesters and loiterers about the hotels in Hartford were laying bets, five to one, that that fellow from the Penobscot would lose his whole drive. A very quiet stranger in brown was going about taking up small amounts.

"Are you a stranger here?" asked a good-natured man, "well, then, take a friend's advice and don't bet against a sure thing; we have lived on this river some time, and that drive's hung up, a dead loss."

Still the quiet stranger kept right on taking up small amounts.

A week later came the word that the drive was safe, down to Springfield, where it could be towed the rest of the way.[142] Then the stranger went around settling bills that brought him in five to one.

"I hate to take money on a sure thing like this," said he apologetically.

A loser hissed, "Cheat! You knew it! You knew what we didn't."

The stranger looked at him; he melted, — it was a hot day. "I guess I *did* know what you didn't," said he very quietly. "I've

---

[142] There might be some who say this is not so, for while some logs were sacrificed to lay in the shallows over the winter, John Ross and the Maine men of the West Branch Drive accomplished what no other crew would attempt. And the bets were they would lose the whole of it. The drive was declared as success as a better portion of the logs made it to the boom.

seen the West Branch Drive before — *I'm Penobscot* myself — and I know John Ross."[143]

But there are no such unsatisfactory people in the world to talk to as the fine and finicky folk who refuse to see by any light but the fox-fire of their own prejudices. The man behind the palm-leaf fan was fast asleep.

The Penobscot men who went over Canaan Falls in 1876 were:

Sebattis Solomon – also known as "Black Sebat." He was the one who started to tell Manly Hardy about the run over the falls. From this, and the conversation with Joe Orson, Manly deduced that Sebat was the bowman in the boat that day. As the reader will already know, the position in the bow is the one of the grandest honor, or responsibility, when running fast water. A picture of Sebat may be found in the final chapter.

Sappiel Orson

Sebat Clossian

Mitchell Soc Francis, the man who drowned that day.

* **Joe Orson** (Sappiel's brother), was not in the batteau, but was the one who told Manly most of the details on the steamer ride back to Maine.

---

[143] Seeing Manly Hardy had told Fannie this story, and she was not apt to make things up, was the stranger in brown – one who lectured against drinking, but was not against a friendly wager?

PORTRAIT OF MANLY HARDY – 1905
Painted by Annie E. Hardy (1839 – 1934).

The Hardy family was one of many artistic talents. The grandfather, Jeremiah P. Hardy was a renowned artist in the Bangor area and some of his paintings survive and are in the collection of the Museum of Fine Arts, Boston. The only son of Manly Hardy, Walter M. Hardy, studied art in New York, Paris, England and Italy. His paintings were shown in numerous exhibits and he illustrated for not only his father's articles, but the work of others.

Image courtesy of Special Collections, Raymond H. Fogler Library, University of Maine.

XVII — A BALLAD ABOUT JOHN ROSS

JOHN ROSS was a lumberman, woods-boss, Head Contractor of the Drive for many years, and a legend of the Maine woods. Men followed him into the woods each year to work in miserable conditions of snow, ice, cold water, black flies, and sleeping in lice infested bunks. Some followed this man into the woods for more than three decades. It was a hard life, but year after year they went, and no one can say they didn't earn their wage. Is it any wonder then that John Ross would have had a ballad written about him? The ballad is added to this edition with commentary from Fannie Hardy Eckstorm who interviewed, Dan Golden, the woodsman poet and composer of this ballad.

In her book, Minstrelsy of Maine, Eckstorm wrote, "When I asked Dan Golden what was the name of his song, he said: 'It don't have no name; you can call it *Old Dan Golden — His Journey Out*. But others call it *John Ross*.'"

Dan Golden told Eckstorm he wrote the song along with his brother, Hughey. To Mr. Golden, it was important that people remembered something about him. He said, "My name is Daniel H. Golden — when you write anything about me again, you will put in my name, won't you? I was born in Paisley, Scotland, and I come to this country in 1865."

Golden said he had worked thirty-six winters for John Ross in the woods and seventeen springs he drove on the West Branch Drive, and other springs on different drives and even rose to 'handle boat.'

Eckstorm noticed that when Golden sung her the song, he went with a heavy beat on the alternating syllables and she noted that if you miss that, the balladry of the tune was lost.

> *Now-ow* the *night* that I was *mar*-ried, *oh*,
> And *laid* on *mar*-riage *bed*,
> Up *stept* John *Ross* and *Cy*-rus *Hewes*
> And *stood* at *my* bed-*head*.

The ballad had its origins, although with poetic license, to sentiment Golden felt from his own life and the boss he was proud to work for. Golden told Eckstorm:
"Yes, when I was married, the very morning I took my wife Mary — she was only sixteen and I was eighteen — I took her to her own door in the coach and left her there. I didn't see her again for ten months because I went right off into the woods to work swampin' for John Ross. I was always one of Ross's men, you see; worked for him every winter till last winter and was on the West Branch Drive for him seventeen springs. Got that down?"

Old Dan Golden — His Journey Out (or John Ross.)
by Daniel H. Golden, Lumberman and River-Driver

Now the night that I was married, oh,
And laid on marriage bed,
Up stept John Ross and Cyrus Hewes
And stood at my bed-head.

'Oh, rise, oh, rise, young married man,
And come along with me
To the lonesome hills of 'Suncook
To swamp those trees for me.'

From the Franklin House we took the stage,
For Moosehead *we* did steer,
And I could not stop for thinking *of*
My charming Mary dear.

When we reached Moosehead
Our sorrows first begun;
Bold Cyrus Hewes was there,
The head leader of the men.

'Boys, tomorrow morning,
Let it be cold or warm,
A five-pound axe and your valise,
You shall start for the Grant Farm.'

Oh, when we heard our sentence
We all hung down our head;
Up stept bold Dan Golden then
And wisht that he was dead.

He says (spoken):
'I told you, if you'd go for Ross
He'd lead you a hard life';
And I wisht myself in Bangor
'Longside of my dear wife.

Now atween Roach River and the Grant Farm
John Murphy's son played out,
And Dan Golden, like a loyal comrade,
Did see his journey out.[144]

---

[144] On the long road from Greenville to the Grant Farm, over rough woods roads, Jim Murphy (John Murphy's son) was unable to keep

I says (spoken):
'Jim, have you any matches?'
('He didn't have any' —
which is spoken without interrupting the song)
'And this night we will camp out.'
We hoofed it through, brave boys,
As you may plainly see.

If ever you see a smiling face
It was John Murphy's eldest son;
'Boys,' an' says he, 'if ever I return to Bangor,
A blacksmith I will be.'

Chesuncook is a lonesome place,
I know there's snow on every tree;
And a woe betue John Ross
For parting of my dear love and me!

In the interview, Golden told Eckstorm what he made for wages: 'Yes, an' when I come out in the spring,' said he, 'I had seven hundred and eighty dollars in my pocket for my year's work.'

This is in line with his statement that he was gone from his wife for ten months and the average salary a woodsman made, particularly one who was a boatman. Now it may seem that Golden is in some way cursing his employer, a man who had

---

up, and Dan Golden volunteered to spend the night with him. In the morning, they pushed on and met the others at the Grant Farm and traveled with them to Chesuncook Dam. In the appendix of this edition, the reader will find this is the same route Eckstorm made with her father and guide Wilbur Webster on departing the West Branch Drive.

just paid the young newlywed with a large enough salary to buy a house and a whole lot more. After this year, he then returns year after year to work for this villain of the woods, or so says the ballad.

PORTRAIT OF JOHN ROSS
Year unknown.
Image courtesy of Special Collections, Raymond H. Fogler Library, University of Maine

Another ballad about Ross. No known title:

Who feeds us beans?
Who feeds us tea?
Who feeds us bread
That hain't sog-gee?
    'Tis Johnny Ross and Cyrus Hewes,
    'Tis Johnny Ross and Cyrus Hewes,
    'Tis Johnny Ross and Cyrus Hewes,
    'Tis Johnny Ross and Cyrus Hewes.

Who makes the big
Trees fall kerthrash,
And hit the ground
A hell of a smash?
    'Tis Johnny Ross and Cyrus Hewes,
    'Tis Johnny Ross and Cyrus Hewes,
    'Tis Johnny Ross and Cyrus Hewes,
    'Tis Johnny Ross and Cyrus Hewes.

Who gives us pay
For one big drunk,
When we hit Bangor
Slam kerplunk?
    'Tis Johnny Ross and Cyrus Hewes,
    'Tis Johnny Ross and Cyrus Hewes,
    'Tis Johnny Ross and Cyrus Hewes,
    'Tis Johnny Ross and Cyrus Hewes.

John Ross was a large, tell man, weighing over 240 pounds who could handle himself on a log and in a batteau. In her journal, Eckstorm added this story about John Ross and his men, as told to her by Dan Golden:

"Once at Greenville, Ross had a big crew going up the Lake and William Strickland, of Bangor, had another crew there at the same time and both lodged at Ivory Littlefield's hotel. Strickland's crew was set down to supper first, which little pleased John Ross. He objected. So, he went to the pigpen and getting a good-sized pig, brought him in under his arm and set it running down the very long table. Everything was in confusion. Littlefield arrested Ross, but since there was no lock-up, confined him in a room in the hotel. In the morning his men, fifty strong, gathered to take the steamer up the Lake - - "the old 'Lumberman' - - was it the Lumberman? No, it was the 'Fairy of the Lake."[145]

No Ross was there. They waited and he did not appear.

Then they all marched down to the hotel, found out where he was, stamped up the stairs and kicked the door down.

They carried off their man and nothing was ever said about it."

---

[145] Meaning the steamer, of which in those days more than fifty steamers, or various lengths and sizes, operated on Moosehead Lake.

> ### THE STEAMER
> # FAIRY OF THE LAKE,
> Remodelled, and thoroughly overhauled, is ready to run regular trips to Mt. Kineo, or the *Head of the Lake;* will also run, when desired, to Spencer Bay, Lily Bay, East Outlet, or any other point on
>
> ## MOOSEHEAD LAKE.
>
> Reasonable terms offered to Excursionists, by the day, or for a longer time. *Address,—*
>
> ### J. H. EVELETH,
> GREENVILLE, MAINE.

An advertisement for the Moosehead Lake Steamship *Fairy Of The Lake*, the ship mentioned by Dan Golden while being interviewed by Eckstorm.

This steamer also played a prominent part in Eckstorm's encounter with Jack Russell. The captain at the time was Louis Gill, an honorable man who assisted Eckstorm and her father. See the appendix.

XVIII — RESCUE

Come all you brave shanty boys, and listen while I relate
Concerning the young shanty boys and their untimely fate,
Concerning these young river men, so manly, true, and brave;
'T was on a jam at Island Falls, two met their watery grave.

adapted from, Jam At Gerry's Rock

THIS is a story Eckstorm had gotten wrong, . . . somewhat. In the chapter, *'Tis Twenty Years Since,* she included commentary from her friend, Penobscot river-driver David Libbey, about the incident. It may have been a small detail to those not familiar with the ways of the river, but to Libbey and Eckstorm it made a world of diffence. She corrected the record based on the new information that came to light. Libbey had died (a victim of a tragedy)[146] the year the original book was published and added what he knew about this rescue. The original story is left as initially written and the reader will find the refinements in the final chapter.

---

[146] The story of Libbey's fascinating life, and untimely death, is given in, "David Libbey – Penobscot Woodsman and River Driver. Annotated Edition," Burnt Jacket Publishing, 2021.

A FORGOTTEN story, a nameless hero.

WHO the man was no one knows, except that he was a Spencer. This in no way distinguishes him; it is but saying, in other words, that he was a riverman, and begs the question of his identity, the Spencers being not a family, but a tribe. We might guess that his name was Elijah, and guess aright most likely; but this is nothing by which he could be discriminated, for every Spencer who was not named something else was named Elijah.

What sort of a Spencer was he? That is just what the story refuses to tell us: good or bad; honest or knavish; lettered or illiterate; a sober, thrifty, useful citizen, or the most worthless ever spawned in Argyle,[147] all that we know for a certainty is that he had in him the right stuff of heroes. For out of all the rescues that I ever heard of, this is the one which had in it the least of bravado and the most of determined courage, the one which the man who started out to make it might have given up with good excuse at any point, and yet that he seems never to have thought of giving up for a moment, but fought through in the face of incredible obstacles.

His reward? To be forgotten so entirely that no one knows his name. Almost is the deed itself passed out of memory. I heard it fifteen years ago (*around 1889*) from Reed McPheters, when we were encamped close by where it happened, and in all

---

[147] Argyle is an unorganized township in Penobscot County. In 1839, it was organized as a town, but was de-organized in 1938. A logging boom along the Penobscot was named for the town. This region north of Old Town was where many a river-driver and lumbermen hailed from.

the years since, asking this one and that one who has spent his life upon the river, I found no one who knew the tale.[148] It sounded all straight, they said, but they had never heard of it, and there were so many Spencers; they couldn't guess which one this was. I despaired of ever learning more, when at last I was directed to the brother of one of the men engaged. He certified to the main points and added new details. This is the story, built up from both accounts; it may be accepted as not far from the facts.

It happened up near Fowler's Carry, where now is the city of Millinocket. Whose wildest dreams ten years ago would ever have fabled a modern city springing up within the fastnesses of that forest? For more than sixty years, the only house between Little Schoodic and Chesuncook had been the Fowler homestead on the lower end of the carry. There or near by there, for fifty-four years, up to the year 1884, when they sold it to Charley Powers, who in turn sold the land to build a city on, no one but Fowlers had ever lived on Fowler's Carry. They were pioneers among a race of pioneers and watermen of superlative excellence. It did not hurt the pride of any man to hear it said that, between the Lower Lakes and Medway, the Fowler boys could do on the river what no other men dared to do. Everybody was free to admit that much. "Those Fowler boys," as Mrs. McCauslin said to Thoreau so long ago as 1846, "are perfect ducks for the water." As well they might be, brought up in the woods with no neighbors within miles, and never a highroad except in winter but such as was afforded by a wild and frothing river, rushing down over endless rapids and falls.

At the time of this story, the two brothers Frank and John Fowler, with their families, were living in the old homestead on the carry. To understand at all this story, it is needful to bear in

---

[148] The mention here of Reed McPheters is from when he guided for Manly and Fannie Hardy on their West Branch Trip in 1889.

mind the lay of the land; for this man Spencer had to swing around a circle of not less than nine miles before he could accomplish what he started out to do, namely to rescue four men who were in great peril on the Gray Rock of Island Falls. The difficulty is that Fowler's, unlike all the other carries of the West Branch, does not skirt the river-bank, but is, or was, a cross-country road from water to water, cutting off a great bend in the river. To one looking up the river from the Forks at Medway, it is as if he held a sickle left-handed, with his thumb stuck straight out where he grasped the handle. At the tip of the blade, like a plum upon the point of the sickle, would be Quakish Lake; the curving steel would be the West Branch of the Penobscot, tearing down a rocky course, some hundred and fifty feet of fall in about four miles; the handle, with the knuckles around it, would be Shad Pond, and the outstretched thumb would be Millinocket Stream coming in from the north. Now Fowler's Carry ran from a point about two miles up Millinocket Stream to a point about a fourth of a mile below Quakish Lake at the tip of the sickle (*see map added to this edition*). The carry was called two miles long, which in Maine always means abundant measure, and yet it was a far shorter portage than would have been required in following the river with all its falls: first, as one leaves Quakish Lake, is Rhine's Pitch of about ten feet; then Island Falls of two miles of very strong water with a heavy fall, — twenty feet in twenty rods in one place, — and Grand Falls, a mile long, with the Grand Pitch, twenty feet perpendicular, just before the river enters Shad Pond. Fowler's, undoubtedly chosen by the Indians ages ago as the shortest and best route from lake to lake, did not go near the river; in most places it was from two to more than three miles away from the river.

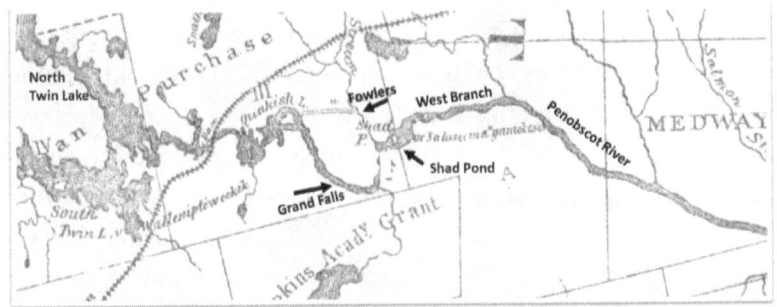

LOCATION OF FOWLER'S CARRY

Today, the town of Millinocket is where Fowler's Carry crosses from Millinocket Stream to Quakish Lake. Notice the closeness to the vicinity of Grand Falls and Shad Pond – where Joe Attien's body was located – see chapter, *Death of Thoreau's Guide – Joe Attien*.
Image from Hubbard's 1899 Map. See: *Hubbard's Guide to Moosehead Lake and Northern Maine, Annotated Edition*, Burnt Jacket Publishing, (2020).

It was the very last day of April, 1867, when Scott and Rollins turned out their logs from the boom on Quakish Lake. Theirs was not the main West Branch Drive, but a private drive, which got into Quakish much earlier and was worked along by a single boat's crew of seven men. That is why no one knows about the matter; for if the success of a jest lies in the ear of the hearer, much more does the memory of a heroic deed depend upon the eye of the spectator. But in this case had there been on-lookers, they never would have permitted Spencer to do what he did; they would have insisted upon helping, and so would have spoiled the story.

The last of April — seven men working on the logs at Quakish, one of them a Spencer. One who knows the place and the season has to stop and think about what it brings back to him, — crisp air; freezing nights; snowdrifts in the shaded hollows, and patches of dark ice, covered with hemlock needles, among the black growth; the chittering of red squirrels chasing each other and the pleasant conversation of chickadees consulting where to dig their nest. The round-leaved yellow violet is out then, even so far north as that, and the brown-winged *Vanessa* butterfly. How they endure the freezing nights no one knows, but for weeks now, fuzzy black-ended brown caterpillars have been crawling around on the snow. The bees are nosing about the woodpiles, their heads close to the sappy ends of the sticks, and the little flies that dance like tiny sprites in the golden light of sunset are treading up and down on air in their bewildering mazes. Out in the fields the sheep sniff the earth, and the cattle bite it for a relish; the ploughed land lies in furrows, wet and rank to the nostril, a wholesome smell — for one must remember again that spring comes late to these northern clearings. Leaves there would be none upon the hard wood; but the red maple might be blossomed like coral and the poplar beginning to fringe itself with silvery tassels, while birch and alder showed their corded catkins of twisted bullion and the "pussies" on the willows were large enough fairly to be called "cats," and were alive with bees. The squaw-bush[149] would have lost something of the scarlet lacquer of its stems, and the big marsh willows would be less golden in their twigs. Already the partridges would have quit their diet of birch and poplar buds and be feeding on the shrubby willows in the lowlands, or foraging for the green leaves of last year's clover and goldthread. Already the fish-hawk would be at work at Shad Pond, carrying sticks to repair his family homestead, while up at Quakish, his natural enemy and bully, the great bald eagle, might be whiling away his idle time in honest fishing from his old station on a boomstick.

---

[149] FHE: A local name for the *Cornus stolonifera*, red-osier dogwood.

One never knows the idyllic charm of our northern woods who has not seen them in April, when it is all a feast of birds and buds and waking life. Midsummer does not compare with this. This month belongs to the birds and flowers; but most of all to the robin. I cannot tell this story without giving the robins the place which I know they must have had in it, — great husky fellows, as red as blood in the lifting between showers that made a golden sunset, sitting high in the treetops and splitting their throats with their rain-carol, singing in jubilance at being back again, glad to find once more the corner of the earth that they were born in, and trolling forth such lusty music that all their pertness and swagger and pilfering of a later date is forgiven in advance. Of all the birds of springtime, I would like best to be the robin just getting back to his old home; for it is brave and blithe and bonny that he is, and he is April to all of us in the far north.

So here there must have been robins, cheerful in the face of all weathers, singing their best when the skies are lowering and the mist drives down the lake. For whatever may be the joys of April at its loveliest, it would seem that this was a bad one. There are evidences in the story that much rain had fallen and was still falling, else why such a rapid rise of water after the most of the snow was gone and the river should have been quieting down to the ordinary driving-pitch? Quakish, then, instead of a sapphire lake girdled with the green of spruces, must have been gray and mist-enshrouded, the nights warmer than on fairer days, and the days alternations of misty sunshine and smart showers of finely sifted rain, — a whole week of wet weather that melted the snows in the woods, that overfilled the bogs, that left all the mosses green and spongy, overflowing in little streams which trickled down all the tiny runlets, and that dripped from the mossy cedars leaning out over Quakish, funereally draped in gray-green moss, — good weather enough for robins, who love the wet, but not such good weather for men driving logs.

The trouble, so Reed said, was in turning the logs out of the boom in Quakish too early. Just what that means is doubtful, if it does not imply long-continued rain, which would swell the river rapidly and make the work of driving the logs more difficult and dangerous than ordinary. Whatever it means, the very first thing they got was a jam on the old Gray Rock just below Rhine's Pitch and about a quarter of a mile above the head of Island Falls. It was a middle-jam, which is the worst to pick, and they had only a single boat's crew to take care of it. Scott, who was one of the head men of that drive, went down to Fowler's at the lower end of the carry at once, with the intent to offer the two brothers, John and Frank, fifteen dollars a day to go up and handle boats and do general work.[150] That was the first day of May, and that very day Frank Fowler had gone up to Big Smith Brook to work for Fowler and Lynch. We hear no more of Scott in this story; it seems likely that, without going back to his men at all, he hastened out to Medway, twelve miles away, to pick up a crew there, and that he did not get back again till the story was over.[151]

Meantime there were but seven men to look after that jam and whatever logs of theirs were running free. They had but their one boat, which it would never do to risk, and so they must have worked short-handed, some on the jam, the rest along the

---

[150] This wage, of $15 a day, in 1867, was significant, even if it were to be split between the two brothers. The fact that this value was included in the story is a testament to the price the skill of a Fowler would command. The earlier footnote on wages of the late 1800s for river drivers ran from $1.75 per day for general labor to $4.00 per day for head boatmen.

[151] Since the story indicates that Scott did not return with at least the one brother, John, we must assume this Fowler declined the offer, or Scott never went to the Fowler residence.

shore keeping the boat by them, ready to rescue the others if anything happened. The water must have been terribly rough then, and one who knows what to listen for in imagination can hear the hiss of the great boils and the bursting of the bubbles in the long white foam-streaks striping the waves which went rushing past, running deep and wicked. Out there in the scuds of rain, one who knows what to see can see once more the piled-up middle-jam and the four men upon it, red shirts and peavies, pulling and prying and pushing to loosen one by one the great jackstraws under their feet and send them darting down the rushing river, — precarious work, this, to pry out the foundations under your feet when you know that there is nothing beneath but water running at a racehorse rate, and below, two miles of dangerous falls.

How long the men had been working on that jam, why Spencer and the others started to take them off, at what time of day the catastrophe happened, neither account satisfactorily determines. Reed understood that the jam hauled suddenly, and left only about twenty logs upon the rock, with the four men on them. Frank Fowler, who should know if any man does, says otherwise, that the jam did not start till some time in the night. Even without the authority of his statement, this would be the better reason; for the former situation is too thrilling by half for a real event, and instead of urging Spencer on to such desperate efforts would, by making it hopeless from the start, have left him nothing to labor for. It seems most probable that the larger half of the crew had been working on this jam since Scott left them the day before (for it is now the second day of May, 1867), other three resting or working near the boat, to be ready in case of accident; that the time must have been not far from six o'clock, the old-fashioned sun-time, which came a half hour later by the light than the railroad standard of today; and that it was now approaching supper-time, and the boat was coming out to take the men off. For it could not have been dark enough to quit work at that season, even of a lowery or a rainy day; but the river-driver's supper hour is seven o'clock, and as these were but a single boat's crew, too few men to carry a cook and separate wangan, they must leave the logs long enough before dark to cook for themselves. It seems likely that it was, as the men would say, "just about half-past hungry time," and the men on the jam saw with pleasure the boat, with Spaulding, Moores, and Spencer in it, dropping down to take them off. Perhaps the rain held up a little and the yellow of the sunset behind the raincloud showed through it, and the robins in the treetops all along the shore were singing, to be seen but not to be heard above the tumult of the water.

"Pretty birds them be to sing," the men might have remarked, leaning on their peavies, "and awful nice in pies." It may sound materialistic, but why is it not better that a robin should be good in a pie as well as out of it? They were willing enough to give him credit for his music, but supper was what was in their thoughts. And here were Spaulding and Moores and Spencer letting the boat down, two with their poles, one at the oars, intending to drop her into the eddy below the jam. Then the four men would tumble in, three of them would take an oar apiece, the boy would sit aft on the lazy seat, and back they would go to campfire, supper, and bed.

Two of those men were doomed to make their bed in a different place that night; and but for a miracle, the like of which I never heard of happening, all seven of them would have been there before morning.

It was but a step more to safety in the eddy, when snap went the stern-pole, and around the boat swung broadside to the current. Before they could straighten her with paddles she was swept down upon the head of Island Falls. She struck a rock, cracked open, and overset, all in the same instant. Quick? A driving-boat is *built* to act quick; that is her special virtue.

There were now three men and a wrecked boat in the water of Island Falls, and four men on a jam in the middle of the river, powerless to save them. If the initial disaster was quick, the final one was to the spectators a prolonged agony. Two of their mates they saw drowned outright, and for the third there was no hope. There were they, four wet, hungry, shivering men, a moment before so near to blankets, supper, and fire, now abjectly miserable on a log-jam in mid-river, no one knowing of their plight, rain falling, night coming fast, the river rising, the jam they were on already beginning to feel the freshet and grow uneasy, their own danger imminent, and their hearts wrung by seeing a catastrophe which they could have in no wise prevented. They were hungry, cold, wet, miserable, disheartened men, in peril of their lives. Did the robin still sing in the treetops? Then they damned his unseemly levity, and in the same breath wished they had the pie he was made for.

The two men who were drowned outright, have nothing further to do with the story. No doubt they were as good men as any of those saved, as good watermen, perhaps, as Spencer was; but it was their fate to lose their lives, not to give them away. Moores was found about a month later down at Jerry Brook, and there was buried. Spaulding was not discovered till sometime in September, under a log where the old mill-pond was, down at Medway, sixteen miles below where he was drowned. 'T is only a sample of what all river-stories are like; in almost all someone loses his life, and no one thinks of him afterward except the family, that sets one less chair at table, and a few mates here and there, who date their stories by the year such and such a one was drowned.

Meantime Spencer, on whom everything depends, is at the mercy of a raging flood on the head of Island Falls. There are two miles of this tumultuous water, but the River helped him. All watermen know — indeed, anyone may observe the same thing by watching even a gutter-current — that all swift water has a pulse-beat; nominally its waves are stationary, but every now and then there comes a larger one, swelling quick and high with a sudden throb, quite different from the ordinary stationary wave. No sooner had Spencer been thrown into the water than one of these great waves took him and lifted him fairly up on the bottom of his overturned boat. It was slippery with wet pitch; it was narrow; it had no keel; he could not have held on at all, bucking and rearing as it did, reeling and rocking, as its long points, bow and stern, ploughed under the great boils, had not the boat when she turned over hit a rock so hard as to split one side open. He got his fingers into the crack, and it nipped them there.

We have four men on a middle-jam waiting to be drowned, two below drowned already, and the seventh man with his fingers caught fast in the crack in a crazy old boat that — upside down, banging into him, overriding him, slatting him against rocks and logs, half drowned with spray and rushing waters, half stunned with being beaten against boat and rocks, his fingers crushed and aching cruelly — towed him the whole two miles down Island Falls.

"And if that wasn't something of an experience, then I don't never want to have one happen to me!" says the woodsman, who can appreciate better than any amateur what it must mean.

It takes a good deal to drown a Spencer. There is a story current about four Spencers and four Province men, a Mattawamkeag crew, going out in 1870 to pick a jam on the upper pitch of Piscataquis Falls. When they saw how bad the water was, two of the Spencers leaped out of the boat and got ashore again; the other two Spencers and the Province men were carried over the falls. The Spencers were all right in the water, of course; they expected to arrive somewhere. Old Lute swam ashore about half a mile below, with his T. D. pipe still in his teeth. He emerged like Neptune, and shook the water off all ready for some more river-driving. Some bystander, a little curious, inquired where he had come from. He answered that he was, "right down from Piscataquis Upper Pitch, and he guessed them four Bluenoses that was in the boat with him was all drownded by that time!" He was right, too. The Spencer whom he did not worry about got ashore on the boat.

This Spencer was dragged down through Island Falls. Just as he reached the point where he did not care to travel much farther because below were the Grand Falls and Grand Pitch, which nothing can go over and live, the boat struck a wing-jam so hard that the crack gaped and let his fingers out. Then the boat went off and left him; for all this time the boat had been holding him rather than he holding the boat. As he was being carried past the jam, he threw one arm over a log, and another of those great pulse-beats of the river came, as before, and lifted him clear up upon the jam.

Reed had heard that at just this moment the jam hauled, that he fell in between the logs as they were moving, grasped two of them, threw himself out upon them, and ran ashore over the tumbling, moving mass. This is requiring too much breath for even a Spencer. Any man, after being dragged through Island Falls the way this one had been, ought to have been grateful enough for the help of that great wave to lie there on the logs, sick and giddy and aching, till he got the water out of him and the woods stopped spinning around him, the noise of the river became a less deafening roar, and he could see the trees and logs in their natural color instead of just the black shapes of logs and trees.

It was getting quite dusk beneath the trees, and here was he, a battered and disabled man, alone on the riverbank, two miles below his comrades in distress and four miles at least from Fowler's, nothing for him to do but to get his legs under him and limp along the best he could to Fowler's Carry. John and Frank would go up and take the men off, and all would come out right.

The water was very strong; it was rising fast; to lose a moment would not do, for no one could tell how soon, under such a pressure as that, the jam on the Gray Rock might give way. He scrambled up, hobbling painfully, perhaps putting his fingers to his mouth to ease them, for they were raw and bloody and still white at the ends from the pinching they had received in the old boat's side; the split board working back and forth had maimed them cruelly. Then he set off down the drivers' path past Grand Falls. There was a boat down below the Grand Pitch, and it was easier, if not shorter, to go by water than to go through the woods, if, indeed he was landed on the left bank at all, which the story does not say. He walked and he ran and he hurried hobbling for a mile, when he reached the place where the boat was. Then he rowed down Shad Pond for a mile, and then poled up Millinocket Stream for two miles more. It must have taken him an hour at least since he was washed ashore below Island Falls, and it was now on the edge of darkness, the time when the robins are flying with sharp *peeps* and *queeps*, jetting their tails and talking about going to bed, for the robin is rather late about his hour of retiring.

At Fowler's landing Spencer hauled his boat up ashore enough to hold her, and then toiled up the hill to the house. He was very much done out. However, he could get the Fowler boys to go over with their boat, and he would have no more worries. He was hungry, too. A woodsman's appetite is not a fickle fancy for victuals, to be lost or forgotten just because he has had some strain upon his nerves. Perhaps, as he dragged himself wearily up the hill in the dusk, he smelled that most appetizing of all the smells of springtime, the odor of smoked alewives roasting before an open fire. He could see in fancy the row of golden-sided fishes, standing on their heads before the bed of coals, as they leaned against the tongs laid across the fire-dogs and gave forth, when they cracked open, a smell so savory that no one who cannot remember smelling it in damp April weather can dream how good it is. Spencer quickened his steps, always supposing that he actually did smell it, for, where the story is silent, conjecture has the right to wander.

He went up to the log-house, finished within and without with rifted cedar, and appeared before the women within like an apparition. It was long after supper; they were finishing the last of the supper-dishes, and the delicious odor was only from the refuse of the feast smouldering upon the coals. He was disappointed, more so than he would have cared to own. He had been planning on being asked to supper, and had anticipated his enjoyment of his share.

"Where's John and Frank?" he asked abruptly, stopping in the doorway, a big, black bulk in the gloaming.

"Lord! how you scared me!" cried one of the women.

"Didn't mean to, mum," was his weak apology, leaning against the door-jamb; he knew that he was faint as well as hungry. "Where's John and Frank?"

"Milking," said John's wife.

"Up Big Smith Brook; went up yesterday," said Frank's wife.

Each one answering for her own.

He dropped into a seat with a groan.

"Why, what's the matter?" asked one of the women kindly. "You do look all beat out! No hat, and — land sakes! you're wet to the skin! Here, draw up close to the fire and get warmed up. What have you been off doing?"

Whether she had ever seen him before made no difference, the cordiality of those pioneer homes being too real for any formality. She drew him up to the fire and bade him rest,

"What's the matter now?" she asked. There was always something the matter on those falls.

"Just been runnin' Island Falls on the bottom of a boat," said he. His fingers almost made him wince when he got them near the fire.

She was a pioneer woman, and could think and act promptly. "Here, Billy and Ann," — or whatever were the names of the first children she could catch, — "just you run out to the barn and tell your father to come right in; there's been a boat swamped up on Island Falls."

"What become of the others?" she asked, turning to the man.

He did not like to say it too bluntly.

"They're where they won't get out till they are taken out, I guess, mum," he answered.

She stood and plaited the hem of her apron. "How many?" she asked.

"Two — there was three of us in the boat. The other four's out on the jam on the old Gray Rock, if so be she ain't hauled yet."

The other woman had stood silent beside her sister-in-law. "And only you and John to do it; and you so used up! How can you ever?"

"Got to," said he.

There is never any fun in being a hero. This man didn't look the hero either, just a worn-out, tired, used-up man, with hair all tossed and tangled, a stoop in his shoulders, a crook in his back, and every rag upon him steaming before the fire. His hands he held down between his knees; he did not wish to have the ladies see them; they were not presentable.

These were women who knew what to do for a man. Already one of them had poured hot water on fresh tea leaves, while the other stooped and stood a herring up against the andiron bar, close to the coals.

"You ought not to, mum," said the man; "I ain't got time to eat; we've got to git right off; there ain't no time to eat." It was a feeble remonstrance. He wanted that alewife; the sight of it put more heart into him than anything else could have done, and to sit and sip his tea and watch that broil would, he felt, make a new man of him.

"You've got plenty enough time to eat," said one of the sisters-in-law, both hospitably busy with laying plates and tea-things and bringing out the food in store.

"It's too bad you are too late for regular supper; things don't taste so good cold, but we'll warm up the biscuit, if you don't mind them a little crusty." No doubt the table was spread with other seasonable food: cold buckwheat cakes, perhaps, with the richest and sweetest of maple syrup, made from their own trees, and spicy dried-apple sauce, as brown as mahogany, flavored with nutmeg and dried orange peel, a delicious spring dainty, or custard pie without stint of eggs, and thick, soft gingerbread, such as woodsmen love best of anything, — "the odds and ends," as no doubt the ladies said, but food enough and good enough for anyone; for these frontier homes were places where there was no lack of good fare, and where no one was allowed to pass without the invitation to partake it.

"Just you rest easy," said the sisters, caring for him. "John has got the boat to see to, and to get the drag down to it, and to yoke up the oxen. You can't help a bit more than the children can till it comes to getting the boat on; then maybe it will take the whole of us, she's so big and heavy. You wait till you are called for and get rested; you'll need all the strength you've got when the time comes." So well did they perform their part, that before the boat was ready he was fit to do his share in helping John Fowler.

Meantime John Fowler was losing no minutes. He understood what his wife meant when he had come in with the foaming milk-pails and she had laid her hand upon his arm. It was: "*Must* you go, John?" — not dissuasion, but wifely concern.

All he said — for he knew that it meant some desperate undertaking — was, "How many? Where are they?"

A rescue is an obligation on all river-men. While a chance remains it is not to be given up, no matter what it costs. "Drown ten men to save two," is the unwritten code of the River. The way in which this has been lived up to is one of the explanations of the willingness of the men to go into all sorts of hard places: they know that if human skill can do it, they are to be saved. Once when two men were adrift on the logs at Piscataquis Lower Pitch, six boats' crews, thirty-six men in all, leaped into their boats and ran the falls to save those two. It was mad folly for them to do it all at once, for the water was terribly rough; but they did it. Sebattis Solomon, good waterman as he was, almost lost his life in the attempt; for a leaping log knocked him out of his place in the bow, and had he not come up like a cork and thrown himself into his boat before his own midshipmen knew that he was out of it, he would not have lived to perform more deeds of water-craft.

This rescue on Island Falls was one of peculiar difficulty; for it must be made long after dark, in the worst of water, with only two men to handle a great Maynard boat whose crew should have been six men, four at the least. It required the most careful preparation for all emergencies. Everything must be provided at the outset. There were poles and paddles to be put into the boat, an axe, a rope, perhaps some dry kindling for starting big bonfires along the shores to light up the river; and there must be torches of birch-bark wound on slender poles to stick up in the boat, lighting more fully the track by which she traveled. Then the boat was too large and heavy for two men to launch, so rollers must be provided, that the pitch might not be scraped off on the rocks in getting her afloat. Then everything within the boat must be lashed in place, that on the rough trip across the carry nothing essential should be lost out. Finally, John Fowler must get on his driving-boots and must hitch up the cattle. Last of all, when the drag was ready and Spencer stood beside it with two of the children, one carrying a lantern, it now being full dark, John Fowler had to go back again to get a little bottle of matches, perhaps to say good-by to his wife. To everyone else those men seemed the same as saved already because he had started to do it, but he and she might have felt the flutter of uncertainty.

So, with the children leading, to light the road with the lantern, to tend the fires, and, if accident were to be piled upon accident that day, as sometimes happens, to bring back home the news of it, they set off up the hill and across the rocky pasture now growing up to pine bushes, with the oxen going at as brisk a pace as was good for either boat or cattle. Ahead the children danced and trotted, their swinging lantern a mere blur upon the misty night. Then came the oxen on the run, John Fowler giving them the gad, while Spencer tried to keep the boat upright. The old drag smashed and bounced on the great gray rocks embedded in the carry road, the boat was tossed more ways than if she were running the roughest water, and in spite of their lashings, the things inside her clattered and clashed. There was the jangling of chains, the shouting to the cattle, the creak of drag and boat, the rattle of the gad on horns and yoke, the racket of the poles inside the boat as they urged that cavalcade along, not sparing their speed. It was two miles to go, over as rough a road as a man cares to walk by daylight unencumbered, and then the offset down to Rhine's Pitch. Half an hour? Well, if they did it in half an hour, that was quick time; the miles in that region are good measure, and the bounces and jounces are thrown in besides.

Meantime there had been four men sitting on a jam out in the middle of the river. Nothing more is known about them. Being merely dummies in the story, whose whole office was to permit themselves to be rescued, no one has thought to preserve their names. Nor would they care themselves if we invent whom we will to take their places.

There were, let us say, a boy of eighteen, off on his first drive, qualifying for the West Branch; an old soldier who would have "seen her through," had not a minie ball through the lungs mustered him out at Gettysburg, — a lean, gaunt man, always chirk and active, with a straggling, thin beard, the type of many a veteran whom we used to see when the war was over; and there was Tom Smith of Old Town, which is no libel, for it used to be reported of the Tom Smiths of Old Town that they named them Long Tom and Short Tom and Chub Tom, and then they began to number them, and they numbered them up to sixteen. This one was Tom Smith number sixteen and a half, the beginning of a new series of Tom Smiths, and not at all a bad sort of fellow; he was probably dark, with curly hair, and having been brought up in Old Town, had never believed that it was going to be his luck to be drowned. The last was a short, thickset, swarthy man, part Inman,[152] who sat silent and smoked. He had nothing to say; he did nothing; he seemed to have no nerves; but in a nook as well protected as any from the drive of the rain and the spray of the river, he sat with his hands in his pockets and pulled at his old pipe, facing death without the quickening of a pulse beat. That was partly because he was a man approaching middle-age, who had been on the river long enough to learn that if a man is

---

[152] There were several families with the surname, Inman, in the area of the Penobscot River who were involved in land purchases and the lumber business. Eckstorm may have been making that connection in her fictional account of the men who were stranded.

born to be drowned, a mud-puddle in the road is deep enough to do it, and if he isn't born to be drowned, the whole Penobscot River cannot keep him under long enough to save him from his natural fate; so there is no use in worrying over what is going to happen to you, even if you do find yourself in a tight place. That is the philosophy of the River. All brave men are fatalistic; the only objection to fatalism is when it is stupid.

But it is no comfortable situation to be where these men were, in a night of rain and mist, out on a pile of logs with the river rushing on all sides, so that it makes one giddy to see the white streaks racing past, like looking out of a train window in the dark at the lane of light which travels beside it, — to be there without fire or food or extra garments, and from hard and heating labor suddenly to have to sit down in a cold spring rain and wait for hours, with nothing to think of but the uncertainty of their fate and the horror of what they had seen. The boy took it hard; silently, of course, for stoicism is the custom of the river, and no one here likes to admit that he has any feelings; but this was the first time he had ever seen anyone drown, and the horror of it shook his nerves, and made the night seem full of noises; he was twice as chilly as he had been, his teeth chattered, and he did not like an old horned owl which kept hooting along the river-bank, audible above the rushing of the water.

What had become of Spencer, they did not know. They had seen him thrown up on the boat by the great wave; he stood a chance, that was all. If he were lost, they were doomed. It was only a question of time before that jam would be carried away by the rising water. Tom Smith took out his pocket-knife, and reaching down among the logs, began cutting into the side of one. It was not dark then, only full dusk, and the rain had given way to mist.

"What you doing, Tom?" asked the soldier.

"Getting spruce gum," replied Tom Smith.

But the man who asked the question was not deceived: one does not look for much spruce gum on a pine log. Tom Smith had been cutting a water-line where he could feel it after dark with his fingers, and judge by the rising of the water when that jam would haul. Then he shut his knife, and put it in his pocket.

"Find any gum, Tom?" inquired the ex-soldier.

"Nothin' good for anything," replied Tom Smith. "That log was all rossy[153] anyway." Then he went dumb again.

The ex-soldier understood the situation. He had the boy on his mind, too; for he had seen enough of raw recruits under fire for the first time, and he did not believe that it helps a man's after-career to let his courage sink too low the first time he is facing peril. One has to see men die more or less, was his notion, and the right thing to do is to think that it is not at all unnatural: it does not follow that one's own turn is coming next. He began telling stories, funny stories, of times when there was nothing to eat and someone sneaked off with the best of the general's dinner, and his mess that day fared all right; of times when in hard places men were supremely comical and kept the others laughing with their drollery; of times when men did such great things that only to hear of them was to applaud, — stories like that of Major Hyde and the Seventh at Antietam, and of Chamberlain at Little Round Top. He had been — where had he not been? — at First Bull Run, at Williamsburg, Chickahominy, Fair Oaks, Antietam, Fredericksburg, Chancellorsville, Gettysburg.[154] At Gettysburg he saw — and then he stopped to cough.

"Quite a cough," said Tom Smith.

---

[153] Rossy, an old word, used for shaggy-barked trees, chiefly of hard wood trees, like swamp maple, but sometimes also of scurfy or scaly barked soft woods. It applies only to the loose, outside bark, which is often called *ross*.

[154] Stories of Civil War battles.

"Keeping that to remember Gettysburg by," replied the veteran, wiping his forehead. "Sometimes when I'm damp it comes on a little to 'mind me of old times."

It did not sound like a cough which river-driving would help to cure; but in that gaunt, thin-faced man with the straggling beard there was a power of grit. Just at present, instead of fretting because he could not get hot tea and warm blankets, he was taking upon himself to be the life of the little group upon the old Gray Rock.

"Oh, cheer up, sonny," said he to the boy, "don't you take it to heart so much; like's not they are all snug somewheres; takes a deal of killing to use a man up, especially an able man at his trade. They'll all come hypering back bime-by when they get 'em another boat; you wouldn't believe what a man can go through and not be hurt a bit; why, I knowed a man . . ." —

Meantime Tom Smith was consulting his water-line.

"Gettin' some more of that same kind o' gum?" asked the soldier.

"Yes," said Smith gloomily. His line was half an inch under water in about an hour, he calculated. At that rate the jam could not hold together till morning. Three inches more, he reckoned, and she would haul.

Already the water sobbed and chuckled higher among the timbers, and one of the big pulses of the river would send it spouting up through the chinks in the centre of the mass where before the water had been almost still. The jam lifted around the edges, too, when one of these big fellows came hurrying past. Of course, there are plenty of youths who never saw anything but a millpond, who will be assured that, had they been there, they would just have caught hold of the biggest log they could find and have serenely floated down to safety: it wouldn't have worried them any, because they always can see easy ways out of sinking ships and burning buildings and dangers which they never experienced. To such a riverman would reply: "Our boys ain't onto them smart tricks o' yourn with logs, but when you try to learn us how, don't start in on a middle-jam on Island Falls."

Tom Smith and the others who were used to the business saw nothing to do but to wait for the end of things right where they were.

"Just the same sort of gum as before?" the old soldier had bantered, trying to get his information lightly.

"And it ain't no good sort, I can tell you," responded Tom Smith bitterly.

The old horned owl on the shore whooped again.

"Blame a owl!" said Tom Smith.

The soldier kept right along with his story, "The awfuliest comical story that ever was about a man that got his head shot clean off; something I seen myself."

His stories had more to do with sudden death than some would think in keeping with their surroundings; but all tales of the river are tragic. These men did not mind mere tragedy. Under their environment, to talk of drowning would not have been etiquette, but there was something almost cheerful in hearing about a man to whom nothing worse happened than getting his head cut clean off with a cannon-ball.

The horned owl hooted again.

"Darn — a — owl!" said Tom Smith, in so ladylike a way that it took off all the objections to strong language. He had to say something. He did not like the hollow mockery of that great voice in the dark that cried, "Oh, who, who, who are you?" He wasn't going to be anybody by tomorrow morning, if Spencer had been drowned with the rest and that water kept on rising half an inch or more an hour; he did not care to be reminded of the fact.

The ex-soldier coughed again, a racking spasm of coughing. River-driving in rainstorms and fitting out all night on middle-jams did not seem to be the sort of health-cure best adapted to a man who has had a minie ball through his lungs. Yet as soon as he could take his hands away from his side where he had pressed them, he began talking again, telling how he once made three men prisoners when he had nothing but an empty rifle; how when he was a vidette he used to trade tobacco with the enemy's outposts; how that first day at Gettysburg, the day before he got *this*, an old fellow in a high-crowned hat and a long-tailed blue had fought all day with the Seventh Wisconsin, and was a blame good shot, too; how at Yorktown, Old Seth of the Berdan Sharpshooters had captured one of the enemy's largest guns, and declared that if they would only bring him victuals enough, he could keep that gun till the end of the game, because not a man could get near to serve it while he had his bead on them. The man had seen life for three years, and there rose in him such a fountain of unquenchable vitality that no vicissitude nor danger could make him feel that he was not going to keep right on living; drown him on Island Falls if need be, and he would turn up somewhere else all alive and kicking, just as when they killed him in the army he had come out a river-driver. He did not worry about that cough even.

"Sometimes coughin' won't kill ye half so quick as ye wisht it would," was his cheerful philosophy.

"This old jam is heavin' now," cried the boy, clutching his arm.

"Don't ye be 'feared o' that, sonny," said he, as cool as ever. "You've been gettin' the water in your head, hearin' the rush of it so long. It's just makin' you dizzy to see them white streaks racin' past. You'll feel a big ram-dazzlefication when this here raft pulls off the old Gray. When I was sharpshootin' down in..."

The old horned owl hooted again sepulchrally and near. "Oh, who, who, who are you?"

"Damn a hoot-owl!" cried Tom Smith, not mincing matters. A loon and a hoot-owl were two birds which he had no use for, always glad to see a man get into trouble.

"And the mock-birds down south," went on the soldier, coughing worse, but bringing himself back to his self-imposed task, for he was intending to talk till the jam broke, just to keep that youngster's courage up — "and the mock-birds so sweetly singing" —

"Hist! Hark! I hear'em comin'!" said the silent man. He had not spoken for almost two hours now.

They listened and could hear John Fowler shouting to his cattle; then they saw the misty glow of the lantern; then Spencer on the shore put his hands to his lips and gave a whoop that scared the hoot-owl out of competition.

Yes, they were all there.

That was good news, and it made the rescuers all the livelier at their work. It was not long before great fires were blazing on the shore, lighting the green wall of forest along the river-bank and the white scrolls of foam upon the water, and turning golden all the haze above the trees. The children fed them with dry brush from near at hand, and with every addition to the fires the blaze threw up an eruption of bright sparks and diffused an orange glare upon the blackness of the night. Then the great Maynard boat was rolled down to the water's edge and made ready, and the blazing torch was stuck up in the peak of the bow. With John Fowler in the bow, Spencer in the stern, they started to drop her down from the eddy below Rhine's Pitch.

The men on the jam saw her coming with breathless eagerness. Supper, fire, and bed were drawing just so much nearer to them every time that the ringing, iron-shod poles telegraphed above the rush of the waters — a foot, a yard, a rod of distance lessened.

The silent man rose and knocked the ashes out of his pipe. He put his hands to his lips. "Take the left of the big rock; don't try her inside!"

He had been studying to some purpose, and now he came to the fore and helped to direct the boat, as dropping her cautiously, feeling their way inch by inch, partly by the light of the blazing torch, glaring red on the misty night, but more by that marvelous knowledge of the river which with the Fowlers was almost an instinct. Fowler and Spencer picked their way in the darkness among the rocks in the rising flood on that wild river.

The men on the jam hardly dared to look, for fear that even John Fowler might not be able to get down safe, and when they saw the boat go below them striving to make her turn and come up in the eddy, and the torch-light dim because it was burning down, they did not breathe for expectation that just as Spaulding's pole had snapped, so Spencer's would break on the same spot and leave them in despair. Then Fowler knocked the shaggy cinder from the top of the torch with his pole; the light blazed bright again; the boat loomed nearer; the flame leaped, and John Fowler swung her side against the jam.

Small time they lost in clambering in, four chilled and weary men of excellent cheerfulness. Then Spencer took the bow and gave the stern to John Fowler, that he might have the place requiring greatest skill, and they poled her back in safety to the eddy below Rhine's Pitch.

Four very wet and weary men tumbled ashore, and a Spencer more done-out than any of them. It is hard work to be a hero; he did not think of anything but going to bed. Some brief but not fulsome thanks were passed, no doubt, some credit for great water-craft was bestowed, and then John Fowler drove his oxen home, the children walking beside him with their lantern.

At the river-drivers' camp the rescued men were thinking of supper. The boy was used up; he had crawled into the spreads and lay shaking in an ague there, because, even covered up head and ears, he could not help seeing things. The silent man took an axe, and the chip-chop of it off one side showed that he was cutting firewood. Tom Smith was getting potatoes out of a bag. The ex-soldier, bent over a little pile of birch-bark and whittlings, was starting a fire. No doubt he was thinking of Moores and Spaulding, for as he worked he sang softly, —

*"We're tenting to-night on the old camp-ground.
Give us a song to cheer."*[155]

Tom Smith, who, when he first landed, had given three great sighs of relief and then had begun to swear, — softly, very deliberately, entirely without animus, like the gentlest summer rain falling upon a roof, just repeating over and over everything which he could remember, — had turned his whole attention to supper.

"Boys," he said, "I've just earned fair a front seat in heaven for not swearing for the three damnedest long hours that ever was tooken out of a man's mortal life; but I'd swap even off with any man who would give me a roasted potato."

---

[155] The song *Tenting Tonight* was written by Walter Kittredge in 1864. It was a popular song with the Union soldiers during the Civil War. For the reader who has never heard this song, the performance recorded by the UCLA University Chorus and R. Lord Conductor (c. 2011) is memorable and is available online. Another composition is the bluegrass rendition by artist Chris Neumeyer. The reference to Moores and Spaulding is likely to the prominent families of the south, which at the time of the rescue in 1867, were only beginning their rise in business and politics. Moores and Spaulding was often referred to as the name of an area of North Carolina where the families were settled.

"Many are the hearts that are weary to-night," chanted the old soldier, paying no attention to anything but his fire and his own thoughts.

Just then, in the distance, far off, a horned owl hooted.

A conscious smirk drew across Tom Smith's face, and he clapped his hand upon his mouth. "O hell, I forgot," he murmured like a child who has been caught. "take it all back again — 'Damn a owl' — that's so; but perhaps they might give me a seat somewheres way back next the door."

The old soldier did not hear him at all; he was keeping on with his song, and had come to the refrain of it: —

> *"Tenting to-night.*
> *Tenting to-night.*
> *Tenting on the old camp-ground."*

Lots of times before, too, the other fellow had been taken, and he had been left.

No other man but one of the Fowlers could have made that rescue; everybody will tell you that. But who else could have done what Spencer did? The water rose that night and carried the jam away. A little less persistence on his part, a little less stubborn courage, a little more thought for his own safety, a little more disregard for other men's, and four men more would have been added to the total of the casualties of the river.

That Spencer man came very near being a hero. Only he was not the fresh, sleek, well-groomed young fellow of books, who never gets wet, or tired, or torn; but just a rough, ragged, dirty, wrinkle-faced, sun-burned, utterly dragged-out man, with lame arms and sore fingers and bruises from rough treatment, the sort of man you pass on the street-corners, spring and fall, and speak of as belonging to the "lower class."

Pray, who knows where St. Peter is going to put you and me and the Spencers when he calls us up by classes and ranks us by the work done in this world?

Will only reading and writing and arithmetic count?

Or will he demand some proof of pluck, persistence, and generous action?

It is likely enough that St. Peter knows by name even all of the Spencers, and for such a deed as this may award his highest honors, something not bestowed upon the nameless ones who make up the "cultured masses."

SIAS HILL

Not all men died on the river. On the road from Kokadjo to Ripogenus, there is a hill named, Sias Hill. It is said the hill received its name from the following incident.
"A man named Sias was driving a six-ox team and sled with poles fastened to the horns of the oxen, over the tote road. In going down this hill, the team got away from him and slewed at the foot of the hill throwing him against a big yellow birch and killed him."

Reported in *The Northern*, 1921.

XIX — DRIVERS' LUNCH

THIS ballad was given to Eckstorm from Mrs. S. M. Crommett, from Derby, Maine, which is a village in the small town of Milo. She wrote the lyrics around 1885. Eckstorm noted this was more of a poem, than a ballad to be sung. It has the ring of truth as in a lumber camp there was no talking during mealtimes. The cook, who had slaved for hours to prepare a meal for possibly a hundred or more men, wanted them to eat and not sit around for longer than necessary. The Crystal Brook mentioned in the ballad could have been the brook north of Patten, Maine that flows to Crystal Lake.

Drivers' Lunch

by, Mrs. S. M. Crommett, Derby, Maine.

I've seen a sight I'll never forget
While Memory holds its sway;
'Twas the drivers camp on Crystal Brook
On a sunny April day,
And seated on a mossy log
I viewed the camp ground o'er
And saw the drivers eat their lunch —
There was full many a score.

The Boss was standing by with ease,
With many a nod and wink,
As he watched his husky lads with speed
Dispose of food and drink.
The Cook was busy with his plates
And knives and forks and dippers,
And tripped around so easy
In his India-rubber slippers.

The pork and beans within the pot
In their midst was set with care,
The cover lifted, and was spread
A tempting banquet there.
And snowy biscuits, flaky brown,
Were tumbled from the baker,
And followed quick the luscious beans,
Great credit to their maker.

And chunks of luscious ginger-bread,
All fragrant shiny-brown,
With quarts of black tea, sweet and strong,
It quickly was washed down,
They ate their lunch in silence,
In silence drank their tea,
Enlivened only by the notes
Of some lone chickadee.

With their hats upon their heads
And their plates upon their knees,
With the river rushing by
And the wind among the trees,
Could they ask for music sweeter
To swell the song of life,
Each one busy with his thoughts
Of sweetheart, mother, wife?

Then T.D.'s were in order
And soon the fragrant smoke
Was wafted to my nostrils
And hid the rushing brook;
Then with cant-dogs on their shoulders
They quickly marched away,
To break the jams and row the boats
From April until May.

(T.D. was a type of clay pipe.)

XX — "JOYFULLY"

DRIVING logs on Sunday has always been accounted as a work of necessity: so many logs to be taken down on only so much head of water, — it is almost a mathematical problem; and if the logs get "hung up," they are spoiled before another year, therefore it is a moral problem also whether it is better to break the Sabbath one's self or to break the owners of the logs financially. On Penobscot the custom is so firmly intrenched that perhaps no argument could avail to change it. Yet upon no point are the heads and the hands of the drive more divided. Some of the men have conscientious scruples about working Sundays; others know that it has been successfully discontinued elsewhere, and cite the example of the Androscoggin Drive, which more than twenty years ago (*by 1884*) had discontinued driving on Sundays; while all are agreed that in seven successive days of labor they cannot accomplish as much work as they could do in six days, if they had Sunday to rest in.

Still, there has never been any open strife upon the subject; the drive pays them seven days' wages when it knows that it is getting but six days' results; the men, realizing that it is not greed oppressing them but the demands of a military necessity, which must snatch the day for fear of the morrow's uncertainties, do their work, take their pay, and grumble privately. They feel that there is room for honest difference of opinion upon the subject, but it is not their campaign. That is the situation upon the Penobscot River.

This brief story relates how elsewhere a Penobscot man, keen to seize his opportunity, changed this established custom. It is a little comedy of conscience. With masterly adroitness Sebattis presses his point home to the other man's conscience, while he dexterously guards his own line of retreat in case he fails. It was no mere lucky fluke. Sebattis was a strategist to whom fine combinations were dear, as anyone must acknowledge who ever sat down with him to a game of draughts, as anyone might guess who noted his resemblance to the pictures of the Marquis Ito.[156] To those who judge by externals only, perhaps he was nothing but a huge, fat, greasy Indian; but in this little tale he reveals himself as a man of heart and judgment, jovial, shrewd, diplomatic, and disinterested, even long years before philanthropy became a fashion.

Dead is Sebattis, and his stories are forgotten. Few could tell you now how he made and recited them, long compositions, requiring sometimes two or three evenings for their full unfolding, yet carefully constructed with an eye to their effects, modeled as only an artist can mould a tale, and told without omissions or alterations because he had a respect for his own artistic creations. They were indeed works of art, and no one who ever hurt his artist's sensitiveness by falling asleep in the middle of an interminable tale will forget his plaintive reproach:

"What for you gone 'sleep? Why you don' gone 'wake?"

Then he would begin some miles back in his story, wherever his listener had lost him, and tell it all over again from that point, because he would not mutilate a work of art.

---

[156] Likely a reference to Ito Hirobumi (1841-1909), a Japanese Statesman and first Prime Minister of Japan.

BIG SEBATTIS MITCHELL
Photograph from the collection of Fannie Hardy Eckstorm.
Caption: "Big Sebattis Mitchell - taken 1891."
*Image courtesy of Special Collections, Raymond H. Fogler Library,
University of Maine.*

Of all the countless stories that he knew, perhaps the following is the only one which can be reproduced at all as he used to rehearse it, and even this is a condensed story. It would have taken Sebattis a whole evening to tell this little story; but even now, shorn of all its divagations, it is still recognizably Big Sebattis Mitchell.

When supper was done and the campfire burned briskly and the blankets were laid out for lounging before the blaze, — how it drew the resinous aroma from the balsam boughs! — then Big Sebattis would begin to untangle the threads of the stories in his memory.

"Never we told you it that story 'bout Old Isaac sung um '*Joyfully*'?" would be his introduction.

Then with slow speech and many pauses he would begin the tale.

"Well, we shall told you all 'bout it. You see that time she live it Old Isaac at Maccadavy" — that is, at Magaguadavic.[157]

"Good many years been lumberin' there –had Old Isaac. We been livin' there ourself eight years, work for Old Isaac, a kind of under-boss, you see.[158]

"One night in fall come Old Isaac to my house, spoke so:"

'Sebattis, we want you go up river tomorrow mornin' berry early.'

"You see on Maccadavy, he don't drove all logs clear down in spring like here;[159] always he left part drive at foot lower lake; then when he want logs in fall, he have um fall drive.

"Well, nex' mornin' we gone with um Old Isaac in wagon. When we come where high bridge cross river, says Old Isaac:

'We want you stay this place pick it off logs so he don't jam on 'butments.'

---

[157] Magaguadavic River in New Brunswick. A Maliseet or Passamaquoddy name, that has been translated to, River of Eels. Sebattis was a frequent traveling partner and guide for Manly Hardy. Between 1873 and 1878, they took at least four trips; two on the Penobscot, one to the St. Croix, and another to the coast and Little Deer Isle (source: the journal of Manly Hardy). Here we have again where a non-native language speaker simply uses the feminine pronoun in reference to himself, a common occurrence in matters of speech.

[158] Old Isaac was a foreman of the lumbering operation in the region for many years. In her book, *Minstrelsy of Maine* (1927, p. 194), Eckstorm reported the name as Isaac Bradley.

[159] The masculine use of 'he' refers here to the Drive, or bosses of the Drive. On the Magaguadavic River, Sebattis explained of the two-season drive, spring and fall.

"You see this bridge he have 'butments, he don' have middle pier. Log he catch on 'butment, suppose we don't pick um off he wing out an' make jam. He give me axe an' peavey, an' coil of riggin', and he points and speak so:

'You'll get good board at that house, you stay here till we come back.'

"Soon, Old Isaac, he's gone, we took it two long logs; we snipe it one end" — illustrating by the pantomime of sharpening his finger-tip — "then we rung it other end, so" — that is, cut a ring around it.

"Then we tied it one end on each side of stream to a stump above the bridge and let it laid out slantin' against 'butment like shear-boom. Then when log struck, she sheer off and gone through bridge hisself. Well, we stuck um up peavey in log. We smoke; we whittle — have berry good time; we go to the boarding house, had nothin't' do. Sometimes we wet it peavey so he don't slip off lings" — that is, rings.[160]

"When we been there 'bout two weeks, Sat'day night come along Old Isaac. He spoke so:

'Sebahttis, you had hard work?'

"We tell um:

'Yes, we had very hard work; had wet it that peavey good many times keep it on lings.'

"Old Isaac says,

'You want to go down home?'

"We tell um,

'Sartin.' (Certain)

"Old Isaac, he says,

'Well, say so then, You get in wagon.'

"Well, we got it in wagon. We start down the river — river an' road he run same way. Old Isaac took out her pipe; then she

---

[160] To wet the wooden handle of the peavey to keep the wood swelled under the metal.

took it out tobacco, an' fill it his pipe; then she stuck it up his feet on fender; then she begun smoke an' sung um *Joyfully*"

Sebattis never said anything more about this song, but it probably was: —

>Joyfully, joyfully, onward we move,
>Bound to the land of bright spirits above.

"We speak so:

>'What for make it you sing um 'Joyfully,' Isaac?'

"He says so:

>'Don't you heard about it? I'm Chreestyun man.' (*Christian man*)

"We ask:

>'Ah-h-h-h! How long first?'

One knowing Sebattis can well understand that his simple interrogation was as full of meaning as Lord Burleigh's nod.[161] It was a caustic comment on all his employer's past, and a pleasantly satiric doubt whether the future was to be any different. We observe how Old Isaac changes the subject; how Sebattis refuses to allow him to escape and still follows with his irony, a grave and delicate mockery in disavowal of his being taken in by such chaff.

"Then Isaac say:

>'Why you no smoke, S'bahtees?'

"We say:"

>'We Chreestyun man, we don't smoke; besides, he charge it dollar and half pound out wangan for tobacker,[162] we cahn't 't'ford it.'

---

[161] In Richard Sheridan's (1751-1816) play, "The Critic," the character, Lord Burleigh, enters during one scene, shakes his head and exits. This gave rise to the expression, "Burleigh's nod."

[162] FHE: "Wangan" (pronounced wong-un) here means the supplies furnished by Isaac and sold to his men at exorbitant

"Then she took it out big piece to-backer; she cut it in two, give me half; Isaac speak so:
'Never you want for tobacker, as long's you work me.'
"We say so:
'Tomorrow mornin' is Sunday, Isaac'
"Isaac answered:
'Yes!'
"We say:
'You goin' drivin' to-morrow?'
"He responded:
'Sartin!'
"Says we:
'Ugh-h-huh!'
Sebattis could put a great deal of expression into a grunt.
"Isaac, she asked:
'Why you ask we goin' drivin' tomorrow?'
'Only we want know.'
Sebattis knew when to be indifferent.
"Asked Isaac:
'You think he ain't right drivin' Sunday?'
'Sartin! Right – <u>me</u> drive um Sunday; we don't sing it Joyfully.'
"Then she keep smoke, smoke Old Isaac. Then bime-by she speak so:
'You think ain't right drivin Sunday?'
'Sartin; right <u>me</u> drivin' Sunday; we don't sung um 'Joyfully.' S'pose we Chreestyun man, we sung it 'Joyfully,' we don' drivin' Sunday.'[163]

---

profits. In most places it is about equivalent to "outfit," and includes the commissary and cooking equipment.

[163] Here Sebattis is making his point, that since he is not Christian, he could drive logs on a Sunday, but he wouldn't be singing,

"Then great while she smoke, Ol' Isaac, she does. Bime-by she spoke so:

'S'bahtees, you ride horse?'

"We speak so:

'Sartin!'

"Says Isaac:

'Tomorrow mornin' he's Sunday.'

"We speak so:

'Yes!'

'Now tomorrow mornin', S'bahtees, very early we want you take it this horse an' go up river. S'pose you find any crews on logs, you tell um stop. When you got up dam, s'pose he been hoist,[164] you tell um, 'Shut down;' s'pose he don't been hoist, you tell um not hoist.'

"Next mornin' berry early, we took it horse, we gone up river, — river an' road he run same way, road close 'longside, of river. Fog on river so you can't see.

"Bime-by we hear it peavey sclatch on ledge; we know crew was pickin' on middle-jam. We left it horse, we gone down river, says, '*Hullo, boys*!'

"Speaks so,

'What you want?'

"We say,

'Come 'shore!'

"He want know what for.

"We tell um,

'Dem's orders, headquarters. Old Isaac she's Chreestyun man, sung it "Joyfully," — no more drivin' Sunday.'

---

especially such a song as *Joyfully*. If he was a Christian man, and he sang such a song, he wouldn't be driving logs on a Sunday.

[164] Meaning the men have the dam up and are releasing water for the log drive.

"Eb'ry crew we come to we told it dat same way. When we got to the dam she been hoist 'bout twenty minutes.

"We speak so,
> 'You shut down, boys; dem's orders, headquarters; Old Isaac she sung it "Joyfully;" no more drivin' Sunday.'

"Speaks so,
> 'We wish you brought it us dat same word ev'ry Sunday.'

"Two more years we work it Old Isaac, no more drivin' Sunday."

Joyfully

IF Eckstorm's hunch was correct, and the lyrics she added were from the song Sebattis heard Isaac sing, this would have been the song *Joyfully Onward*, by William Hunter. Hunter was born in Ireland (1811-1877) and arrived in America in 1817. In 1855 he was appointed Professor of Hebrew at Alleghany College and subsequently Minister of the Methodist Episcopal Church in Ohio. Some of his 125 hymns were translated into various Indian languages. A review of Eckstorm's original book introduction may remind the reader that the lyrics, singing of joyfully reaching heaven, could be the anthem of the Christian river-drivers depicted in this book who seemed to do their work on the river without fear.

Joyfully, joyfully, onward we move,
Bound to the land of bright spirits its above;
Jesus, our Saviour, in mercy says, Come,
Joyfully, joyfully haste to your home.
Soon will our pilgrimage end here below,
Soon to the presence of God we shall go,
Then, if to Jesus our hearts have been given,
Joyfully, joyfully, rest we in heaven.

Death with its arrows may soon lay us low,
Safe in our Saviour, we fear not the blow;
Jesus hath broken the bars of the tomb,
Joyfully, joyfully, we will go home.
Bright will the morn of eternity dawn.
Death shall be conquered, his scepter be gone;
Over the plains of sweet Canaan we'll roam,
Joyfully, joyfully, safely at home.

XXI — 'TIS TWENTY YEARS SINCE

IN 1904, when Eckstorm published this book, she was thirty-nine years old. Twenty years later, she purchased the plates, and issued a new edition with the following chapter. With the re-issue, she took the opportunity to respond to a few of her critics in a refreshing and somewhat humorous way. There have been more critics of her work following her passing, and while critical reviews of an author's work is not the core issue, for since books were first published there have been critics; however, a good number of her critics missed the point of these stories and thus their reviews were more of the comical kind, for those who were familiar with the subject matter. The most annoying critics, as Eckstorm so rightfully points out, were those who did not understand the subject, or reviewed her writing with a narrow and specific lens. She not only took on those poaching with a rifle, but also those who unfairly mischaracterized her with the pen, and she did it with style and wit. A current-day review of this book is certain to elicit some unfair reviews, for these stories are from another age; an age when times were different, and many modern-day critics will mistakenly review the words, or the morality of the men depicted, through their aberrated lens and not from a historical period perspective.

Thankfully, the book wasn't written to please critics. When this book was first published, Eckstorm knew the times had already changed for the riverman. She knew the large independent log drives of the Penobscot were coming to an end, and likewise the men who drove those logs would cease to exist. She knew her characterization of the lumbermen, river-drivers, and woodsmen, might be unfairly treated by some who thought the depictions were crude. This did not concern her. It was not her purpose to please everyone reading at the time, or in the future. Her intent was to document what she knew, and what she had been told in stories as true to fact, so others could learn what these men were made of, and what they made of their job as river drivers. In further defense of a stereotype, she pointed out more than once in this book, and her other publications, how she found many woodsmen to be men of honor, courtesy, sentiment, and some even well-read when it came to literature. She also noted their dressing smartly when not working in the woods.

This book was the first of its kind and Eckstorm was a pioneer researcher who took the reader behind the scenes of a Maine log drive. She was the first to document the West Branch Drive, carrying her camera and glass plates tens of miles to bring the story to readers. If sleeping on the ground, and dealing with the Maine blackfly were not enough, she went to the woods even as Jack Russell had threatened her life. Yet, the unknowledgeable critics called the work fiction, their limited experiences not being able to see the craft of her story from the facts or the "hinting style" of Eckstorm's writing.

Ah, but Alas! There are elements of fiction in this book. In her essay, "Rescue," she plainly states where her addition of dialogue gave dimension to the men who were stranded on the jam. With her expert knowledge of the woods and the river, she brought us a thrilling story that likely isn't far off the mark of what a conversation may have been like between those men whose lives were at the mercy of the river.

In this added chapter, Eckstorm didn't 'explain' her writing, but rather she proved the shortcomings of the critics, who unfamiliar with the experiences of the river, had blundered their reviews by missing the meaning for the stories and the significance behind them. In the end, what did it matter what some book critic thought? She had received the recognition of the men who worked the river, who sang the ballads, and who risked their lives. And above all, she earned the endorsements from John Ross and David Libbey!

'TIS TWENTY YEARS SINCE
THE WRITER CHATS WITH THE READER
1924
FANNIE HARDY ECKSTORM

WHEN "The Penobscot Man" first appeared twenty years ago it met with a most indulgent reception from critics all over the country and locally with greeting more than kind. Through several years it has been out of print the call for it has been so strong that its author has been encouraged to buy the old plates and issue the new edition. There are some changes which she would gladly make – chiefly of "is" to "was" almost throughout; but electrotype plates are stubborn things, and faults of phrase and pointing, even of grammar here and there, must be left unaltered. Some of these corrigenda will be pardoned by the kindly reader who knows that, owing to exceptional conditions, the writer was correcting the proofs of the first stories before the last were written.

At the time of publication, Mr. Bliss Carman, then editor of *The Literary World*, wrote editorially: "It seems to us that 'The Penobscot Man' should in twenty-five years, be a valuable 'human document,' for despite the form and fiction, the life, the men, the deeds, ring true. To those who would know a strong and fine side of New England manhood, this book is to be heartily commended for present reading – and, what is more for preservation."

It is of the "human document" that this belated chapter would speak. Twenty years have so utterly changed the Maine woods and all that they sheltered, that it must be said explicitly that these tales are not fiction; that they are facts very carefully wrought out, without exaggeration, understated if anything, and accurate even in the details of no importance. Three times Joe Attien's batteau was painted over before a man could be found who said: "She was white inside and blue outside."[165] It is not of the least consequence that she was not red, brown, or gray; but to the men who saw that tragedy it would have been an unpardonable blunder to get her color wrong. Before writing the scene in "Rescue" of Spencer at the Fowler house, Frank Fowler was consulted as to his wife having offered food, and he wrote that he "rather thought the women *did* give him something to eat." What it was might be left to imagination, but not the act of hospitality. These were not just stories, not even just true stories, but what architects would call "a measured drawing," and authentic record of the act and spirit behind it.

It took some understanding of the situation to know what to include and what to leave out. A good story might be left out entirely rather than hurt someone's feelings, but it was not altered to save them. It would have pleased John Ross, I think, not to have had Sebattis Mitchell's comment at the end of the first tale included; but that was Sebattis's story and it was told as he saw it.

---

[165] In the chapter, *Death of Thoreau's Guide – Joe Attien*, Eckstorm noted Attien's batteau to be, 'blue without and painted white within.' The men who knew Attien, and his boat, would never forget the color and Eckstorm was sure to get her description correct through their critical eyes.

On the other hand, the story of Joe Attien's death was re-written and wholly recast to satisfy John Ross. He was the head of the drive and an eye-witness, and his testimony outweighed all the rest. Every man I had ever talked with blamed Prouty in no measured terms, and the story was written on that theme. But when Ross said: "I never blamed Prouty," although the tale had been bought and paid for by the *Atlantic Monthly* and was in their keeping, I called it back and re-wrote it. And yet, I understood that it was only officially, as head of the drive, that Ross said that. Technically, of course, Joe was responsible for what he did with his own boat; there he was not accountable to Ross. Morally every man I ever talked with blamed Prouty in outspoken terms; and no doubt privately Ross felt with them. But so magnificent was the morale of the old West Branch Drive that the head of it was honor-bound to stand by the men who had stood by him. And I confess to being enough a part of that old order of things to be willing to spoil my best story rather than fail of that standard. The reward was John Ross's praise when he handed back the manuscript after second reading of it, with the words: "That reads very good now. That is very inter-*est*-ing."

To show how close to facts this story lies, I will give the chief sources of information. I had it first from my father, who knew all the facts at the time and who never forgot anything; then from Jot Eldredge,[166] who was on the West Branch Drive that year; then from Lewis Ketchum, the best-known Indian guide in Maine, who had left the drive only two days before; from

---

[166] Jot Eldredge, guide, but also friend, often accompanied Manly Hardy on woods trips, not so much to be a guide, for Hardy needed none, but as a second hand. He was along with Manly Hardy, and Fannie, when they took their Machias Lakes trip. See, *Exploring The Maine Woods – The Hardy Family Expedition to the Machias Lakes*, Burnt Jacket Publishing, 2021.

Roderick Sutherland, head lumberman, who worked two years in Joe Attien's boat; from Daniel Golden, expert river-driver, who was there at the time; from Waldo Davis, veteran West Branch boatman; and last from John Ross himself. If all historical facts were as well authenticated, history would be an exact science.

One detail, which I got too late to use, is worth recording. It is how the river-drivers on the logs in Shad Pond, far below the accident, first learned of the disaster. It was a calm, hot morning, without a ripple on the pond; for the current from the Grand Pitch draws under the surface there to a great distance, at high water, and leaves no tailings.[167] To these men on the logs near the shore, suddenly, without warning, out of the smooth bosom of the lake, shot up Joe Attien's long, blue-bladed stern paddle, handle first, with the eagle carved upon it, lifting half its length from the lake. They knew the paddle, all of them, and great fear fell upon them.

In "Lugging Boat" I hinted at something in connection with Joe's death which I did not then wish to enlarge upon out of regard for the feelings of Steve Stanislaus. They were cousins, fast friends, physical counterparts of each other and they always handled boat together. Both were heavy men of great strength and in a boat they worked "just like one man." But when Sebattis Mitchell ran Sowadnehunk and the others failed to do it, Steve, who was bowman, criticized the way Joe handled stern on a boil – (John Ross told me this) – and the rupture did not

---

[167] From Eckstorm's journal, we know that Jot Eldredge was on the West Branch Drive the year Attien died. However, he was at the head of the drive and heard of Attien's death from the men arriving in Bangor. He told Eckstorm he believed there to be 200 feet of fall between Quakish and Shad Pond, a number that is not that far off the mark.

heal. At the Lower Lakes,[168] Steve left the drive and Joe took on Prouty, "a little, rattle-brained fellow, with no more strength than a musquash," as Lewey Ketchum told me. It was partly because Joe was unconsciously relying upon his cousin's strength and weight at the bow that the batteau did not swing to the current as it ought to have done.

Since this chapter is reminiscent, it may be owned that "A Clump of Posies" was a personal experience, which explains why "I never met the lady face to face." Pete Ronco said once of one of his bear stories: "You see, Manly, we got two t'ree way we told it dat story. Dis way she's troof. Some ways she's more wusser dan dis way."[169] This also might have been "more wusser" and still have been the truth; for in the encounter with Jack Russell there was some rather plain speaking, though his respect for the West Branch Drive kept him civil. The dedication of the book acknowledges the friendly interference of the Drive in an otherwise personal matter.[170]

The story of "Rescue" is the only one so far as I know, which ever called out any correction. Had I dreamed that my old friend David Libbey knew the facts he would have been consulted before it was written. In the *Bangor Daily Commercial* for June 14, 1904, under his pen name of "Penobscot," he adds a section which is necessary for the full comprehension of the situation and which must be made a part of the record.[171]

---

[168] The lower lakes here are meant to mean in the area of Ambajejus and North Twin Lakes.
[169] There are two or three ways to tell a story. Some ways are better than others.
[170] The words of the dedication are yet another hint that more was said, even if the interaction was classified as civil. (See Appendix)
[171] Earlier, Eckstorm noted that Frank Fowler was consulted to see if his wife had offered any food to Spencer. The reader will recall from the "Rescue" story that Frank was not at the house at the time,

"In reading Mrs. Eckstorm's intensely interesting book, "The Penobscot Man," I find a few points in the story of the "Rescue," which are lacking and which explain why Spencer was not considered a hero; but instead was blamed for disobedience of orders.

"When Scott (the foreman) turned out of Quakish, he found that he had no boatmen who he considered qualified to handle a boat in such water as in found in Rhine's Pitch to Shad Pond. Therefore when starting for the Fowler place, he said to his crew: 'Boys, don't lift a cant-dog till I get back.' This was no perfunctory order, but being a skillful boatman himself he well knew the danger of attempting to drive in such water without their presence.[172] Of course when he gave the order he expected to get back that day; but the force of it was in nowise weakened when he failed to do so. However, the men became restless the next day and decided to pick off a big wing jam, just below Rhine's Pitch. That it was a wing is proved by the fact that the boat was on the shore. If it had been a middle jam, it is self-evident that the boat must have been used to get the men on to it, and if so how came it ashore? For it is inconceivable that men could be so idiotic as to take a boat ashore and leave four

---

it was his brother John who led the rescue. Here, David Libbey is about to explain that John Fowler, did not take Spencer with him in the boat for the rescue. The only explanation here is that Eckstorm had not shared the full story with Frank Fowler, or had not asked him other questions beyond food, otherwise the reader must believe that Frank Fowler would have told Eckstorm the same information that David Libbey here writes. Unless, Frank never made much of his brother's handling the boat alone to save the men from the jam. The Fowler men were rivermen and did what they had to.

[172] Meaning, a crew of skilled boatman.

men working on a middle jam at the head of three miles of the worst water on the West Branch.

"So these men hauled their boat up on the shore and began picking off the wing.[173] While thus engaged, it suddenly hauled from the inside. Spencer, Moores and Spaulding, the three most experienced, instantly started for the shore; while the other four huddled around the rock, a piece of folly no good driver would be guilty of, as the chances were the balance of the jam would swing out and carry them to destruction. However, enough of the jam clung to the rock to afford them a resting-place, and then followed the attempt to take them off, which Mrs. Eckstorm so graphically describes; but Scott declared that John Fowler took them off alone.[174]

"When Spencer wanted to go with him he answered, 'No, it is better for me to go alone than to have a man

---

[173] A wing jam is a jam of logs that extends from the shore, typically to a rock. Whereas a middle jam is one, as the name implies, hung on rocks in the middle of the river with no option to run to shore.

[174] The story, "Rescue," by Eckstorm's own admission had color added, around how the men stranded on the rock passed their time in conversation. As to the earlier critique of the book being one of fiction, this story certainly has the most fictionalized elements in the book. Even with this new information from Libbey that Fowler went alone (as told by Scott, the foreman), the story is not far from the mark. Here, we declare Fowler an even bigger hero than if he had help; for if he went out in such a large boat alone, at night, and saved the men from the torrent of the river where a jam was about to break, he certainly was a Penobscot Man. It should be noted that the Fowlers of this area were already famous river-men by this date. They had been operating in the region before Thoreau visited and wrote of them. Spencer was still a hero, for without his determination to get help, the men may not have made it off that jam.

with me who does not know exactly what to do.' This was the simple truth. In all my experience river-driving I never heard a single word passed between boatmen in times of dire extremity and danger. Each man must know just what to do and do it instantly. There is no time for instructions or conversation.

"The old Penobscot river-drivers, to whom this book most strongly appeals, do not as a class haunt bookstalls; but it is to be hoped that it will be read by every one of them.[175] To the writer, who knew personally almost every character mentioned in it, it possesses a greater interest than any book he ever read."[176]

David Libbey worked twenty-five seasons as a river-driver and seventeen of them he handled boat as a master boatman. If he and John Ross and others like them found the volume "interesting," what did it matter what the ordinary book reviewer thought if it? The very technicalities which were a bane to the reviewer, they demanded. Many of the critics did understand and responded with unexpected sympathy; others were kindly but a little beyond their depth in this sort of "fiction." They pointed out the faults of "wordiness," "formlessness," "lack of story interest," "too slender incident," "too much sentimentality," and suggested what an improvement a certain amount of "love interest" would have been.

---

[175] David Libbey may have been an extreme outlier in the river-driver class. He was self-educated in many trades and had a large library of his own. Eckstorm paid tribute to his legacy in a separate book where she published his journal notes with permission from his family.

[176] Considering the facts that Libbey was extremely well-read in all matter of classics, a fact to which Eckstorm was well-aware, this must have been a wonderful compliment to her.

A few of these, even at this late date, may be amusing. One Chicago journal called it, "A rattling story of the open air and muscular red-shirted activities by perhaps the only woman in the world qualified to write from experience of the rough life of the logging jam . . . One infers that she has roughed it through bitter struggles with wind and flood, worked on heavy carries in the turbulent log-jam, and knows the pinch of hunger which half rations implies."

What an idea of river-driving the writer must have had when he thought that "carries" were laid out over log-jams in motion!

Another wrote, "The author also tells the original story of 'The Gray Rock of Abol' and the man who died there, suddenly, by the hand of God, for blasphemy. Poe based one of his tales upon this incident."

Page Mr. Poe! He died in 1849, eight years before Goodwin was drowned at the Gray Rock.[177]

This from the *Milwaukee Free Press* taxes our credulity. "It is in the shadow of Katahdin, below the Gray Rock of Abol, that all this lumber-driving takes place, where the giant pines of the Maine forest are guided, dismembered, down the Connecticut to the sea."[178]

The innate philistinism of the city-bred man comes out in his cock-sureness upon what is outside his own experience. A Boston paper remarked, "It is doubtful if any of these woodsmen or any of their descendants ever go out of sight of the Penobscot, excepting perhaps to go back to the Provinces whence many of them came."

---

[177] Notes were added to the chapter about how Eckstorm made selective use of Poe's poem.

[178] The editor thinks the words of all reviewers should come under such a lens! For this reviewer's comment, no further explanation is necessary for the knowledgeable reader.

Then there rose in memory those nights in camp at Ripogenus. Good was the talk, varied, humorous, wide in its range, and to it Webster contributed not only the comments of an expert woodsman and hunter, but the experiences of a sailor, cowboy, cotton stevedore and alligator hunter.[179] There was another guide of ours who went to Arizona and turned cowboy for a time and, coming back, hung up his spurs and quirt and went into the woods again. I remembered others who had hunted in Pennsylvania and the Ozark Mountains, who knew Michigan and Minnesota and had lived within the Arctic Circle. And there was David Libbey, thoroughbred woodsman and waterman, one of the most notable of our hunters, who, going to San Francisco, took a place in a stationer's store and handled paper by the quire and arranged perfumery on the closet shelves; and from there to the deserts of Nevada, in the seventies, when it was rough there, where he set up mining machinery and met western bad men, and he unarmed and unruffled made them behave themselves.

"It is doubtful also," went on the Boston paper quoted, "if the citizens of Bangor, where the Penobscot man spends his holidays and money, would give him as good a recommendation as the author."

Just here the Lord delivered this Philistine into my hands! If anyone knew what the river-driver did with his time and money when in Bangor, it was those of us who lived in Brewer, where I was born and brought up. No one from Brewer, in those days before electric cars,[180] went to any part of Bangor without going through either the Exchange Street tenderloin or the Devil's Half Acre. We had to see all the worst of it. As a school-girl, going every day through one or the other of these water-front districts, I had to pass through the midst of the crowds of

---

[179] Wilbur Webster, the guide in "Clump of Posies."
[180] The trolleys had a different route than the walking route.

woodsmen who at certain seasons thronged those parts. Sometimes the riverman was lively. Among the news items of June 5, 1903, in the Bangor papers, is the story of the police getting four calls in such quick succession from Hancock Street that the patrol went on the gallop, picking up an officer at every corner, others following in private teams. And the riot turned out to be only one young river-driver enjoying himself. It is illuminative to learn that this one was let off with a suspended sentence "on account of his previous good record." We who lived in Brewer saw all these things, but were not disturbed by them. If there was a fracas on the sidewalk we merely stepped into the street and regarded it as not existing: it was nothing belonging to us. Never in my life did I experience any annoyance in passing through these woodsmen and never did I hear of any other woman being affronted by them. Yet they were somewhat daunting to look at – no two alike, no one like anything else in heavens above or the earth beneath (and therefore, as our local saying ran, "no sin to worship if you wanted to"). Such a medley crowd of gaunt, haggard, sun-baked, mosquito-bitten, bearded men, each one wearing heavy spike-soled driving boots and nearly every one with a meal-bag, rather shrunken, tied end and corner, and hung around his neck. Their clothing passed description. But they soon sloughed all this. Before me is a picture of a group of our best Indian river-drivers, taken about the close of the Civil War.

There is Attean Soc, the wag of the tribe, and Sebattis Solomon ("Black Sebat"), with his dark, eager face, Lewis Ketchum, a well-bred gentleman, and John Stanley, serious but alert – a group of able-looking young men. And the clothing of two of them appears to be broadcloth; one waistcoat is certainly black satin, and another a bright-striped velvet, while three of the four wear gold watch-chains. One must not generalize too much upon either the clothes of the behavior of these woodsmen being uniformly bad.

FOUR *TERRIBLY ABLE* RIVER-DRIVERS
Modern day publishing allows us to insert the very picture Eckstorm was describing within this edition.
Standing: Sebattis Solomon ("Black Sebat"), and Lewis Ketchum
Sitting: Attean Soc and John Stanley
Photo taken around the close of the Civil War, c. 1865.
These men, all Penobscot Indians, worked for Manly Hardy around the close of the Civil War. Lewis Ketchum, was also a guide for Hardy, but Manly refers to him in his journal notes as a friend, for the two spent a good deal of time together hunting and trapping in the woods.

Photo from the Hardy Collection files
Image courtesy of Special Collections, Raymond H. Fogler Library, University of Maine.

"One cannot help thinking that he is pictured in these stories as just a little but too much of a hero," says the Boston reviewer.

Well, he isn't made out to be a saint! But the lengths to which these men would go out of pure daring are incredible. Take it all in all, a story of their deeds would be a book of golden follies. The stranger, coming once and looking at us, says: "This is superb darling." He cannot know, as we do, that, every year for a hundred years, something quite as good has been done not once but many times, it is likely, every year. One man is in danger – a dozen volunteer to save him. A dozen? Two score; twice that. I know where two men got adrift on some logs. Only one boat's crew could help them, but six boats' crews jumped in, thirty-six men in all, and risked their lives to save two. Again and again I have heard of one man daring another to sure death, believing the dare would not be taken, and every time it *was* taken; usually, too, both came out all right, by pure miracle. I have known men to be so greedy of supremacy that they were a menace to all around them, and I have been told of a case where a boss had to discharge a good man, whom he needed, to save the man's life, or he would have been drowned by another who could brook no rival.[181] Life had no meaning to some of these men apart from the name and the frame of being "crack watermen."

Yet so far as I can observe river-driving did not breed a type. The hunter was a type – you could tell him at a glance; the lumberman was a type – he was easy to distinguish; but I cannot recall that, after he had shed his particular clothes, the river-driver was a marked man. It was the life they lived the rest of the year, rather than the few weeks on the drive, that classed them as types. With most of them river-driving was a

---

[181] This reference is to the description David Cremins relayed to L. I. Flower about Charles 'Dingbat' Prouty. See earlier chapter – *Death of Thoreau's Guide – Joe Attien.*

metamorphosis rather than a profession. The more reckless either died young or reformed, the more intelligent and ambitious worked into other occupations and became head boatmen, head lumbermen, mill-owners, or land-owners. I have known a few to enter the learned professions and come out doctors and lawyers. As a trade, river-driving is not without a parallel. After a long trip through the southwest forty years ago, my father came back and delivered an ultimatum. "Come to think it out," said he, "a cowboy is only a river-driver on a horseback." Anyone who understands the old cowboy can understand the river-driver as he used to be. A log – the old, big log – was as much a brute beast as any steer, and acted like one.[182] It could do anything a steer could do, and much worse when it piled up in those huge jams that had to be cleared out at no matter what risk. The similar work bred men of like type, who worked hard and played hard, but not always judiciously, and then went back to work again.

But there was always play mingled with their work. I remember years ago of sitting on the high river-bank near home, watching the men rafting logs on the Bangor side. One day as they worked, they amused themselves by jumping into the water, clothed and booted, leaping sometimes forwards, sometimes backward, and coming out dripping and laughing. Another day they were doing tricks with their pick-poles, balancing and twirling poles on one hand or upon the chin, sometimes with a cap revolving upon the top of the pole, they all the time having to keep their balance upon the loose, floating logs. Sometimes a trick would call forth a round of applause.

---

[182] A reference to when massive trees were floated down the Penobscot, as opposed to the more recent (as in 1924) when four-foot pulp-wood logs had already appeared, destined for the paper mills. The shorter logs were in no comparison to the logs on the drives of yesteryear.

The woman with me was used to the life of large factory towns. Suddenly she exclaimed, "But they have no boss over them! They are working just by themselves." Head-men there had to be to take responsibility; but there was no time-clock but the sun, and he was not of much use, for they were at work long before he rose and long after he was in bed.

They had a pride in their work too. Would any cattle-man have his cattle-brand put on his tombstone as a matter of pride? But a head lumberman would do it. Not long ago I was standing with Mr. Tefft before his working model of the great Peirce Memorial Fountain, soon to be erected in Bangor as the gift to his hometown of Colonel Luther Peirce, of Chicago.[183] Three river-drivers breaking a jam is the sculptor's subject and we were discussing the technical details of this work.

"Why have you scratched that mark on the end of the log they are cutting?" I asked the sculptor.

"A decorative touch; to relieve the bare surface," he replied.

I said, "That is the right place for a log-mark. Why not use the real one, one that means something to people here?"

He assented, the Committee on the Memorial approved, and then one of them, a kinswoman of the donor, made a suggestion so fit that only the native will appreciate its aptness.

"Colonel Peirce was a lumberman; why not put his own log-mark there?" said she.

And the one man among us who knows everything that used to be, standing in front of the model, told the story of a mill-owner and lumberman who is buried at Mount Hope. He lies between his two wives, a triple arch over the three, and upon the central arch, his own, are carved the letters V Y V. Not an emblem of the faith, not the formula of a classic phrase, but just

---

[183] Luther H. Peirce was a lumber baron and his descendants donated money to have the memorial made. The actual statue, was completed by sculptor Charles Tefft in 1925.

Joab Palmer's log-mark! I am told, though I have not seen it, that the inventor of the "peavey," who lies in the same place of rest, had a peavey cant-dog carved on his tombstone. These men were proud of their trades. They felt that they were artists and creators, working at something that was inspiring.

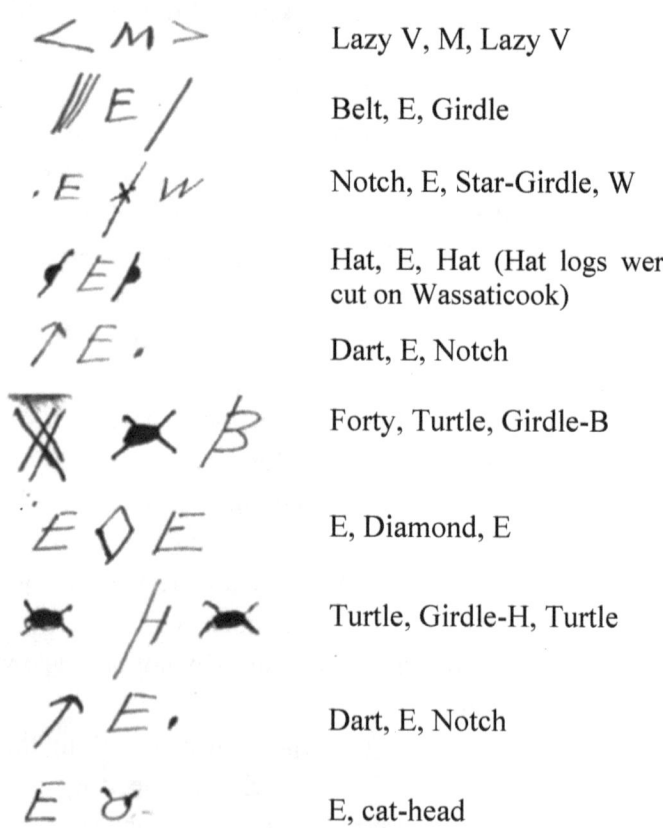

Lazy V, M, Lazy V	
Belt, E, Girdle	
Notch, E, Star-Girdle, W	
Hat, E, Hat (Hat logs were cut on Wassaticook)	
Dart, E, Notch	
Forty, Turtle, Girdle-B	
E, Diamond, E	
Turtle, Girdle-H, Turtle	
Dart, E, Notch	
E, cat-head	

LOG MARKS

A sample of Log Marks from Eckstorm's journal. "1927, Sept. 30. Conversation with Mr. Charles H. Adams, for twenty-five years clerk of the Penobscot Log-Driving Association. From his books I copied the following log marks, with his rendering."

Too late sometimes we realize that we have been moving among great events; when we are out of the woods we find that we did not see the forest because the trees were in the way. The era just past was a period which bred men who were great in their grip upon realities, who wrestled with unwilling circumstances until they compelled it to do their work for them. Hardly a greater story is there on record than this of a few common men, isolated in their location, many of them with neither capital nor education, taking hold of an engineer's problem of subduing a most unmanageable river and finally biting and bridling it and training it to be *their* River, that brought their logs to market at their bidding. Few but the remnant who remain of those who did this, know how tremendous was the task of organizing and equipping the army that every year invaded the woods and brought the lumber down to the shrieking mills below. The happiness of this Penobscot region in those days was that it was doing creative work, realizing an idea born in its own brain, wrought out by its own hands. It was Bangor and the sister towns of Orono, Veazie, Bradley and Oldtown – (Brewer having its own problem of building the lumber into ships) – that brought river-driving to the highest perfection it ever reached, that worked out all the details of its complicated technique, invented the peavey, perfected the axe, developed the batteau, and bred and trained the men who could handle them. Then it produced the one sculptor in all the world who, understanding these things by intuition, could rightly interpret them. And finally, not too late, Bangor gave to him an opportunity, uniquely inspiring, by which he could declare the achievement through art, realistic to the least detail, yet classic in the rhythm of its symbolism and spiritual in its interpretation. In Bangor, mother of men, the Peirce Memorial Fountain of the River-Drivers soon will tell in living bronze the great story of the plain men who were bred upon the banks of the Penobscot, to whose memory this little book was dedicated twenty years ago like a withering flower.

THE PEIRCE MEMORIAL

Located outside Bangor Public Library.
The inscription reads:
PRESENTED TO THE CITY OF BANGOR BY LUTHER H PEIRCE – ERECTED 1925
(Editor's Collection)

APPENDIX — THE PENOBSCOT RIVER

The four branches of the Penobscot River cut the state West to East and North to South. It was this river that helped build Maine and in some ways the shipping industry and even a nation. This was the river that made, *The Penobscot Man.*

The North Branch begins in Township T6 R17 WELS, roughly near what is known as "The Big Bog" and close to Fifth St. John Pond. This branch flows south for roughly twenty miles to Seboomook Lake where it meets the South Branch.

The South Branch begins at the Canadian border in Sandy Bay Township, with additional feeds from Penobscot Lake. This Branch flows about twenty to thirty miles, through numerous bends, to Canada Falls Lake. From there it enters Seboomook Lake where it joins the North Branch.

After the Seboomook Dam, these two branches of the River become the West Branch. The West Branch flows past the Northeast Carry Road where many explorers and lumbermen carried their gear to reach the river; then it passes Lobster Stream which sometimes flows into the river, and sometimes the river flows into it. From there it enters Chesuncook Lake and onto Ripogenus Lake. At Ripogenus Dam the river takes on its most wild character with rapids, falls, canyons, and a bottom full of boulders and in places rattled with Katahdin granite. This branch also runs through various deadwaters and empties into Ambajejus Lake, North Twin Lake, and then Quakish Lake. Following Shad Pond and Dolby Pond (near Millinocket) the West Branch meets the East Branch at Medway and becomes the Penobscot. The reader unfamiliar with the river can find videos online of the Class IV and Class V rapids in the vicinity of the Ripogenus Gorge, the Crib Works, and the churn of the Nesowadnehunk Falls. A favorite bird's-eye video was published by North Country Rivers, titled, *Aerial Tour of Maine's Penobscot River*, September 26, 2010 (available as of 2021). The segment covering the rapids following the Ripogenus dam begins about three minutes into that video. It may not be apparent, but much of the flow of the river through the Ripogenus dam is passed through underground tunnels until the power station. So as impressive as the flow is, it is meager to what full power lies behind the dam.

Over its course, the West Branch may be said to have flowed for one-hundred and fifteen miles, a very inaccurate measurement considering its winding path and the various lakes the river flows through.

The roughly seventy-five mile long East Branch can be said to begin in Township T7 R11 WELS, at East Branch Pond, which is north of the South Arm of Chamberlain Lake. This branch meets Webster Brook and then flows through Grand Lake Matagamon. From there it races through some of the most picturesque river scenes in Maine, such as Stair Falls, Haskell Rock Pitch, Grand Pitch, and Spencer Rips, with the Traveler Mountains in view to the West. At Medway this branch joins the West Branch.

The Penobscot continues southward 109 miles from Medway to the Atlantic. Along the way it winds past Mattawamkeag, Lincoln, Passadumkeag, Old Town, Orono, Bangor & Brewer, Winterport, Bucksport, and Castine; finally ending in Penobscot Bay.

Combining the four branches, the Penobscot River runs a total of about 270 miles. This length makes the river the longest entirely within the borders of Maine. The stories of this book might be mainly about the men who worked the West Branch Drive, but certainly, there were Penobscot Men on the other branches, and its many tributaries. No matter what branch they *drove logs* on, or *handled boat* on, they all were *The Penobscot Man*.

APPENDIX — A CLUMP OF POSIES

THE GIRL, THE GUIDE, AND THE POACHER

THE personal narrative of "Clump of Posies," along with the hint of danger Fannie Hardy (yet to be Eckstorm) and her father faced during the Ripogenus trip, made for a captivating essay. There clues in the essay about the threat from Jack Russell led to further research on the segment of the trip following their separation from the men of the West Branch Drive. For all the descriptive writing Eckstorm provided, something was left untold in the book about what occurred between the Hardys, Wilbur Webster, and Jack Russell.

It should be noted that the Ripogenus trip took place eight months after the Hardy family expedition along the Passadumkeag to the Machias Lakes. In the same series of Forest and Stream articles, Fannie Hardy called out the Downeast poacher Jock Darling, for his illegal hunting of deer with dogs. The account of that trip with information on Darling is covered in, *Exploring the Maine Woods – The Hardy Family Expedition to the Machias Lakes*. Although, Eckstorm wasn't shy about calling out poachers and those who hunted illegally, for this book her purpose was to observe the West Branch Drive, and not to find evidence of poaching or to confront known lawbreakers. However, the interaction with the renegade Russell is now explained with additional details. The information for the following account is based on two, never before published, sections of Eckstorm's journal, to which commentary has been added by the editor.

While Eckstorm did not elaborate on the Jack Russell situation in the chapter, a hint of the seriousness of the threat was discovered in the obituary notice Fannie Hardy wrote for Wilbur Webster. In her written eulogy of Webster (included in the main chapter of this edition), there is a clue, somewhat buried, about their return trip to Greenville. After the men continued down the Penobscot with the logs, Webster guided the Hardys on an excursion looking for sheldrake nests. Manly Hardy as a bird collector, and his daughter, a naturalist who was considered an ornithologist later in her life, were both always engaged in studying bird behavior. It would not have been out of character for them to want to observe the nests, however, sheldrake are common mergansers that frequent both the coast and inland lakes of Maine at various times of the year. Certainly, the two of them had seen plenty of these species, and going far out of their way to see nests, even if not in a nesting location typical to their experience, seems to be suspect.

The reason for the side-excursion was given in the Webster obituary, where Eckstorm wrote, "I remember one day a question came up about the nesting place of sheldrakes. Father and I said, "in old stubs;" Webster said, "on the ground." We knew that we were right, and did not doubt that he was also, but still he was anxious to have us see for ourselves. If we went back by way of Caribou Lake and the Grant Farm, said he, not once nor twice, but many times, he would agree to show us all the sheldrakes' nests we wanted to see, and all on the ground. And so he did. We scudded about in Caribou Lake, making from one rocky islet to another between the flaws — until we saw under the little spruce bushes, as he had said, the big nest full of eggs wreathed with down and feathers."

It would appear, from this note, that Webster lobbied for taking this revised route, which would require the three of them to walk many miles, instead of a return over water. It is likely he had specific reasons for doing so; reasons beyond seeing a bird's nest.

Even though the chapter concluded with a poke at Jack Russell, Eckstorm's journal notes described the days after the two-hundred, or so, lumbermen and river-drivers had moved on to drive the logs downstream. There was no longer the 'safety in numbers' she had written about in the story, and if the Drive's message to Russell had been a deterrent while the Hardys were in their company, now, a choice in direction had to be made to put as much distance between themselves and Russell as possible.

In the journal, the story continues and began with: "That Sunday night, the eighth of June, 1891, we encamped alone on Ripogenus Carry. The night before two-hundred men had been there or near at hand. But the last of the logs had been sluiced, the boats had been dragged across, the wangan, that is the commissary of the Drive, had been wearily transported on men's shoulders three miles to the Big Eddy at the end of the carry, and the whole Drive was well on its way down the Penobscot. In six weeks more, with good luck, the logs would arrive at the boom. And we, not wishing to follow a river packed for miles and miles with logs, must go back up stream, some eighty miles if we went as we came, by water all the way, or about fifty if we left our canoe at Caribou Lake and travelled out through the woods."

The first mentioned choice of direction home would have required a month of camping all the way to at least the train station at Mattawamkeag; a journey they were logistically unprepared for. To avoid this, they could have returned the way they came, which was their original plan, but that route would have taken them straight through Russell's hunting grounds and back to Chesuncook where he had made the initial threat. This left a third, and final, option; a route that while shorter in direct miles, was all the more difficult by the terrain.

If they only desired to see the promised bird's nests on Caribou Lake, a side-trip paddle would not have been far out of the way, and it would have been easy to return to Chesuncook in order to continue back to Northeast Carry. But this is not what they did. The direction they chose to go, and the editor's knowledge of what such a walking route would entail in the year 1891 (and near the same even currently), led to further research and discovery about possible fears the retribution from Jack Russell would bring.

Eckstorm's notes on distances were yet another clue the land route was not of the original plan, and are modest in the estimation. The "eighty" by way of Northeast Carry included the forty miles of steamer travel over Moosehead Lake, for which the traveler would do nothing but watch the scenery or take a nap. By the land route, catching a steamer from Lily Bay merely eliminated ten miles from the fifty of the woods walking trail. This direction resulted in a significant number of miles on foot, rather than paddling a canoe and resting on a steamer.

The direction of their travel to and from the Ripogenus Dam are shown on the map. On the way to the Dam, the Hardys took a steamer from Greenville to Northeast Carry where they met their guide Wilbur Webster. From there, they went by canoe, paddling down the Penobscot, to Chesuncook Lake and Ripogenus Lake in order to reach the Drive camp near Ripogenus Dam. For their return, they went by way of Chesuncook, to Caribou Lake, then to Grant Farm, Kokadjo, and finally Lily Bay. This route required the carrying of gear over land, which is an anomaly for travel in those years when water routes were available. Note that this map predates the modern dams, and the thoroughfares between Ripogenus Lake, Caribou Lake, and Chesuncook are now wide expanses of water.

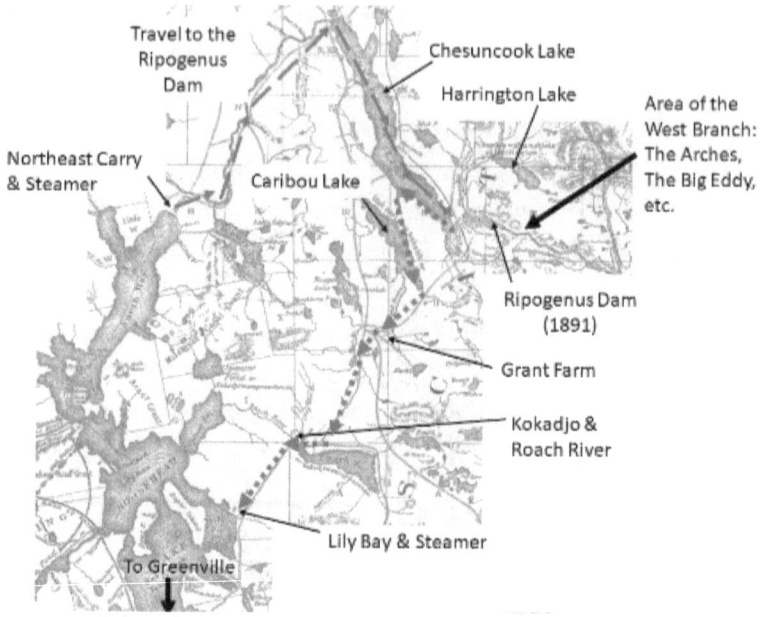

AREA FOR THE RIPOGENUS TRIP, 1891

Based on Hubbard's 1899 Map.

For reference of scale, Moosehead Lake (not shown in entirety in this image) is forty miles long from Greenville to Northeast Carry.

- - - - -

Before leaving the tent site, Eckstorm said goodbye to the hermit thrush who had nested along the carry. "I have wondered since if she did not miss her human associates and feel more fear of the prowling skunk and fox that came to sniff the relics of the drivers' camp, than she did of the scores of busy men who for weeks had been tramping back and forth."

Of the men she wrote, "Not one of them, rough men as they were, ever startled her purposely, that I know, though I sometimes saw them stand and gaze at her little tent."

On the morning they departed from the campground near the dam, Eckstorm made a point about how early they had risen, took down their tent, canoed across Ripogenus Lake before sunrise, and carried their gear a half a mile on Chesuncook carry. Walking along the carry she recalled, "We came upon some Chesuncook bear-hunters just eating breakfast, and these are men who are wont to be up betimes." In a different section of her journal titled, "Started for Grant Farm," she wrote, "Met Jack Russell and the two Smiths eating breakfast at the end of Chesuncook Carry." From these notes, we can deduce that the "bear-hunters" were the Smiths, and they were in the company of Jack Russell!

Eckstorm's word choice in using "wont to be up betimes," is specific and is an old phrase meaning these hunters were in the habit of being up before what might be considered a more usual morning hour. She writes this to further make her point on how early a start they had made, for to find *the hunters* had only recently risen and were having their breakfast is a testament to what her, her father, and Webster had accomplished already by that early hour of the morning. It seems, the Hardys and Webster had figured if they were up earlier than most, they'd be through the area before they might come across anyone. With the meeting of Russell on the carry road, when supposedly he was hunting near Harrington Lake, the alternate woods route Webster had negotiated was now compromised.

There are several pages in Eckstorm's journal where she details bird sightings on their way to Grant Farm. A selection of her observations are included here to illustrate that she was not dwelling on Jack Russell. It is as likely she was yet to know the extent of Russell's threat against herself and her father. Her notes indicate she was her typical observant, naturalist-self, as the three of them made their way through the woods. On the canoe paddle to Caribou Lake, she mentioned seeing a pileated woodpecker and wrote, "or as we call him here, the log-cock. I like the homely name. It confers a well-merited distinction, for he is a masterly fellow, easily cock of the woods or cock of the walk in his own line of work. As the guide puts it, 'an awfully able bird.' To *be able* is about the highest praise a guide can give; it implies skill, energy, strength, and initiative."

Eckstorm also documented the scenery. Her notes included her opinion, or statement of the facts, on the Maine lumber trade. While she had an appreciation for the lumbermen and the river-drivers for what they did, the impact on the land did not go unnoticed from her eyes. The water from the dam, held in reserve for the log drive, had backed up onto the shores and she observed, "This back-water had flowed and killed the trees along the lower levels of Caribou and they still stood, gaunt and bare, sufficient evidence that the white man had been there with his 'improvements.' This ghastly ruin of forest, killed by water is his mark. But it is not the lumberman who does it; he is but a man sent by the consumer. The building of your house made these lakes shores unsightly."

(Today Maine's sustainable forestry industry utilizes the renewable resource with better management of the forest for wildlife habitat and protection against forest fires. The forest shores around these lakes are now some of the most pristine in the country protected by required setbacks.)

Further commentary was written about a loon and a gull sighting. As they canoed the thoroughfare between the lakes, she wrote, "A head without a body, leaving neither wake nor ripple. There is always something a bit eerie about the sight of a head navigating without bodily assistance. Anyone who understands a loon will admit that it is a most un-bird-like creature and that it is just as spooky on a bright June morning as when backed by all the accessories of wind and darkness." She goes on, "We took the sight of the loon as a sign that the lake was near and soon it opened up, a fine expanse of water, perhaps seven miles long, with good shores and a few rocky islets."

She continues, "The last of my camera plates had been expended upon our friends the river-drivers and their works, but in memory I can recall the stately retreat of the great herring gull, the share-winged terns rising in clamorous alarm, the quick flight of the brooding sheldrake startled from her nest, the loud peet-weet of the frightened sandpiper, just skimming the water as she flew, and on all sides the nests. Along the rocky, mossy margins were seven tern's nests, each one built rather neatly of small twigs and each containing two or three eggs."

Of all the nests mentioned, one in particular was satisfying for them to discover as it was the one they had come in search of. "Of the red-breasted sheldrake we found three nests, all rather near together and one of them but eight feet from the herring gull. One contained three eggs, one seven, and one had no less than sixteen. A pretty nest it was, not neatly made but well located, half hid under the side of a low spruce bush, and rich in its abounding treasure of smooth green eggs, as large as hens' eggs and pearly smooth of surface, whereas the gulls and terns were rough. The eggs in this nest were partially covered with down, a sign that the complement was full and the bird was ready to brood. But though this was well into June, the eggs were not at all incubated. We knew – well, we ate of them. Three hungry people who have been up since summer dawn and still nearly forty miles from market shouldn't be choosers as to what they eat. If they can't get anything better than sheldrake eggs, they can support life on those. And there is a proverb against putting all ones' eggs in one nest which might be profitably studied by sheldrakes having sixteen to lay." In this statement is another clue that going in this direction was not in their original plan, as the three travelers did not have food supplies to sustain them on this longer route. Had they gone by way of Chesuncook, the farm and supply store there would have been a place to re-stock their food stores, or to have a meal. Being in the woods for extended periods of time, with little food other than what they could hunt, was nothing new to the father and daughter, but it was the only time they were being threatened by a notorious poacher and outlaw.

> **CHESUNCOOK FARM AND TAVERN.**
>
> Situated at the head of CHESUNCOOK LAKE, on its Western Shore. Magnificent Panorama of Mt. Katahdin and the Sourdnahunk Mountains.
>
> Meals and lodging furnished at all times on short notice. Fresh milk constantly on hand.
>
> Campers going down the *St. John*, or *Penobscot Rivers*, or up to *Caucomgomoc Lake*, supplied with Pork, Flour, and Potatoes.

1880s Advertisement for the Chesuncook Farm and Tavern, where meals and lodging were available.

The three moved to an adjacent island, and Eckstorm mentions seeing a blue-backed swallow and the nest of herring-gulls. There they built a fire and had fried eggs, cooked by the guide, "with a more liberal allowance of pork fat than seems hygienically required with the thermometer up in the eighties – and we sat in the sun, which ungallantly blistered our noses, and tried to call the breakfast a feast. 'One might fare worse,' was the general verdict."

Webster then entertained them with a story, that Eckstorm recorded as: "No doubt sheldrakes' eggs are delectable (and) we could appreciate the story the guide told us of old Con Doherny, a man of those woods, who ate seventeen sheldrakes' eggs at one meal – mind you, they are as large as a hens' eggs and more hearty – and then he remarked, 'Some folks call 'em good but I thought they always tasted kinda fishy.' The story may seem to some to have the same flavor, but the guide who told it was ever a most truthful man."

While on the island they have a visit from who she describes as, 'two Chesuncook bear-hunters.' At this, she gives her view on bear hunting. "Cruel as the trapping of bears in steel traps necessarily is, it is the only practicable means of keeping down their numbers. And our Maine bears do not "want to be good," they are very bad little bears and do a deal of mischief, and they are perfectly capable of taking care of their pretty black hides. It would be a great mistake, for any sentimental reason to prohibit the bear-hunters from following their trade."

When they reached Ragged Stream, they left the canoe, and started their first leg of the chosen land route towards Kokadjo. Walking, as they did in June of 1891, the fourteen or more miles from where they left Caribou Lake, lugging their gear along blackfly infested moose swamps, could not have been by clear choice for a pleasant hike through the woods. It should be noted that, Manly Hardy was familiar with this route. In the journal of his 1857 West Branch Trip made with Hiram Leonard, he included daily notes on his hunting in the opposite direction from Grant Farm to Caribou Stream.

The editor will also inform the reader that this was not Ms. Hardy's first canoe trip to a branch of the Penobscot River for a wood's excursion. In August of 1888, she traveled with her father, and guide George Leonard, via Northeast Carry for a trip down the East Branch of the Penobscot River. They traveled to this region again in August of 1889 with guide Reed McPheters, going from Northeast Carry and then down the West Branch, a trip in which they took time to climb Katahdin. From those excursions, Eckstorm noted of the caribou, "In 1888 we saw two (caribou) near Second Lake at head of East Branch, and in 1889 found two shed horns from different animals on the top of Katahdin. About 1896 the last were disappearing and none seen since."

There is an additional clue in Eckstorm's writing that the woods walk they were taking was not a pleasurable experience, especially carrying all their gear. It was not her style to complain of anything about the woods, for even when she poked fun about the miseries of Fourth Lake, or being wind-bound on the shore of Chamberlain Lake, she saw the beauty and bounty of the woods. Furthermore, in her essay, *Winter Fishing*, she told how, with her father, she walked over ten miles on a brutally cold winter morning to a lake which they were to ice fish. Once at the lake, their fire did little to keep them warm, the fishing holes were freezing over quicker than they could clear them, and they caught no fish to mention. Yet, she wrote of a wonderful day in the Maine woods for the chickadees came to share their lunch and left her with a vibrant memory.[184] This woods walk to Kokadjo seems to be the only writing the editor has discovered with what might be considered a complaint by Eckstorm. She wrote, "I believe the distance to Roach River (from Caribou Lake) is called about fourteen miles. And a miser in miles must have measured them, for the measure has been stretched more than ordinary. Whoever hopes a Maine woods mile of the old

---

[184] In, *Exploring the Maine Woods – The Hardy Family Expedition to the Machias Lakes*, and, *Katahdin, Pamola & Whiskey Jack – Stories and Legends from The Maine Woods*.

tenor will not hold to one and a half or even two, or in exceptional instances rising three of the standard mile, has 'never entered here.' Those who have, abandoned all such vain hopes long since. It used to be said that the way some of these miles were measured was to start a fast hound running in the gray of dawn and to let him go till he dropped of hunger and fatigue, when they calculated that he had run 'pretty near a mile.'" She wrote that, all in all they walked four hours to reach Grant Farm, which was somewhat south east of the lower end of Ragged Lake; and then six hours more the next morning to reach Roach River, "at a three-mile gait or better, with less than an hour stop in all."

Maybe the anticipation of a warm meal and a night's rest in a bed at Grant Farm, a resting stop along the way, was enticing enough to make the extra effort of walking worth it. The reader may be the judge based on Eckstorm's description:

"I carried eight boxes of camera plates, not wishing to trust them to even the most cautious guide, and this may explain my lack of zeal about not adding a heavy field-glass in a sole-leather case to the outfit. *(An earlier journal entry explained the weight being the reason she was without such a glass to use for bird observation.)* That night we had planned to stay at the Grant Farm, a lumberman's supply farm, part way through on the road to Roach River. The old house was on the eve of being torn down, and it was no part of its charter to board ladies; but the keeper did all the hospitality he could do. He gave up his own room and assigned my father and myself not only to the same room, but to the same bed. This somewhat extraordinary politeness was fully explained by the condition of the house which, outside that room, was overrun with individuals much smaller than Macbeth, but equally able to "murder sleep."[185]

---

[185] In Macbeth, Act II, Scene II, Macbeth says, "Methought I heard a voice cry, 'Sleep no more! Macbeth does murder sleep.'"

Our guide said he did not sleep at all. There was a barn full of nice hay, but to permit a lady to sleep in a barn – why, there are some things that would shock the gallantry of a Maine woodsman much more than others."

The next morning, Eckstorm tells how they trudged ten more miles, or what was so called ten, "Over a road too deeply gullied by the spring rains to be practicable to any conveyance known in Maine." The *smoothness* of this road was noted by many travelers to the region. A visitor, six years hence, in 1897 wrote in, *The Industrial Journal*, "We had a load on our buckboard of grain and corn, but before reaching the farm (Grant Farm), three bags and most of the fourth were left along the roadside, thrown from their position en route."[186]

On their next to final leg of the journey they were transported on a road of similar roughness from Kokadjo to Lily Bay. At this point, they traveled without Webster who only accompanied them as far as the Roach River, allowing him to save the expense of a rough round-trip carriage ride for which his services would not be needed. As Webster did not accompany the Hardys to Lily Bay, he backtracked to retrieve the canoe that was left near Ragged Stream. In doing so, he had added sixty miles (thirty each way), lugging his clients gear over rough roads, only to return to his canoe and take the water route back to his starting point of Northeast Carry. If he was going to ultimately go that way, why did the Hardys simply not go that way as well? He had gone far off course to see Manly and Fannie would have safe passage to Greenville. If this doesn't speak to his character, nothing else matters.

Of the travel to Lily Bay Eckstorm wrote, "(the ride was) largely over fresh corduroy, on a Maine buckboard of the

---

[186] As noted on page 9 of the book, *Hidden in the Woods – The Story of Kokad-jo*, by Shirley Duplessis, Moosehead Communications, Inc., 1997.

springless variety, which was like being tossed in a blanket for an hour." A few years prior to Eckstorm's trip, Lucius Hubbard reported, "A buckboard can be procured at the Lily Bay House to haul one to Ray's at Roach Pond, where there is a substantial hotel with all the comforts," to which he added, "the ride is rather rough, and occupies about two hours and a half."[187]

Kokadjo Sign

*Population –
Not many.*

(Editor's Collection)

Moosehead Lake.

HOTELS, STORES, AND STEAMER.

ROACH RIVER HOUSE,

Twenty miles by road from Greenville, at the foot of *Roach Pond*. Reached comfortably by steamer to Lily Bay, thence by team, seven miles, over a good road.

The Trout-Fishing in its neighborhood is unexcelled by any on Moosehead Lake.

The hotel, a new and commodious two-story building, can accommodate a goodly number of guests, and the wants of visitors will receive careful attention.

TERMS EASY.

Canoes and Boats to let.

LEVI DAVIS, Proprietor.

1890s Advertisement.

Given Eckstorm's protection of her glass camera plates, the reader may imagine how concerned she must have been should the jostling buckboard damage her documentary evidence of the river drive, and what was the entire reason for the trip. As they

---

[187] *Hubbard's Guide to Moosehead Lake and Northern Maine, Annotated Edition.*

neared Lily Bay following ten canoe miles, nearly twenty on foot, and six more miles in a buckboard, the anticipated steamer ride must have been a great relief. They'd be safe from Jack Russell at last. However, the journal indicates an initial setback. "There we found that the steamers were not running regular trips so early (in the season) and we might have to wait a day or two." Here they were, so close to safety but had now become boxed in between the lake and the single narrow road back to Kokadjo.

With no steamer, and without a guide to carry their gear, they did not consider walking the remaining nine miles to Greenville, for that was known to be the worst of "roads," it being full of stumpage and in most places swampy mud. The lumber companies had yet to improve the road south from Lily Bay for anything more than winter travel, since going by water was easier, faster, and the steamers towing log booms transported passengers as well.

They may have considered camping out, but because of oncoming rain, the journal makes mention of having the need to spend money on two nights lodging at the tavern at Lily Bay. This choice became inconsequential.

"Toward night a steamer came in unexpectedly. But it was a special boat; had only come in for the night so as to be on hand bright and early to tow logs; couldn't think of going back to Greenville. Now it is of very little use to attempt to buy a Maine woodsman; if he will not work for love, he won't for money; and when he says no he means it, until he thinks better of it."

In true Eckstorm fashion, her journal is full of clues, without outright writing what transpired. The reader can imagine, Manly Hardy, with a father's concern, spoke to the good captain. Their voices were probably muted, while the small crew of the steamer stood waiting, not knowing if they could pull out their bedrolls, or would be shoveling more coal into the engine box. Manly Hardy probably explained why they had come down the east side of the lake, through swamps and over rough roads, not giving the reason to look for sheldrake nests, but at his desperate hour he explained to the captain the true situation. The captain surely knew the kind, and in all likelihood the specific names of the "early-riser bear hunters," and particularly the name Jack Russell. Men in those parts knew the reputations that preceded a man and you could bet a captain of a Moosehead Lake steamer knew the guides, the trappers, the bosses, and the troublemakers. And because of this knowledge, the captain had a change of heart.

"And so it happened, as it is ever likely to do with one of these men if he knew your grandfather, or a man you had been with, if he had heard of you favorably, or even if he took a fancy to your poor self." After this sentence, there is another in which Hardy uses the Latin terms, vir (man) and homo (humans), but it is crossed out, as if she expected to edit it out of the journal. It reads, "and they can read the difference between vir and homo out of all rifle range." This sentence appears to be the strongest clue that by the time she was writing her notes, she'd come to understand they were not safe from Russell, especially beyond the protection of the West Branch Drive, and the captain came to the same conclusion.

Eckstorm noted, "Why it happened that Capt. Louis Gill without any talk of doing favors, changed all his plans just because he knew my father, and he saw a storm coming on, and he ordered her about and down to Greenville. No bargain was struck, and one does not expect to charter a steamboat for nothing; but when given a good sized bill he passed back note after note, saying that, 'for two of us he thought a dollar and a half would be about fair.' About fair for the time of himself and crew, the coal of his steamer, for coming twenty-six miles out of his way (including the return trip), and saving us one or two days hotel bills in a rain storm! This sort of fairness, of which I have known a great deal in the Maine woods, looks suspiciously like generosity. But it is what you may expect if you are recognized as belonging to the confraternity of the woods."

Captain Louis Gill

The Fairy of the Lake Steamer

The steamer *Fairy Of The Lake*, captained by Louis Gill, is photographed docked near Rockwood with Mount Kineo in the background. This steamer was a side-wheeler, one hundred and forty feet long, and twenty-five feet wide amidships. It had two decks, gangways fore and aft on the main deck, and could carry three hundred people. The engine was two-hundred horse power and she ran eight to ten miles an hour.

(from, *The Northern*, 1922)

The fact that a large steamer took two passengers on a special delivery from Lily Bay to Greenville is a testimony to the danger that was conveyed. This is further highlighted since the captain took his ship over the lake at night, apparently convinced the Hardys required added distance between them and Jack Russell. While steamers did operate in the open water of the lake on calm nights booming logs, Eckstorm's note of rain coming on indicated it was not a cloudless night, and such darkness would make travel through Lily Bay even more a challenge. Anyone familiar with Moosehead Lake and the narrows between Sugar Island and the shore (now Lily Bay State Park) will know this is not a place for a pleasure cruise in a large steamboat in the dark of night.

Eckstorm concluded the chapter with, "(the laughter being) disturbing to Jack Russell's ears that by the time the leaves were falling, he turned his canoe prow northward, and was last seen going down the Allegash[188] in search of a climate more congenial to his health." It appears more was said between the months of June and October and relayed to Eckstorm, maybe from the men of the Drive, maybe the Guide, maybe a Hardy friend, such that she added this mention of Russell heading _farther north_ to the book. In doing so, Eckstorm felt she was not further 'poking the bear.' When the book was published in 1904, thirteen years after that June at Ripogenus, it is not known if Jack Russell was still living. If he was, and if he had been made aware of the statements about him in the book, it is certain he would have considered the portrayal in "Clump of Posies" as

---

[188] An older spelling of Allagash; here meaning the Allagash River.

damning of his character as Eckstorm's *Forest and Stream* article on his game poaching.

The journal notes end in typical Eckstorm fashion. "After all the best thing to see in the Maine woods is the woods, unless you are able to go straight to the hearts of the people in them, which is better yet. But the birds are of little enough account, except for a few unusual species, and the bird-lover will do far better to stick to his familiar hedgerows within city limits than to go so far afield and perhaps see nothing. If the record of this one day seems to disprove this, remember that it is far and away the best bird-day I ever had in the woods, and I took it just on that account. It also illustrates the point that there is some hard work to be done whether there are any birds or not any birds." (*the entry in this book has been abbreviated and not all bird sighting notes have been mentioned*)

Following the final page of the journal entry Eckstorm placed a letter in which she introduced the essay on exploring for sheldrake nests and her bird observations for submission to a magazine. In the margin she added a note, many years later during the typing of her hand-written journal, where she speculates the article was for *Bird Lore* magazine, to which she scribbled, "but I do not know."

Overall, there are enough clues in the writing to realize Wilbur Webster and Manly Hardy took the Russell threat against Fannie as serious business, causing them to take a direction of much more difficult travel. It was a tragic conclusion that Wilbur Webster drowned on Moosehead Lake seven months after he guided for the father and daughter.

MERGANSERS ON MOOSEHEAD LAKE

A family of young mergansers sticking close to their mother. They were over one-hundred yards from the shore when the photo was taken with a zoom lens during the month of July.
(Editors Collection)

Sheldrake (or sometimes shelldrake or shelduck) is a common Maine woodsmen's name for Merganser americanus, the American Merganser. The females will have from six to upwards of over twelve young in a season (source: Birds of Maine, Ora Willis Knight, 1908).

Eckstorm, in her journal notes specifically wrote, "Of the red-breasted sheldrake we found three nests, all rather near together and one of them but eight feet from the herring gull."

The red-breasted sheldrake (Merganser serrator), is similar to Merganser americanus, but there are differences noted by Knight. According to Knight, both of these mergansers may be found along the Maine coast from fall to spring, and then they migrate to the inland lakes soon after ice break-up. That author reported that for the merganser americanus, "the nest is built in some hollow stub which is near to or overhanging the water." Whereas for Merganser serrator, "the nest is composed of dry grass, often lined with down from the breast of the female, and is almost always on the ground and well hidden in the grass or under growing plants on some island."

It appears the differences Webster had with the Hardys on the nesting ground of sheldrake may have been a case of confused identity and the reason, as Eckstorm alluded, they were both correct.

On Moosehead Lake the editor has observed yearly broods of mergansers in groups of ten or more. They are more cautious than the common duck, and when not near their nesting site they navigate a good distance from the shoreline. When young, that is for most of their first season, they stick close to their mother, always in a tight formation. This behavior is in contrast to the common ducks, who frequent the lake shallows and along the rip-rap; even beginning to explore at distances from the mother by early summer. It is not uncommon to see the number of young in a duck family reduced from eight, in June, to only a few young remaining by middle of August; most likely attributed to turtles and other shoreline predators. Whereas, the editor has observed the number in the merganser brood remains close to the original all the way into the fall. The lesson of putting some distance between you and your enemies is well-learned by mergansers, and terribly able woodsmen alike.

DAVID STONE LIBBEY
HE *WAS* PENOBSCOT

Not only was David Stone Libbey born and raised along the Penobscot River, he was a Maine river-driver, and a writer that signed his essays, *Penobscot*. Eckstorm's *The Penobscot Man* was about many men, this book is about a man. This annotated edition of Eckstorm's book about Libbey, includes the writings from Libbey himself, and ballads the men sang on the river. It is a tribute to the pioneer, the inventor, the writer, a true American type, and a terribly able Penobscot Man.

I AM PENOBSCOT

America had many pioneers. The stories of some of those men have been exaggerated when told and retold. The story of the life of David Stone Libbey needs to embellishment. In this book, based on a true American pioneer, Maine author Tommy Carbone brings the characters of the Maine woods to the reader. This is the telling about the life of adventure, danger, and exploring David Libbey led. The novel will bring you to the deep Maine woods with the moose, the bear, and the trout; to the battle fields of the American south; the icy-cold waters of the Penobscot River, and to the hot arid deserts of the West. This may be historical fiction, but you'd only get a more accurate portrayal of this Penobscot Man's life if you had been there.

Edition Editor and Author - Tommy Carbone

Tommy Carbone lives in Maine and spends a wicked amount of his time exploring the waterways and trails of the north woods. He writes from a one room cabin, on the shores of a lake, that is frozen for almost six months out of the year, and moose outnumber people three to one.

His first novel, "***The Lobster Lake Bandits – Mystery at Moosehead***," has made those 'from away' want to visit Maine. It's a big state – come explore.

BOOKS FROM MAINE'S NORTH WOODS

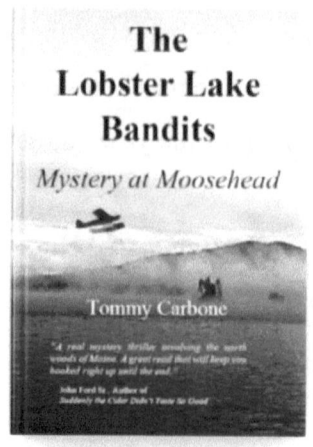

A Maine Novel

The second novel in the

Moosehead Mystery

series

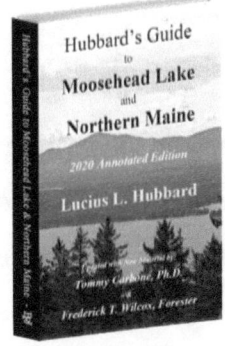

Hubbard's Guide to exploring Northern Maine.

2020 Edition

Hubbard's adventure through Maine to Canada.

2020 Edition

"Thomas S. Steele's Maine Adventures."

Two book collection.

A BURNT JACKET PUBLISHING CLASSIC RELEASE

Based on the writing of **Fannie Hardy Eckstorm** this memoir is a wonderful tale of the Maine woods and history from the 1800s.

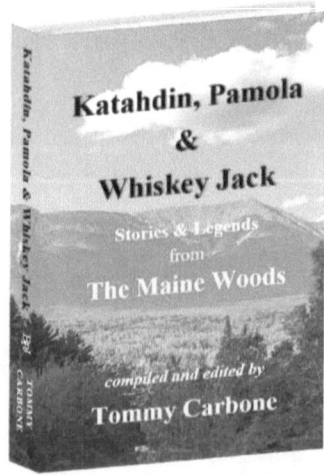

An annotated edition of additional stories from:
Fannie Hardy Eckstorm
Manly Hardy
&
Other Writing on Maine

www.ingramcontent.com/pod-product-compliance
Lightning Source LLC
LaVergne TN
LVHW092013090526
838202LV00026B/2631/J